Undergraduate Topics in Computer Science

'Undergraduate Topics in Computer Science' (UTiCS) delivers high-quality instructional content for undergraduates studying in all areas of computing and information science. From core foundational and theoretical material to final-year topics and applications, UTiCS books take a fresh, concise, and modern approach and are ideal for self-study or for a one- or two-semester course. The texts are authored by established experts in their fields, reviewed by an international advisory board, and contain numerous examples and problems, many of which include fully worked solutions.

The UTiCS concept centers on high-quality, ideally and generally quite concise books in softback format. For advanced undergraduate textbooks that are likely to be longer and more expository, Springer continues to offer the highly regarded *Texts in Computer Science* series, to which we refer potential authors.

Michael McCarthy • Barry Burd •
Ian Pollock

Concise Guide to the Internet of Things

A Hands-On Introduction to Technologies,
Procedures, and Architectures

 Springer

Michael McCarthy
Heinz College
Carnegie Mellon University
Pittsburgh, PA, USA

Barry Burd
Department of Mathematics
and Computer Science
Drew University
Madison, NJ, USA

Ian Pollock
Department of Art
California State University East Bay
Hayward, CA, USA

ISSN 1863-7310   ISSN 2197-1781   (electronic)
Undergraduate Topics in Computer Science
ISBN 978-3-031-57341-5   ISBN 978-3-031-57342-2   (eBook)
https://doi.org/10.1007/978-3-031-57342-2

This Springer imprint is published by the registered company Springer Nature Switzerland AG
The registered company address is: Gewerbestrasse 11, 6330 Cham, Switzerland

If disposing of this product, please recycle the paper.

PREFACE

In July of 2017, I led a working group in Bologna, Italy as part of the 22nd Innovation and Technology in Computer Science Education (ITiCSE) conference. The group's report, *Courses, Content, and Tools for Internet of Things in Computer Science Education*, identified challenges in bringing the emerging field of IoT to students at many levels and in many parts of the world. Drawing on experiences from distinguished educators, the report offered suggestions for meeting the challenges posed by the rapid growth of IoT technologies.

The following summer, the ITiCSE working group reconvened in Larnaca, Cyprus, creating a second report entitled *Internet of Things in CS Education: Updating Curricula and Exploring Pedagogy*. Beyond writing the report, each working group member left the conference with a strong belief in the value of IoT education and a deep commitment to the task of promoting that education.

With that in mind, two other working group members and I decided to push onward and write a book about the Internet of Things. We set our sights on a textbook for undergraduate students because those students will see a future in which IoT serves the common good. They'll develop new technologies, new ideas, and new modes of living while they spread the word about the impact of IoT.

Naturally, our vision of the future with IoT was upbeat and optimistic. But we took care to consider the possible pitfalls. We decided to introduce security issues as early as possible and to infuse the book with applications that promote sustainability. We believe that IoT education goes hand in hand with considerations about the future of society and the future of our planet.

                                                                    - Barry Burd, July 2023

Who Should Read This Book?

This book provides a hands-on introduction to modern IoT systems and does so in the context of building systems that promote sustainability. We, the authors, believe in building toward a sustainable future. We are also excited about the Internet of Things (IoT). We believe that the latter may help with the former.

We have written the book for a wide audience. Each chapter contains solutions that are created in a step-by-step manner and will be well within reach of any motivated undergraduate. The book asks that the reader deploy software to various systems and configure hardware in several ways. This requires some "stick-to-itiveness," and it would help to have some prior exposure to programming computers.

The activities described in each chapter should be doable by those without backgrounds in sustainability, computer science, or digital electronics. Our goal is for students to increase their interests in these fields and, perhaps, design IoT systems of their own.

We do not neglect the reader who may have a background in computer science. Our exercises include a subset of challenges that are appropriate for this group.

In some exercises, we encourage the use of generative AI as a starting point for solving complex problems. We structure the exercises so that students think critically about the responses they get from AI bots. Students correct the AI tools' mistakes and enhance the corrected code with ideas of their own. In this way, generative AI is a tool to stimulate further thinking.

What's in Each Chapter

Chapter 1 Introduction

Chapter 1 introduces a smart city application and a system model that describes many of the IoT systems we see today - and will likely see tomorrow. Many of the examples in the book can be understood by referring to this model.

Chapter 2 Setup

Chapter 2 provides hands-on instructions for setting up the software and hardware used elsewhere in the book. It is designed so that the active reader will become familiar with the technologies. It provides step-by-step instructions on setting up a microcontroller, writing a sketch using Particle's Web Integrated Development Environment (IDE), writing a first sketch, installing Node.js, using the command line, installing Node-RED, adding Express to Node.js, and building a web site.

Chapter 3 Securing IoT Data

Chapter 3 takes the view that IoT security and data privacy are essential parts of a sustainable future. It provides step-by-step instructions on configuring a light sensor and transmitting its data privately on the open internet. The data is received by a web service written in Node.js and Express. Two famous cryptographic algorithms are used: the One-time Pad and the Tiny Encryption Algorithm. The chapter serves as a hands-on introduction to cryptography and web services.

Chapter 4 Web API's

Chapter 4 provides hands-on instructions on the building of a smart city application. It promotes the use of mass transit and makes good use of the Bay Area Rapid Transit Application Programmer Interface (BART API). It demonstrates how a microcontroller can use data available from the World Wide Web. It introduces the reader to the Representational State Transfer style of API design.

Chapter 5 Designing Smart Connected Products

Chapter 5 demonstrates how solar energy can be used to heat a meal. The reader is taken step-by-step through the construction of a pizza box oven and a system that sends email when the food is cooked. It introduces sensors and how sensors can communicate with the World Wide Web. It makes use of the "If This Then That" (IFTTT) service to alert users (via email) when a meal is cooked.

Chapter 6 Publish Subscribe Using MQTT

Chapter 6 takes the view that IoT reliability and failure detection are fundamental parts of many IoT systems. These parts will play an important role in IoT systems designed for sustainability. It introduces the publish subscribe style of communication using MQTT. It shows how MQTT messages can be displayed graphically on the World Wide Web using Google Charts.

Chapter 7 Actuation Using MQTT

Chapter 7 describes a remote control application that could be employed to save the lives of migrating birds. It also makes good use of MQTT— this time for actuation rather than sensing. It introduces the need for authentication and how password based authentication can be implemented. Along with Chapter 3, it exposes the reader to some fascinating topics from cryptography.

Chapter 8 Identification Technologies

Chapter 8 illustrates how the sensing of QR codes can help protect us from viral transmission. It takes the reader step-by-step through the process of constructing and scanning a QR code. The QR code may be used to identify and visit a GitHub based website. It illustrates how a modern website is built and how the web can interact with the ubiquitous QR code.

Chapter 9 Constrained Networking

Chapter 9 discusses how telemedicine systems can be designed to transmit vital signs in real time over the web. Proceeding step-by-step, we connect a temperature sensor to the microcontroller and learn how to transmit and visualize the data on the World Wide Web using Google Charts. This chapter is the first that illustrates how a constrained network, such as one based on Bluetooth Low Energy (BLE), can be leveraged to provide data over a local wireless network. It illustrates all of the salient components of a modern IoT architecture.

Chapter 10 Persistence and Visualization

Chapter 10 discusses how climate change is impacting the global water supply. It describes how IoT systems can be utilized to help save water. The chapter introduces the reader to persistence and time series databases. In a step-by-step fashion, the reader is guided in using the popular SQLite embedded database. The system that is built uses data coming from a water sensor. BLE networking is used to communicate with a gateway running Node-RED, MQTT, and SQLite. The system uses the World Wide Web to access the database.

Chapter 11 Machine Learning and IoT

In the past, people said, "Computers do only what you tell them to do." But, in recent years, researchers have gone beyond rote-instruction computing and marched into an era in which computers modify their behavior. In other words, machines can learn.

In Chapter 11, we take advantage of recent developments in which machines have learned to recognize faces. We connect facial recognition software to a local network and trigger reactions from a microcontroller.

Chapter 12 Cryptocurrency and IoT

The original World Wide Web (Web1.0) was mostly concerned with reading data. The Web evolved to a system providing read and write capabilities – Web 2.0. Some believe that we are experiencing the beginning of Web 3.0 – where we read, write, and own resources. Chapter 12 discusses how smart cities may incorporate smart devices that own resources and recognize when cryptocurrency payments have been made to a blockchain. The environmental impact of proof-of-work blockchains is also discussed.

On The Web

For late breaking information about this book's content, visit:

https://github.com/sn-code-inside/guide-to-iot

Author Acknowledgements

Throughout the creation of this book, we've benefitted from so many peoples' advice and assistance. First and foremost, we thank Wayne Wheeler, our editor at Springer. We also extend thanks to other ITiCSE IoT working group members, including Lecia Barker, Monica Divitini, Felix Armando Fermin Perez, Ingrid Russell, Bill Siever, and Liviana Tudor. A special thank you goes out to the organizers of the 22nd and 23rd ITiCSE conferences -- Panayiotis Andreou, Michal Armoni, Janet Carter, Renzo Davoli, Michail Giannakos, Mikey Goldweber, Stephan Krusche, Stan Kurkovsky, Cary Laxer, Roger McDermott, Irene Polycarpou, Janet C. Read, Guido Rößling, Simon (who goes by a first name only), Bruce Scharlau. and Mark Zarb.

For artwork and drawings, we acknowledge the work of Marissa Dunlap (from MezzoJD Graphics Design) and Erin O'Reilly (Drew University).

For his significant contributions to Chapter 8 on QR codes, we acknowledge the excellent work of Kieran Walsh while he was a student at Carnegie Mellon University.

For his help in investigating the intersection of IoT and machine learning, we acknowledge Sagar Vijay Baviskar while he was a graduate student at Carnegie Mellon University.

Michael McCarthy

I would like to acknowledge Marci McCarthy, Robert McCarthy, Jen Espinosa, Cristina McCarthy, and Benjamin Peters.

For pointing me to IoT in the first place and for his continuing interest and support, I would like to acknowledge and thank Ramaya Krishnan.

I dedicate my portion of this book to Kade Emmet McCarthy. His joy for life helped his loved ones to get through the pandemic.

Thanks to my colleagues Andy Wasser, Marty Barrett, and Joe Mertz in the Information Systems Management program at Carnegie Mellon's Heinz College, as well as my former colleagues Robert Daley, Roger Flynn, and George Novacky from the University of Pittsburgh.

Barry Burd

Thanks to my colleagues, the faculty members in the mathematics and computer science department at Drew University: — Sarah Abramowitz, Chris Apelian, Seth Harris, Emily Hill, Steve Kass, Diane Liporace, Yi Lu, Ziyuan Meng, Ellie Small, and Steve Surace. As always, I thank Richard Bonacci, Cameron McKenzie, Gaisi Takeuti, and William Wisdom for their long-term help and support.

I dedicate my portion of this book to Abram and Katie, Benjamin and Jennie, Sam and Ruth, Sam and Jennie, and Harriet.

Ian Pollock

I want to recognize the kindness and collegiality of my colleagues Barry and Michael on this project as well as the support of my colleagues in the Graduate Program for Interaction Design in the Art Department at the California State University East Bay in Hayward, California. I also want to give special thanks to my students whose creativity and spirits inspire and teach me daily.

I dedicate my efforts in this book to the creatives who will use this to make the world a better place and to my love P.

CONTENTS

CHAPTER 1

Introduction

This chapter covers
Modeling the Internet of Things
Hardware requirements

M. McCarthy et al., *Concise Guide to the Internet of Things*,
Undergraduate Topics in Computer Science,
https://doi.org/10.1007/978-3-031-57342-2_1

Songdo Central Park, South Korea

"Machines take me by surprise with great frequency."

Alan Turing

Songdo, South Korea

Songdo, South Korea is a smart city. City planners have used green spaces and smart technology to reduce pollution, traffic congestion, and waste.

Introduction

Imagine wearing a small device which measures air pollution or toxic fumes. The device might use a network based on Bluetooth Low Energy (BLE) to communicate with your cell phone. Your phone could communicate with a cell tower to transmit data on to the internet. Once there, the data from many users could be stored and analyzed. What purpose would this serve? We measure what we treasure and we treasure clean air. This small device which collects data on air pollution may serve as one part of a system of systems that helps us to improve the quality of air in our cities.

Systems are being built that reduce air pollution, improve agriculture, reduce food waste, help prevent the spread of viruses, improve transportation systems, protect wildlife, improve the efficiency of buildings, reduce energy consumption, and improve healthcare. Many of these systems are built upon the Internet of Things (IoT). The evolution and impact of IoT on our daily lives is continuing and dramatic. It is an exciting time to be thinking and learning about IoT.

A deeper understanding of how the "things" in our world can be connected to the internet is invaluable. The reader may one day play a role in the design or construction of such systems.

The question is how do we start to study IoT? We begin with a model of all of the systems that we will build in this book.

Our Model and an Example

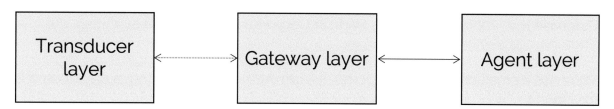

This is the model that we would like for you to keep in mind as you read this book. It describes the architecture of many modern IoT systems.

In this model, there are three layers and two networks. In the box on the left, the transducer layer, we find devices and gadgetry of various sorts – sensors and actuators. These devices are able to communicate over a constrained network with devices in the gateway layer. Devices in the gateway layer are able to bridge the two different networks. They are able to communicate with the transducer layer and the agent layer. In the agent layer we find applications that are on the internet and are available to many potential users.

Consider the air quality example from above. The transducer layer holds our pollution sensor. A constrained network carries signals over Bluetooth Low Energy to our phone. Bluetooth Low Energy is a constrained network – only able to communicate over a short distance. The phone is in the gateway layer and is able to communicate over a far more capable network to the internet. Applications in the agent layer are able to store, analyze, and process these data from sensors throughout our city. They may be used, for only one of many examples, by a city government to issue alerts if the air quality is poor in a particular area.

What's next?

Chapter 1 is the only chapter in our book which is not based upon a hands-on exercise. This book will provide hands-on experience with each of these layers and all of these technologies.

From Chapter 2 on, we will build small systems that illustrate how these components can be organized and exactly how they can be built. Before we get started, be sure to have purchased the necessary hardware.

Hardware Requirements

In order to work through the examples in this book, you will need to purchase the following hardware:

Purchase the "Photon 2" made by Particle Corporation. At the time of writing, the Photon 2 costs 17.95 USD.

Purchase a small breadboard. 8.5 cm X 5.5 cm. At the time of writing, a breadboard is less than 1 USD.

Purchase one Phototransistor (Everlight ALS-PT243-3C/L177) 5mm T1 ¾. Be sure to buy one that has a flat top. At the time of writing, this light detection sensor is less than 1 USD.

Purchase one 220Ω resistor. At the time of this writing, this is less than 1 USD.

Purchase a SHT30 Temperature And Humidity Sensor - Wired Enclosed Shell. At the time of this writing, this thermometer is available on the web at a cost of about 10 USD.

Purchase a DGZZI Water Level Sensor. At the time of this writing, a pair of these sensors is available on the web at a cost of about 6 USD. You only need one.

Purchase three jumper cables that fit into the breadboard. Z&T sells Solderless Flexible Breadboard Jumper wires in packages of 100 for 7.29 USD.

You will need an Android or IoS phone capable of BLE communications and QR code scanning.

You will need an Apple Mac or Windows PC capable of running Node.js and Node-RED. These devices will, of course, also need to run a modern browser such as Chrome, Firefox, or Edge.

Check Your Understanding

1. Provide an example of a transducer.

2. Provide an example of a gateway.

3. Provide an example of an application that would run in the agent layer.

4. Describe an IoT system that you are already familiar with in the terms of the model described in the chapter.

Make More / Explore Further

1. Do some research and describe how sensors are used in Songdo, South Korea.

2. Do some research and learn about actuation. Describe how actuators are used in Songdo, South Korea.

3. Do some research and describe how systems in the agent layer are used in Songdo, South Korea.

Summing Up

In this chapter, we learned how IoT systems may be described with a model. We learned that we should keep that model in mind as we explore the systems that are built in the remaining chapters.

We also reviewed the required hardware for this book.

Looking Ahead

In Chapter 2, we need to install software and configure our hardware so that the systems in the remaining chapters can be built.

CHAPTER 2

Setting Up
Your System

This chapter covers
Registering your IoT device
Writing simple code
Responding to events
Creating a web page

M. McCarthy et al., *Concise Guide to the Internet of Things*,
Undergraduate Topics in Computer Science,
https://doi.org/10.1007/978-3-031-57342-2_2

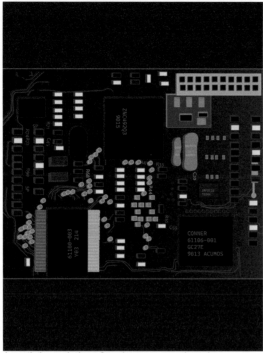

An artist's rendering of a microprocessor board.

"Your best and wisest refuge from all troubles is in your science. "

Ada Lovelace

Forging Connections

To paraphrase the poet John Donne, "No one is an island entire unto itself; everyone is a piece of the continent, a part of the main...." The same is true about today's technology. If you lived in the mid 1980s and used a personal computer, your computer had little or no contact with other hardware. You could create documents. But to distribute a document, you'd save the document on a removable disk and insert that disk into another computer. Very few people had email accounts. But if you had an account, you'd couldn't send an email without squeezing your phone into big, clunky modem.

Fast forward to today's home environment. When diabetes patients measure their sugar levels, the glucose meter stores each reading. The patient brings the meter to the physician's office, where a special device copies the readings from the meter. That works, but some patients forget to bring their meters to the physician's office. Other patients visit their physicians rarely because of limited mobility.

To solve this problem, some glucose meters come with mobile connectivity. Each sugar reading is automatically uploaded to a central service. Then, with an eye toward privacy and confidentiality, the central service relays the patient's readings to the patient's physician. If necessary, the physician can monitor the readings in real-time

Connectivity makes things better. When you build IoT systems, you start by putting computing power in a strategic place. You put a transmitter into a glucose meter, a water sensor on a basement floor, or a crash sensor in an automobile. Then you use that chip to communicate with other devices. If a patient's glucose levels are too high, a physician calls the patient. If your basement starts to flood, you see a notice on your mobile phone. In case of a car accident, emergency help is notified immediately.

This chapter is about making connections. It starts with a development board that you put in a strategic place. For this book's examples, the device we use is a Photon 2 -- a device sold by a company named Particle. For details, see Chapter 1.

Along with the Photon 2, you will need a breadboard, a cable, and an optional antenna.

The following paragraphs describe each component in detail.

The Breadboard

Figure 2.1 has a picture of the *breadboard*. When we refer to the top and bottom of the board or to the left- and right-sides of the board, we are referring to the board as it's shown in Figure 2.1.

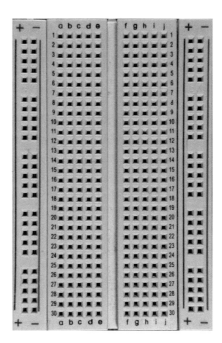

Figure 2.1: This breadboard that we use with the Photon 2.

The board has 400 holes.

- Along the left side of the board, there are two columns of holes with 25 holes per column. The columns are labeled + and -.
- Along the right side of the board, there are also two columns of holes with 25 holes per column. These columns are also labeled + and -.
- The middle of the board has ten columns, with 30 rows in each column. The columns are lettered a to j, and the rows are numbered 1 to 30.

You can plug a wire into any of the board's 400 holes. Beneath the board's surface, the holes are connected by the pattern shown in Figure 2.2.

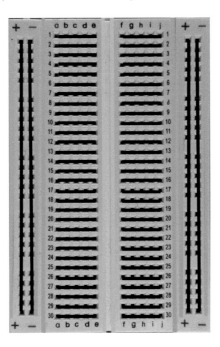

Figure 2.2: The yellow lines in the diagram depict electrical connections.

- Imagine that you plug one wire into hole b2 and another into hole e2. A straight line in Figure 2.2 connects holes a2 through e2. So, any current going through the b2 wire will reach the e2 wire as well.
- Imagine that you plug one wire into the upper-left corner hole and another wire into the lower-left corner hole. A straight line in Figure 2.2 connects all the holes along the board's left column. So, any current going through the upper-left corner wire will also reach the lower-left corner wire.

Here's a fun fact: According to legend, the earliest breadboards were made of wood -- just like the board in a kitchen that you use to cut bread.

The USB Cable

The cable that we need has two connectors -- an *A-connector* on one end (Figure 2.3) and a *micro B-connector* on the other (Figure 2.4).

Figure 2.3: USB-A connector

Figure 2.4: USB Micro B-connector

The micro-B connector will go into a slot on the Photon 2. The A-connector will go into one of two places.

- In most cases, you can plug the A-connector into any compatible power source.
- In rare cases, when you need to set up direct communication between the Photon 2 and a laptop, you plug the A-connector directly into the laptop.

If your laptop doesn't have a slot that accepts a USB-A connection, you can add an adapter cable. The adapter goes between your laptop and the Photon 2's USB cable.

The Wi-Fi Antenna

Figure 2.5 shows the optional antenna for the Photon 2.

Figure 2.5: Wi-Fi antenna for a Photon 2

Depending on the strength of your Wi-Fi signal, the Photon 2 may or may not need an antenna. But, when you start working with electronic connections, you have enough to think about without worrying about Wi-Fi connectivity. A wire that's fastened to the antenna ends in a female *U.FL connector.* In the next section, you snap the U.FL connector onto the Photon 2.

The Photon 2

Your Photon 2 is one of the many "brains" of the IoT operation. When we refer to the top and bottom of the device or to the left- and right-side of the device, we'll be imagining the device as it's shown in Figure 2.6. There's a column of 16 pins along the left side of the device and a column of 12 pins along the right side. We describe other components (the user LED, and so on) later in this chapter.

Figure 2.6 The Particle Photon 2

The device's components rest on a rectangular base made chiefly of fiberglass.

Part 1: Set Up Your Photon 2

What you need:

- Photon 2, USB cable, breadboard, and optional antenna
- Access to Wi-Fi. (Your Wi-Fi hotspot should have a captive portal. That is, the hotspot should not display a sign-on page each time you attempt to connect.)

What to do:

1. Place the breadboard on a flat, stable surface.

2. The Photon 2 may come with its pins pressed into a piece of anti-static foam. If so, remove the device from the foam.

3. Line the pins of the Photon 2 device along holes in the breadboard. The precise position of the device on the board isn't critical. If in doubt, have one end of the device's fiberglass base covering Row 6 of the breadboard, while the other end of the base covers Row 25. (See Figure 2.7.)

4. Press down evenly on the device so that the device's pins sink into the breadboard's holes.

   You have to apply some pressure for the pins to go all the way into the holes. Try to press only on the fiberglass base, not on any of the components on the base. It may help to slightly rock the device from side to side as you press down.

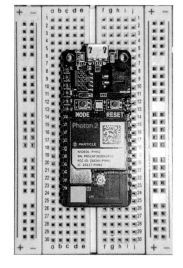

Figure 2.7: Positioning the Photon 2 on the breadboard.

5. Look for a U.FL connector near the bottom of the Photon 2 device. Press the antenna's connector onto the Photon 2's connector. See Figure 2.8.

   Before you start pressing, try to align the antenna's connector so that it sits squarely on the Photon 2's connector. Avoid aligning the antenna connector at an angle. Apply pressure until the antenna clicks into place.

   Later, if you have to remove the antenna from the device, try not to pull the connector at an angle. Instead, use a small pair of pliers to pull the connector upward.

Figure 2.8: The Wi-Fi antenna fastened to the Photon 2.

6. Plug the USB cable's micro B-connector into the device.

7. Plug the USB cable's A-connector into a power source.

   If your computer has a place to plug in a USB A connector, you can plug the cable in there. If not, any USB-A power source will do for now.

When you power up the Photon 2, the status LED (labeled in Figure 2.6) will light up. The LED's color and blinking behavior may change a bit. But, after a few seconds, there will be no more changes.

By the way, the acronym LED stands for *light emitting diode*.

8. When the status LED settles into a constant pattern, take note of the LED's color and blinking behavior. At the moment, the Photon 2 is in one of many possible modes. The status LED tells you which mode the device is currently in. Table 2.1 lists some of the possibilities.

If the color is ...	... and the blinking speed is ...	... then ...
blue	medium	The device is in listening mode. It's waiting for you to configure it via USB from your computer.
cyan	slow	The device is connected to the Particle cloud and is ready to receive instructions.
green	fast	The device is trying to connect to Wi-Fi.
green	slow	The device is not connected to the Particle cloud.
red	SOS	The device is in an Error state.

Notes:
- Medium blinking is roughly 16 times every 10 seconds.
- Slow blinking (also known as *breathing*) is roughly two times every 10 seconds.
- Fast blinking is roughly 40 times every 10 seconds.
- SOS blinking is three short blinks followed by three long blinks, three more short blinks, and finally a number of blinks to indicate the nature of the error.

For a list of all the Photon 2's modes, visit https://docs.particle.io/tutorials/device-os/led/photon/.

Within half a minute, the device settles into one of the modes described in the first two rows of Table 2.1.

- **Blue, medium-speed blinking:** If the Photon 2 isn't configured to work with a particular Wi-Fi hotspot, the device goes into *listening mode*. It's listening for instructions about joining a Wi-Fi hotspot. Beginning in Step 9, you'll issue those instructions by connecting it to a computer and following step-by-step instructions.
- **Cyan, slow blinking:** If the device has already been configured to work with your current Wi-Fi network, the device connects automatically to that network. Beginning in Step 9, you'll register the device with an account in your name.

  In some cases, you may not have access to whatever Wi-Fi hotspot the Photon 2 is configured to use. In those cases, you can reconfigure the device by forcing it to go back into listening mode. To do so, hold the device's mode button. You can release the mode button when the device's status LED starts blinking blue. (Under normal circumstances, you hold the mode button for approximately three seconds. The mode button is pictured in Figure 2.5.)

9. Visit https://setup.particle.io/ and follow that site's step-by-step instructions.

When you do, the app walks you through the steps to connect your Photon 2 to your current Wi-Fi network and register the device with your Particle account.

Particle's publicly-available computer power goes by several different names. You may see the terms *Particle device cloud*, *Particle server*, *Particle cloud*, and possibly others. Each of these terms refers to computers belonging to the Particle company.

If all goes well, Particle's setup web page says your device is connected to the Particle cloud, and the LED on your device is breathing cyan. Your device is ready to receive further instructions. (For details about the Particle cloud, see this chapter's "What the Particle App Does" section.)

A Photon 2 has no shutdown procedure. When you've finished working with the device, you can simply unplug it.

What Did You Do, and How Did You Do It?

The previous section lists 11 steps. When you're finished, you should have a usable connection between your device and the Particle cloud. But following steps is only part of the story. You must also understand the reasoning behind each of the steps. This section describes some of those behind-the-scenes details.

What is a Microcontroller?

Deep inside the laptop or desktop that you use is a small but powerful microprocessor. The *microprocessor* is your computer's "brain" with sections to do calculations, a handful of registers, and some input/output ports. The section that performs calculations is called the *Arithmetic Logic Unit (ALU)*. Less than 100 *registers* store the intermediate results of the calculations, and a *Control Unit* coordinates operations. (See Figure 2.9).

Today's microprocessors work at speeds above 1 Gigahertz -- a billion operations per second. On average, they consume about 20 watts of power. (For comparison, a typical household LED consumes only 10 watts.) A decent microprocessor may cost a few hundred dollars.

A microprocessor may have many more components than the ones shown in Figure 5.23. For example, a *Graphics Processing Unit (GPU)* may enhance the capabilities of the ALU with special circuitry for producing images. Even so, a microprocessor lacks some of the things that a computer needs in order to function. For example, *random access memory (RAM)* -- possibly billions of locations for storing data and instructions -- is connected from outside of the microprocessor.

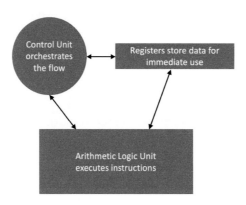

Figure 2.9: The parts of a microprocessor.

What about a smart lightbulb? Does that need a microprocessor? It doesn't. The computing tasks required of a smart bulb are tiny compared with the programs running on a laptop computer. A smart bulb runs only one program -- the program that turns the light on and off. But a laptop computer runs hundreds of programs at once. Under the hood, an ordinary laptop may juggle 300 programs -- all to manage only five apps that the user sees running.

An IoT device's smarts should be small and inexpensive with very low power consumption. Most IoT devices have no screens or keyboards. A smart lightbulb performs all of its input wirelessly.

A typical IoT device doesn't have its own microprocessor. Instead, it has a *microcontroller*. A microcontroller has more parts built into it than a microprocessor, but a microcontroller's components are less powerful than their microprocessor counterparts. The microcontroller on your Photon 2 runs at only two hundred million hertz. That's roughly one-tenth of the speed of a laptop computer's processor.

A microcontroller combines some of a microprocessor's logic with peripherals such as RAM all on one chip (See Figure 2.10).

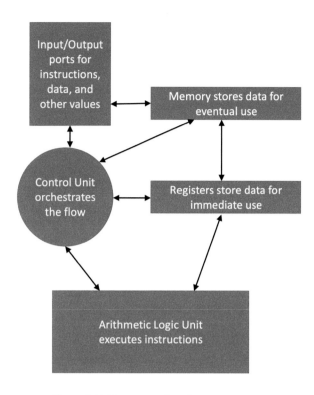

Figure 2.10: The parts of a microcontroller.

Particle's Photon 2 board has 4.5 Megabytes of RAM compared with the 8 Gigabytes of RAM that you find on many laptops. A typical microcontroller consumes between one-tenth and one-hundredth of the amount of power consumed by a microprocessor. To top it all off, a microcontroller costs about $20 -- much less if you buy them in bulk. This combination makes microcontrollers suitable for embedded systems and IoT applications.

Microcontrollers are sometimes called *embedded processors* because they tend to be hidden inside coffee pots, refrigerators, automobiles, and other devices that we don't normally think of as computers.

What the Particle App Does

Imagine yourself sitting at a restaurant table talking to a friend. The two of you are exchanging information. You're *communicating*. What's involved in the act of communicating?

- You're using an agreed-upon set of rules to exchange information.

  You wouldn't communicate very effectively if you didn't speak the same language. So, the language that you're speaking is an element in these rules. The social conventions that you follow (for example, don't spit in your friend's soup) form another part of these rules. Taken as a whole, we call these rules a *protocol*. Without a protocol, successful communication would be nearly impossible.

- Something carries the information that travels between you and your friend.

In a typical restaurant discussion, you exchange information by talking -- making sounds that go from your mouth to your friend's ears. The air in the restaurant carries your sound waves across the table. The air is an example of a *medium*.

Of course, there are many different protocols and media. The people at the next table are from another country. Their protocol involves a different spoken language and some different social customs. Instead of talking out loud, they could be passing written notes back and forth. In that case, the medium would be ink on a napkin.

In the same way, all information that's passed among parts of a system involves protocols and media. Follow along in Figure 2.11 as you read about the kinds of communication involved in Part 1: Set Up Your Photon 2.

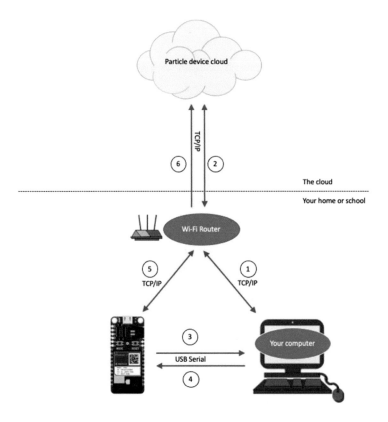

Figure 2.11: Setting up the Photon 2

1. Your home or your school has a Wi-Fi router that enables you to connect to the Internet. The Wi-Fi router has a name (a *Service Set Identifier*, also known as an *SSID*) and a password. When you log in with this name and password, you begin a session with the router.

The medium for connecting to your router is a wireless radio signal. The communication protocol is called *TCP/IP*, which is short for *Transmission Control Protocol/Internet Protocol*. It's the protocol you use when you visit a website, send an email, or do almost anything else involving the Internet.

2. The router requests content from https://setup.particle.io/. A computer that the Particle company manages sends a response containing the Setup page, and the router forwards this response to your computer.

Throughout this process, the protocol is TCP/IP.

3. After a few preliminaries, Particle's website sends instructions that make your computer communicate with your Photon 2. The Photon 2 sends information about itself to your computer, and your computer forwards this information to Particle's computers.

The medium for communication between your computer and the Photon 2 is the USB cable.

Early computers used a specialized piece of hardware called a *Universal asynchronous receiver-transmitter* (*UART*) to exchange data. The protocol was called *serial* communication because the data traveled only one bit at a time. Today's Universal Serial Bus (USB) connectors are much faster than the old UARTs, but your Photon 2 uses its USB cable to mimic the behavior of the older UARTs. That's why, in Figure 2.11, the arrows in Steps 3 and 4 are labeled *USB Serial*.

During this step, Particle's website asks you to assign a name to the Photon 2 -- a name like *guerilla_picklefish* or *jane_smith_photon2_01*. When you finish this step, the device delivers the name to the Particle device cloud. Particle registers the name with your account along with your device's device ID -- a 24-character string that's stored on your device. No two Particle devices have the same device ID so, as far as Particle's cloud is concerned, this device is yours.

4. With your router and computer as intermediaries, Particle's website tells the Photon 2 how to communicate with your router. In particular Particle gives your Photon 2 your router's SSID and password.

5. Using the information that you supplied in Step 2, the Photon 2 connects to your Wi-Fi router.

6. The Photon 2 connects to the Particle device cloud by sending data through your Wi-Fi router.

Now that your Photon 2 can communicate with the Particle cloud, you can start programming the Photon 2.

Part 2: Program Your Photon 2

What you need:

- Photon 2, USB cable, breadboard, and optional antenna
- Access to a computer

What to do:

1. Plug the Photon 2 into a power source.

   After thirty seconds or less, the device's status LED should be breathing the cyan color. This indicates that the device is connected to the Particle cloud. (See Table 2.1.)

2. With your computer's web browser, visit https://build.particle.io.

3. Sign onto your Particle account (the account you created in Part 1).

   After signing in, the Particle website shows you a page named *Particle Web IDE*. Most of this page is taken by a black region called the *editor*. The editor contains the following text:

Figure 2.12: The Devices icon.

```
void setup() {

}

void loop() {

}
```

4. Hover over the icons in the lower-left region of the Web IDE page. Look for an icon whose hover tip is *Devices*. (See Figure 2.12.)

   When you click the Devices icon, the web page shows you a list of devices registered to your account. (See Figure 2.13.)

Figure 2.13: A list of Particle devices registered to a particular account.

5. Make sure that the star associated with your Photon 2 is yellow. If not, click that star.

   Figure 2.13 lists three Particle devices -- *barry_argon01*, *Barry_boron*, and *Photon_2* We've touched-up Figure 2.13 so that the yellow Photon_2 star stands out a bit more than it does on the real web page. The yellow star indicates that any code we write should run on the Photon_2 device. The barry_argon01 and Barry_boron stars are greyed out. So, for now, we won't be sending code to the barry_argon01 or Barry_boron devices.

6. Add a few lines (the lines shown in boldface type) to the code in the editor.

```
void setup() {
   pinMode(D7, OUTPUT);
}
```

```
void loop() {
  digitalWrite(D7, HIGH);
  delay(1000);
  digitalWrite(D7, LOW);
  delay(1000);
}
```

Type these lines *exactly* the way you see them in the box. In particular, make sure all the words are capitalized the way you see them here. For example, type `pinMode`, not `pinmode` or `PinMode`. Make sure to put a semicolon at the end of each of your lines. You have some leeway in the way you write this code but, for now, it's best to type it exactly as you see it.

This code that you type in the web page's editor is a complete program -- a set of instructions for a processor to execute. When you write a program for a Photon 2, you sometimes call that program a *sketch*.

7. Hover over the icons in the upper-left region of the Web IDE page. Look for an icon whose hover tip is *Verify*. (See Figure 2.14.)

Figure 2.14: The Verify icon.

When you click the Verify icon, the web page checks your code for certain kinds of errors. If you see some red error markers along the bottom of the page, something is wrong. Make sure you've copied the code exactly as it's shown in Step 6. If you don't see any error markers, you're good to go.

8. Just above the Verify icon, you'll find the *Flash* icon. (See Figure 2.15.)

When you click the Flash icon, the Particle cloud starts sending the code to your Photon 2. For a short time, a message at the bottom of the Web IDE says, "Flash successful!" The Photon 2's status LED blinks in various ways for about 30 seconds. But then, the Photon 2's user LED begins to blink -- on for one second, then off for one second, then on for another second, and so on. (Remember that the device's user LED is at the top of the device's base. See Figure 2.6.)

Figure 2.15: The Flash icon.

Congratulations! You've sent a program to your Photon 2! Let's make sure that you're really in control. Here's how you can tell:

9. In the editor, change the first `delay(1000)` to `delay(5000)`.

10. Click the Flash icon again.

About 30 seconds later, the user LED's behavior changes. Now the user LED is on for five seconds, then off for one second, then on for another five seconds, and so on.

Sure, you haven't written code that benefits people around the world yet. But remember the old Chinese saying, "A journey of a thousand miles begins with a single step."

11. Look for a folder icon near the upper left corner of the Particle Web IDE. Click that folder to save your work.

What Did You Do, and How Did You Do It?

What really happens when you follow the previous section's steps? This section provides some insight.

Sending Code to the Photon 2

In Part 2 of this chapter's experiments, you write code and send it to the Particle 2 device. Figure 2.16 shows you what lines of communication you used.

1. When you type the code or make any changes to the existing code, any characters you type go from your computer to the router in your home or your school.

2. The router sends these characters to the Particle device cloud.

In Figure 2.16, the arrows labeled 1 and 2 go only one way to emphasize the fact that you send computer code to the cloud. But, in a more nuanced view of this action, your computer and the cloud exchange information in both directions. For example, when you click the Verify icon, the cloud checks your code and sends its verdict back to your computer screen.

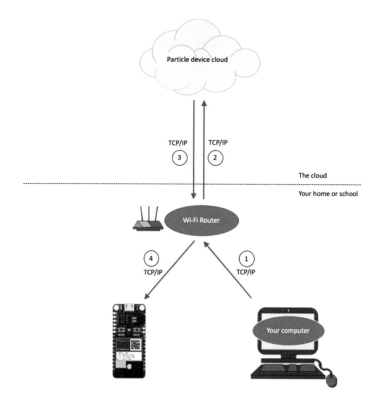

Figure 2.16: Sending code to the Photon 2.

3. When you click the Flash icon, the cloud sends instructions back to your Wi-Fi router.

4. As the router receives instructions, it forwards them to your Photon 2.

   When the device digests all the instructions it's been given, it starts executing those instructions, making its user LED blink on and off.

Writing Code for the Photon 2

When you say, "Go to the store and buy some bread," you're instructing someone to do something. The instructions are written in the English language. Now look back at the code in Step 6 of Part 2. When the Particle device cloud flashes your device, the cloud instructs the device to blink its user LED. The instructions are written in a language named *C++*.

Bjarne Stroustrup developed C++ in the early 1980s. It's a *general-purpose programming language*, which means you can use it to program computers, microcontrollers, phones, watches, and just about any kind of device you'd want to program. C++ is one of the world's five most widely used programming languages.

You can type C++ code in any plain old editor, like Windows Notepad or the Macintosh TextEdit app. But it's easier to type code in an integrated development environment (IDE). An IDE is an editor that has special features for writing and delivering code. For example, in Part 2, you click the Web IDE's Devices icon to tell the cloud which device will eventually be executing your code. Later, you click the Flash icon to send your code to that device. Plain old editors, like Notepad and TextEdit, don't have these icons.

To run some IDEs, you download and install an app on your computer. But you don't install Particle's IDE. Instead, Particle's IDE is a page in your computer's Web browser. That's why Particle's IDE is called a *Web IDE*.

A C++ program, like the code in Step 6, is just ordinary text with no formatting whatsoever. Particle's Web IDE displays colors and italicized text, but that formatting is only to help you read and understand the code. The IDE never saves any of that formatting.

In fact, the Particle cloud never sends the text in Step 6 directly to the Particle. Instead, the cloud *compiles* the text. That is, the cloud translates the text into another language -- one that the Photon 2 can easily understand. The formal name for this device-friendly language is the *ARM® Cortex®-M33 Processor Instruction Set*. In this book, we'll refer to a set of instructions in that language as *firmware*. Depending on the context, you may also see the terms *object code*, *compiled code*, or *executable code*.

Object code isn't suitable for reading or writing by ordinary human beings. For one thing, object code instructions are expressed in bits rather than characters. You can make sense of text such as

```
delay(1000);
```

but you'd have trouble making sense of bits such as

```
00000000 00000000 00001010 00001000 00110100 00001110
00001010 00001000 00000000 00000000 00000110 00000000
00000110 00000000 00000101 00000001 00000100 00000010
00110101 00001000 00000000 00000000 00000000 00000000
01010100 00001100 00001010 00001000 00001001 01001000
00001010 01001001 00001000 10110101 10001000 01000010
00000101 11010000 00001001 01001010 10000010 01000010
```

In addition, object code instructions are much more detailed than the instructions in Step 6. Even if you could make sense of the object code's 0s and 1s, you'd still have trouble understanding the code's overall purpose.

The Instructions in a Program

Here's an enhanced version of the code in Part 2, Step 6:

```
/* This sketch makes the
   Photon 2's user LED blink. */

void setup() {            // Do the following once:
  pinMode(D7, OUTPUT);    //   Make D7 send output to the user LED
}

void loop() {             // Do the following repeatedly:
  digitalWrite(D7, HIGH); //   Have D7 turn the user LED on
  delay(1000);            //   Wait for 1 second
  digitalWrite(D7, LOW);  //   Have D7 turn the user LED off
  delay(1000);            //   Wait for 1 second
}
```

You can flash this enhanced code to your Photon 2. When the cloud compiles this code, it ignores all the text between `/*` and `*/`. It also ignores the rest of the line after each occurrence of `//`. Each piece of text that the cloud ignores is called a *comment*. Well-written comments help people understand how the code works.

Here are a few more facts about the Part 2, Step 6 code: Each pin on the Photon 2 has a name. On the left side of the device, the fifth pin from the top is named D7. When the D7 pin has been set to `OUTPUT` (as opposed to `INPUT`), the D7 pin controls the user LED. Writing `HIGH` to the LED turns the LED on; writing `LOW` turns the LED off. The Part 2, Step 6 code tells the device to send `HIGH` to the LED, then wait one second (1000 milliseconds) and send `LOW` to the LED, and then wait another second before repeating the whole process.

In Step 7 of Part 2, you asked the Web IDE to verify your code. As a result, the Particle cloud tried to compile your program. If the cloud couldn't compile the code, the IDE displayed an error message. Maybe you had accidentally typed an uppercase letter `D` instead of a lowercase `d`:

```
Delay(1000); // This is incorrect!
```

The accidental uppercase `D` is called a *compile-time error* because the cloud detects this error when it tries to compile your code. But what if your code had no compile-time errors? Would that mean your code was completely correct? Unfortunately, it wouldn't. In addition to compile-time errors, there's another kind of error called a *run-time error*, also known as a *logic error*. With a logic error, the cloud can compile your code, but the code doesn't tell the device to do exactly what you want it to do. It's like saying, "Go to the store and buy some bread," when you have plenty of bread, but you need more butter.

To see a run-time error in action, make a small change to the code in Part 2, Step 6. Move the `digitalWrite(D7, HIGH);` line below the `digitalWrite(D7, LOW);` line, like so:

```
/* This sketch has a run-time error. */

void setup() {
  pinMode(D7, OUTPUT);
}

void loop() {
  delay(1000);
  digitalWrite(D7, LOW);
  digitalWrite(D7, HIGH);
  delay(1000);
}
```

Particle's Web IDE verifies your code because you have no errors on any of the lines. But when you flash this code to the Photon 2, the user LED never seems to blink. With the `digitalWrite(D7, HIGH);` line out of place, the device isn't pausing after sending `LOW` to the LED. Instead, the device sends `LOW` to the LED and then immediately sends `HIGH` to the same LED. Without a one-second delay, the time when the LED stays in the *off* state is imperceptible. The LED may go off for a tiny fraction of a second, but you can't see it.

Assuming that you want the LED to blink, the above program contains a run-time error. When you verify the code, the Web IDE says the code is OK. But when you run the code, it doesn't do what you want it to do.

Part 3: The Command Line Interface

What you need:

- Photon 2, USB cable, breadboard, and optional antenna
- Access to a computer

What to do:

1. Visit https://nodejs.org/en/download/ to install Node.js.

   Node.js provides an environment that allows us to run JavaScript programs outside of the context of a browser - where JavaScript normally runs. When you visit the download page, you might see two versions of Node.js -- a 32-bit version and a 64-bit version. Most people select the 64-bit installer for their computers' operating systems (Windows or macOS).

2. Find out how to launch your computer's *shell application*.

   - In Windows, the shell application is called *Command Prompt.* Type *Command Prompt* in the Windows search box, and then press Enter.
   - On a Mac, the shell application is called *Terminal.* Press Cmd+Space. In the resulting popup, type `Terminal` and press Return.
   - In Linux, the shell application is called *Terminal.* Each desktop environment has its own way of launching new apps. If you have a Linux system, find out how to launch an app and launch the system's Terminal app.

3. What you do next depends again on your computer's operating system.

Windows: Visit https://binaries.particle.io/cli/installer/windows/ParticleCLISetup.exe. Your web browser will offer to download an installation file. Download the file. Then run the file by double-clicking the file's icon. Your computer will install Particle's *Command Line Interface* (CLI).

macOS and Linux: In the Terminal app's window, type the following command exactly as you see it here. Then press Enter.

```
bash <( curl -sL https://particle.io/install-cli )
```

As a result, your computer will install Particle's Command Line Interface (CLI).

4. Close and then reopen your computer's shell application (named Terminal or Command Prompt).

5. In the shell application window, type *particle login*, and then press Enter.

   In response, the shell prompts you for your email address and Particle password. After you've entered this information, the shell responds with a message like `Successfully completed login!`

6. Using the USB cable that comes with your Photon 2, connect the device to your computer.

   Depending on the availability of slots on your computer, you may need an adapter that goes between your computer and the device's USB cable.

7. With your computer's web browser, visit Particle's Web IDE.

   It's time for you to create a brand-new program.

8. Find a panel with the title Particle Apps along the left side of the Particle Web IDE.

   If you don't see the Particle Apps panel, click the Code icon in the lower-left corner of the Particle Web IDE. (See Figure 2.17.).

9. Near the bottom of the Particle Apps panel, click the CREATE NEW APP button.

   When you do, the Particle Apps panel displays a blank field for the name of your new app.

10. Type a name for your new app.

    A few lines of code appear in the editor part of the Particle Web IDE.

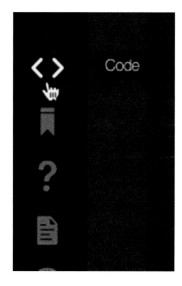

Figure 2.17: The Code icon.

11. Add two lines (the lines shown in boldface type) to the code in the editor.

```
void setup() {
}

void loop() {
  Serial.println(Time.format());
  delay(1000);
}
```

12. In the Particle Web IDE, click the Flash icon.

Your Photon 2 receives the new code and starts running it. To see what's happening while the device runs the code, proceed to the next step.

13. In your computer's application, type the following line and then press Enter.

```
particle serial monitor
```

After a brief pause, you'll see the following text in your computer's shell application:

```
Opening serial monitor for com port: "/dev/tty.usbmodem1434301"
Serial monitor opened successfully:
Fri Sep  3 00:53:33 2022
Fri Sep  3 00:53:34 2022
Fri Sep  3 00:53:35 2022
Fri Sep  3 00:53:36 2022
Fri Sep  3 00:53:37 2022
```

Every second, the device sends a current-time message to your computer's shell application. It might not be the same time where you live because the device displays *Coordinated Universal Time* (UTC) which is roughly the same as the time in Greenwich, England.

Here's a useful tip: You can set the device to display your local time. Visit https://www.timeanddate.com/time/difference/timezone/utc to find your region's local time offset. It's a number between -12 and +14. Then, run a program containing the line `Time.zone( );` with your region's offset number in the space between parentheses.

14. To stop the flow of new numbers in the terminal, press Ctrl+C. If pressing once doesn't work, press a few more times.

15. Log out of your Particle account. To do so, type `particle logout` in your computer's shell application.

What Did You Do, and How Did You Do It?

With a real-life IoT application, you seldom connect a computer to a smart device. Think about an air-quality sensor on a busy city street. To share its readings with the central station, the sensor connects to a Wi-Fi or to a mobile phone network. Rarely do you see someone standing on the street, plugging a laptop into the sensor's USB port. Once in a while, someone does this in order to diagnose a problem and repair the sensor. But, in general, the connection between computers and the sensor is wireless.

In Part 4 of this chapter, you forged a direct, wired connection between the Photon 2 and a laptop computer. You did this to get practice for occasions in which a wired connection is useful or necessary.

Talking Directly to the Photon 2

In Part 3, the lines of communication are almost the same as the ones in Part 1. The only change is the order in which things take place. (See Figure 2.18.)

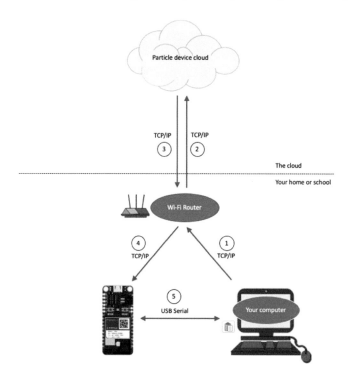

Figure 2.18: Computer-to-device communication.

Your computer uses TCP/IP to compose the code and instruct Particle to send that code to your Photon 2. The Particle cloud uses TCP/IP to flash the code onto your Particle 2 device.

In the code, the text `Serial.println` tells the Particle 2 to send information along its USB cable. The information to be sent is `Time.format()`, which is device-speak for the current time.

In the shell application on your computer, the command

```
particle serial monitor
```

tells your computer to display any information that's sent along the USB cable.

Part 4: The Particle Console

What you need:

- Photon 2, USB cable, breadboard, and optional antenna
- Access to a computer

Figure 2:19: The Console icon.

What to do:

1. Flash the following code to your Photon 2.

```
void setup() {
}

void loop() {
    Particle.publish("Traffic Light", "Green");
    delay(5000);
    Particle.publish("Traffic Light", "Yellow");
    delay(1000);
    Particle.publish("Traffic Light", "Red");
    delay(5000);
}
```

In this code, your device repeatedly executes `Particle.publish` commands. The word `publish` means "tell the Particle cloud that something just happened." The thing that just happened is called an *event*.

2. In the lower-left corner of the Web IDE, click the Console icon. (See Figure 2.19.)

When you click the Console icon, your web browser
takes you to a page of the Particle device cloud.

3. Look along the left side of the page to make sure you're
viewing the Console's Events tab. (See Figure 2.20.)

When you select the Events tab, the console shows you
each of the events that your device is sending to the
Particle device cloud. (See Figure 2.21.)

Figure 2.20: The Console's Events tab.

Events

NAME	DATA	DEVICE	PUBLISHED AT
Traffic Light	Green	Photon_2_A	6/22/23 at 2:10:00 pm
Traffic Light	Red	Photon_2_A	6/22/23 at 2:09:55 pm
Traffic Light	Yellow	Photon_2_A	6/22/23 at 2:09:54 pm
Traffic Light	Green	Photon_2_A	6/22/23 at 2:09:49 pm
Traffic Light	Red	Photon_2_A	6/22/23 at 2:09:44 pm
Traffic Light	Yellow	Photon_2_A	6/22/23 at 2:09:43 pm
Traffic Light	Green	Photon_2_A	6/22/23 at 2:09:38 pm
Traffic Light	Red	Photon_2_A	6/22/23 at 2:09:33 pm
Traffic Light	Yellow	Photon 2 A	6/22/23 at 2:09:32 pm

Figure 2.21: A list of the most recent events.

According to the console, the Photon 2 mimics a quickly-changing traffic light.
The light starts by being green. After only five seconds, the light turns yellow.
Then, after only one second, the light turns red. For more realistic traffic light
timing, you can change the numbers in the code's `delay` calls.

To give real meaning to the messages "Green", "Yellow", and "Red", you can
experiment with the Photon 2's status LED. Proceed to Step 4.

4. Flash the following code to your Photon 2:

```
LEDStatus status;

void setup() {
    status.setActive(LED_PRIORITY_IMPORTANT);
```

```
}

void loop() {
    Particle.publish("Traffic Light", "Green");
    status.setColor(RGB_COLOR_GREEN);
    delay(5000);

    Particle.publish("Traffic Light", "Yellow");
    status.setColor(RGB_COLOR_YELLOW);
    delay(1000);

    Particle.publish("Traffic Light", "Red");
    status.setColor(RGB_COLOR_RED);
    delay(5000);
}
```

When the code runs, your device's status LED changes color the way a traffic light does. (If only small insects would obey traffic signals!) Whenever the light changes, the device sends an update to the Particle console.

What Did You Do, and How Did You Do It?

An air-quality sensor sends readings to a central monitoring station. A heart-rate monitor sends a runner's pulse rate to the runner's coach. An accelerometer sends safety warnings to an automobile driver's phone. In the same way, your Photon 2 sends news of its events to the Particle cloud.

Sending Information to the Cloud

Figure 2.22 shows the exchange of information in this section's example. To keep Figure 2.22 uncluttered, we don't show the role of the router. And, since all communication uses the TCP/IP protocol, we label the arrows with nothing but numbers.

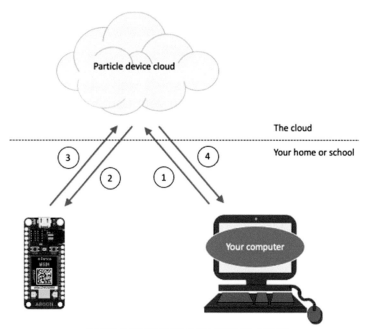

Figure 2.22: Capturing the device's events.

Here's what happens along each of the figure's arrows:

1. With instructions in Particle's Web IDE, your computer tells the Particle cloud to flash the code in Part 4.

2. The Particle cloud flashes the code to your device.

3. Your device publishes an event to the cloud (an event like `"Traffic Light"`, `"Green"`).

In computing terminology, the word *event* has a special meaning.

- An event is something that happens.
- A *source* initiates the event, and one or more *targets* receive notification of the event.
- The targets don't have to be waiting idly for the event to occur. The targets can be running other code (code having little to do with the event) while they listen for notifications.

In this section's example, the event is your device's executing a statement like

```
Particle.publish("Traffic Light", "Green");
```

Your device is the event's source. The Particle cloud (the event's target) handles input from users all over the world, So the cloud isn't waiting idly for your device to publish events. The cloud's computers are performing lots of other tasks.

When the cloud receives notification of your event, the cloud updates your console's web page, and another event occurs. For this new event, the source is the Particle device cloud, and the target is your computer.

4. The cloud publishes a change in your console's web page to your computer. Your computer responds by showing the change on your computer's screen.

Part 5: Using Node-RED

What you need:

- Photon 2, USB cable, breadboard, and optional antenna
- Access to a computer

What to do:

1. Launch your computer's shell application. (See Part 3, Step 2.)

2. Type a command in the newly-opened shell application window:

If you run Windows, type

```
npm install -g --unsafe-perm node-red
```

If you run macOS or Linux, type

```
sudo npm install -g --unsafe-perm node-red
```

Doing this will install Node-RED software on your computer.

3. Close and then reopen your computer's shell application. In the new shell application window, type

```
node-red
```

This command launches the Node-RED application on your computer. You see some `Welcome to Node-RED` text in the command window, but no additional windows will open. (See Figure 2.23.) The Node-RED application is making its own website on your computer.

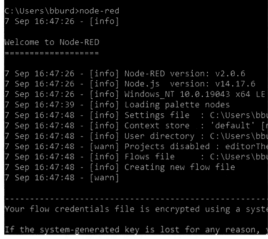

4. In a web browser window, visit http://localhost:1880.

The Node-RED window appears in your browser. (See Figure 2.24.)

Figure 2.23: Launching Node-RED.

The list of items on the left side of the page is called the *palette*. Each of the items (labeled *inject*, *debug*, *complete*, and so on) in the palette is called a *node*. In this set of steps, you'll be dragging nodes onto the big, white area that consumes most of the Node-RED screen. This big, white area is called the *flow-builder*.

Node-RED doesn't automatically come with any nodes that are specific to Particle devices. So, you must add some Particle-specific nodes to Node-RED's palette.

Figure 2.24: Visiting Node-RED in your web browser.

5. Click the hamburger icon (three vertical lines) in the upper right corner of the Node-RED window. In the resulting list of menu items, select Manage Palette. (See Figure 2.25.)

When you do, Node-RED shows you a User Settings panel with two tabs, labeled Nodes and Install. (See Figure 2.26.)

6. Select the Install tab.

7. In the Search field, type *particle*. (See Figure 2.26.) The panel shows you some collections of nodes.

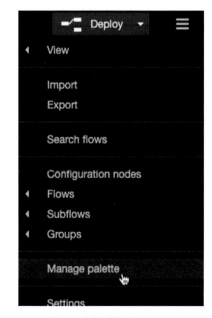

Figure 2.25: The Manage Palette menu item.

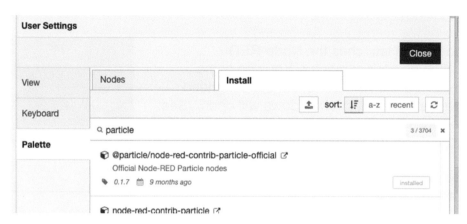

Figure 2.26. The User Settings panel.

8. In the list, look for @particle/node-red-contrib-particle-official. Click the Install button next to that list item.

   As a result, Node-RED installs the Particle-specific nodes.

9. Click the Close button at the top of the User Settings panel.

10. Scroll down to the bottom of the palette.

   Notice the nodes labeled *publish*, *subscribe*, *variable*, *function*, and *particle api*. These are the Particle-specific nodes. (See Figure 2.27.)

   In this section, your Node-RED application will get information from the Particle cloud. Node-RED can't do that without first getting permission. To grant that permission, you create authentication information in the Particle Console, and copy that information to Node-RED. Here's how you do it:

11. From the Particle Web IDE page, visit the Console. (See Figure 2.19.)

12. On the left side of the Console, select the Authentication tab. (See Figure 2.28.)

13. In the top-right corner of the Particle Console, click the NEW CLIENT button. (See Figure 2.29.)

14. In the resulting dialog box, select Two-Legged Auth (Server). Then type a name for your client, and click the GET CLIENT ID AND SECRET button. (See Figure 2.30.)

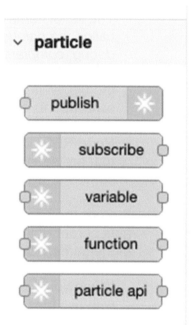

Figure 2.27: Particle nodes on the Node-RED palette.

Figure 2.28: The Authentication tab in the Particle Console.

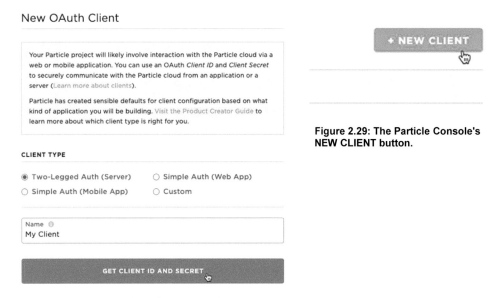

New OAuth Client

Your Particle project will likely involve interaction with the Particle cloud via a web or mobile application. You can use an OAuth *Client ID* and *Client Secret* to securely communicate with the Particle cloud from an application or a server (Learn more about clients).

Particle has created sensible defaults for client configuration based on what kind of application you will be building. Visit the Product Creator Guide to learn more about which client type is right for you.

CLIENT TYPE

◉ Two-Legged Auth (Server)   ○ Simple Auth (Web App)
○ Simple Auth (Mobile App)   ○ Custom

Name ⓘ
My Client

GET CLIENT ID AND SECRET

Figure 2.29: The Particle Console's NEW CLIENT button.

Figure 2.30: Creating a client.

After clicking the button, you see a box showing you the ID and the secret.

15. Copy these two values. Save them to a place where you'll be able to find them later and where other people won't be able to find them.

Saving the secret is particularly important because this is your only opportunity to see it. Later, if you lose the secret, there's no way to get it back.

Now you return to the Node-RED window, where you'll use the client ID and the secret.

16. Drag a *subscribe* node from the Particle section of the palette onto the flow-builder.

You want this subscribe node to listen for events from your Photon 2, so you have to tell Node-RED where to look for those events. Here's how:

17. Double-click the subscribe node that you've placed in the flow-builder.

When you do, Node-RED shows you a panel labeled Edit Subscribe Node. This panel is the *node configuration editor* or *node editor*, for short. (See Figure 2.31.)

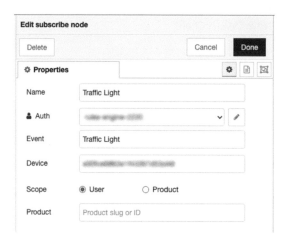

Figure 2.31: Editing the subscribe node.

18. In the node editor's Name field, type a helpful reminder phrase.

    In Figure 2.31, we type *Traffic Light*. That happens to be the same name that appears in the code in Part 4, but it doesn't have to be the same. Whatever name you type will eventually appear on the subscribe node in the flow-builder.

19. Type *Traffic Light* into the node editor's Event field. (See Figure 2.31.)

    In this step, you're telling Node-RED the name of the event it's subscribing to. What you type in the Event field *must* be the same as the name you used in the code in Part 4 of this chapter.

20. With Add New Particle Config appearing in the Auth field, click the pencil icon to the right of the field.

    When you do, an Edit Particle-Config Node panel appears. (See Figure 2.32.)

Figure 2.32: The Edit Particle-Config Node panel.

21. In the Edit Particle-Config Node panel's fields, paste the Client ID and Client Secret that you copied in Step 15.

22. Click Update to save your changes and dismiss the Edit Particle-Config Node panel.

Once again, Node-RED displays the node editor. (See Figure 2.30.)

In Part 4 of this chapter, you create an event named Traffic Light, so ...

23. In the node editor, make sure that the User radio button is checked.

Before leaving the node editor, notice the Delete button in the editor's upper left corner. If you wanted to get rid of the subscribe node, you'd double-click the node and then click this Delete button. But, for now, don't click the Delete button.

24. Click Done to dismiss the node editor.

You now have a node that will receive the Traffic Light events published by your device. In the flow-builder, this node's label is now Traffic Light.

You want another node that displays these events.

25. Drag a *debug* node from the common section of the palette onto the flow-builder.

26. Double-click the flow-builder's new debug node.

This opens the node editor for the debug node.

27. In the node editor, make sure that the node's Output is msg.payload and that the Debug Window checkbox is checked.

Take a moment to look at the flow-builder, and notice the msg.payload label on the face of that Debug node.

28. Click Done to dismiss the node editor.

In the flow-builder, notice the little circles on the sides of your two nodes. These circles are called *connectors*. The Traffic Light node's connector is on that node's right side, and the msg.payload node's connector is on that node's left side.

29. Drag your mouse from one connector to the other.

When you do, you see a line going from one node to the other. (See Figure 2.33.) Events received by the Traffic Light node will be sent to the debug (msg.payload) node.

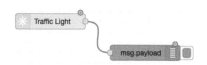

Figure 2.33: Connecting two nodes.

(If, at any time, you want to remove a connection, shift-click one of the nodes' connectors and drag the line away from the node.)

You're almost ready to display your device's Traffic Light events in the Node-RED window.

30. Use the USB cable to plug your device into a power source. Make sure that the Photon 2 is running one of the programs in Part 4.

31. Click the Deploy button in the upper-right corner of the Node-RED window.

When you do, the Debug Messages panel appears along the right side of the Node-RED window. See Figure 2.34. (If you need to tease out this panel, look for an icon of a bug near the window's upper-right corner.) As your device publishes events to the Particle cloud, Node-RED displays those events in its Debug Messages panel.

What Did You Do, and How Did You Do It?

In this part of the chapter, you created a virtual wire between your Photon 2 to a piece of hardware that responds to events. Imagine that the Photon 2 is part of a real traffic light while Node-RED runs on a computer that monitors traffic signals. The computer may be miles from the traffic light. It may even be halfway around the world. A computer that listens for events is called a *client*. If you have three computers that monitor traffic signals, you have three different clients.

To understand the roles of the device, the Particle cloud, and Node-RED, think about a conversation whose parts are portrayed Figure 2.35.

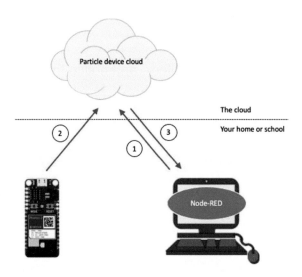

Figure 2.35: Sending events from the Photon 2 to Node-RED.

1. Node-RED sends a message to the Particle cloud asking to be notified about your device's events.

In response to this request, the Particle cloud asks "What client wants to be notified, and how do I know that the client has the right to be notified?" Fortunately, this question has a nice answer. In Steps 10 to 14, the Particle cloud created a Client ID and a Client Secret for you. The *Client ID* is like a username, and the *Client Secret* is like a password. In Step 19, you shared the ID and Secret with Node-RED. So, when Node-RED asks about your Photon 2's event, the Particle cloud recognizes the ID and the Secret. The cloud grants permission for Node-RED to be notified about your device's events.

It's important to remember that a Client ID identifies two things. In addition to naming a particular client, the Particle cloud remembers whose account created that Client ID. When Node-RED requests event notifications from the cloud, the cloud sends only those notifications that come from your own device. Other people's Particle devices play no role in this interchange.

2. Your device runs the code in Part 4, Step 4. When the device executes one of the `Particle.publish` statements, the device sends notice of that event to the Particle cloud. If you're watching the Events page of your Particle Console, you see each event listed on that page.

At this point, you may ask if the Particle cloud can be called a "client." And the answer is "Yes, but...." It's "yes" because the cloud is receiving information from your Photon 2. But in this game of events and responses, the Particle cloud is a special kind of player. The cloud doesn't consume your events. Instead, the cloud acts as a clearinghouse to gather your events and distribute them to "real" clients -- clients that analyze your data and draw conclusions from the data. So, in general, we don't refer to the Particle cloud as a client.

3. Your computer receives notification of the events gathered by the Particle cloud. Your computer relays these events to the subscribe node in the Node-RED flow.

In that flow, a connecting line sends events from the subscribe node to the debug (msg.payload) node. (See Figure 2.33.)

In Step 27, you checked Debug Window. Because of this, the information received by the debug node is echoed in the panel along the right side of the Node-RED screen. (See Figure 2.34.)

Part 6: Make Node-RED Work for You

What you need:

- Photon 2, USB cable, breadboard, and optional antenna
- Access to a computer

What to do:

1. Follow the instructions in Part 5 of this chapter.

2. Drag a *function* node from the Node-RED palette to the form-builder.

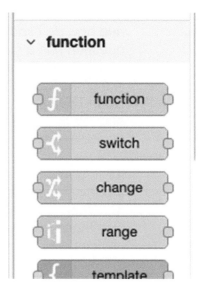

Figure 2.36: The function node in the palette's function section.

   Your Node-RED palette has at least two nodes labeled *function*. One of them belongs to the palette's Particle section. Oddly enough, that's not the one you want. The one you want is in a section of the palette named *function*. (See Figure 2.36.)

3. Shift-click the little circular connector on the left side of the msg.payload node, and drag the connecting line to the left side of the function node.

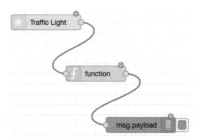

Figure 2.37: The function node acts as a go-between.

   Doing so deletes the direct connection between these two nodes.

4. Draw a connection from the right side of the function node to the left side of the msg.payload node.

   Now you have a flow with three nodes. Messages sent from the Traffic Light node will be modified by the function node and then sent on to the msg.payload node. (See Figure 2.37.)

5. Double-click the function node to reveal its configuration editor.

   A function node's editor has four tabs -- Setup, On Start, On Message, and On Stop. (See Figure 2.38.)

Figure 2.38: The function node editor.

6. In the Edit Function Node panel, select the On Message tab.

7. In the space below the row of tabs, type the following code:

```
if (msg.payload == "Green")
    msg.payload = "Go"
else
    msg.payload = "Stop"
return msg;
```

Figure 2.39: The messages from your function node.

8. Click Done to dismiss the function node editor.

9. Plug the Photon 2 into a power source. Make sure that the device is running one of the programs in Part 4.

10. Click the Deploy button in the upper-right corner of the Node-RED window.

   When you do, the Debug Messages panel repeatedly displays "Stop" and "Go". (See Figure 2.39.)

What Did You Do, and How Did You Do It?

In Part 5, the subscribe node gets the words "Green", "Yellow", and "Red" directly from the Photon 2, and passes these words straight to the debug (msg.payload) node. That's why Node-RED's Debug Messages panel displays the words "Green", "Yellow", and "Red".

But here in Part 6, you place an additional node between the subscribe node and the debug node. That additional node changes the words before sending them on to the debug node. In particular, the instructions in Step 7 change "Green" to "Go" and change everything else to "Stop". With that additional node in the middle, the original color words never reach the Debug Messages panel. Instead, the Debug Messages panel receives the instruction words "Go" and "Stop".

When you drive a car, your brain acts like that function node in the middle of the Node-RED flow. You see a traffic light's colors, and you translate those colors into explicit commands for vehicles and pedestrians.

Part 7: Build a Tiny Website

What you need:

- Access to a computer

What to do:

1. If you run Windows, open a Command Prompt window and type the following lines:

```
mkdir %homepath%\simplepage
cd %homepath%\simplepage
npm init
```

If you have a Mac, open the Terminal app and type

```
mkdir ~/simplepage
cd ~/simplepage
npm init
```

When you do, your computer will prompt you for several values, such as a package name, a version, a description, and so on. Press Enter in response to each of these prompts. (By doing so, you're accepting all the default values.) The last of these prompts is

```
Is this OK? (yes)
```

Once again, press Enter.

2. With either Windows or a Mac, type the following shell command:

```
npm install express --save
```

Your computer should respond with a message like `added 50 packages, and audited 51 packages in 1s` and possibly some other text.

3. If you run Windows, type `notepad index.js`, and then press Enter.

If you have a Mac, type the following two lines (pressing Enter after each line):

```
touch index.js
open -e index.js &
```

In either case, your computer opens up an application in which you can enter text.

4. Paste the following text (exactly as it appears here) into the apps empty window:

```
// index.js
// Simple demonstration using Node.js and Express
// run at the command prompt with
// node index.js
// Visit at http://localhost:3000/HelloWorld

const express = require('express');
app = express();
const port = 3000;

app.get('/HelloWorld', (req, res) => {
  console.log("We have a visitor");
  res.send('Hello World From Node.js and Express');
})

app.listen(port, () => {
  console.log(`Example app listening for GET at
http://localhost:${port}/HelloWorld`);
})
```

5. Save your new text.

On most systems, you do this by selecting File->Save in the app's menu bar.

6. Return to your computer's shell application, and type the following line:

```
node index.js
```

If all goes well, your computer should respond with a message like `Example app
listening for GET at http://localhost:3000/HelloWorld`.

7. In a web browser, visit `http://localhost:3000/HelloWorld`.

When you do, your browser displays the words "Hello World From Node.js and
Express." Your tiny website has only one page, and that page contains only one
sentence. It may not be much, but it's a very good start.

8. Look once more at your computer's Command Prompt or Terminal window. In that
window, you see the words "We have a visitor."

The computer is reporting that you're serving up a web page.

9. Stop serving web pages. To do this, type Control-C in the Command Prompt or
Terminal window.

What Did You Do, and How Did You Do It?

Imagine that you're visiting your favorite website. You start by typing the site's URL in
your web browser's address field. After pressing Enter, your browser makes an HTTP
request.

The letters HTTP stand for *Hypertext Transfer Protocol*. Like any other protocol, HTTP is a set of rules to enable communication between two or more entities. An *HTTP request* is a collection of data that includes a URL, information about the web browser, a description of any content (whether it's text, sound, images, or something else), a return address, and other useful details. Among other things, the URL specifies the request's destination. Where should this request be sent?

The answer to the "where" question is called a *server*. A server receives the request and formulates a *response*. An outgoing response has much of the same information as an incoming request. The response has a destination, information about the server, and most importantly, a body. Typically, that body describes the text and images that you see when you visit a web page.

The request/response cycle doesn't end there. A response's body may contain links to other pages. When you click such a link, your web browser sends another request to get more content from a server. In turn, that server sends a response back to your web browser.

This brings us to the specifics of the Express framework. When you run *Express*, you create a server that runs on your own computer. Your server accepts requests and sends responses. In Step 4, the code

```
res.send('Hello World From Node.js and Express');
```

tells your server to respond to every request with the words `Hello World From Node.js and Express`. That's why, when you visit `http://localhost:3000/HelloWorld`, you see those words in the web browser's window.

But what kind of a URL starts with `localhost:3000`? Why not `http://springer.com` or `http://particle.io`? Web browsers recognize that the word `localhost` always refers to the same computer as the one running the browser. In essence, the word `localhost` means, "look for a server on this very machine." In this exercise, we run a browser and a server on the same computer. That way, you can learn about web servers without juggling two computers in two different locations.

In this section's URL, `3000` is a port number. You can think of a *port* the way you think about a television channel. A provider of television content can send programs along Channel 2, Channel 3, or in some locations, Channels 500 and 1000. You tune a television to whatever channel you want to watch. In the same way, your `localhost` server can listen for requests on ports 80, 443, and many other ports. In Step 4 above, you tell your server to listen on port 3000 for incoming requests. So, when you type `localhost:3000` in your web browser's address field, the browser sends a request to the expected port.

Check Your Understanding

1. With your Photon 2 in hand, identify as many parts of the device as you can.

2. How can you find your Device ID?

3. List some of the ways in which a microcontroller differs from a microprocessor.

4. List the ways in which a Photon 2 may communicate with other kinds of hardware.

5. When you flash code to a Photon 2, how many times does the device execute the `setup` function? How many times does the device execute the `loop` function?

6. What's wrong with the following line of code?

```
digitalwrite(D7, high);
```

Is this a compile-time error, a logic error, or some other kind of error?

7. Is anything wrong with the following lines of code? If so, what?

```
void loop() {
    digitalWrite(D7, HIGH);
}
```

If this code contains an error, is it a compile-time error, a logic error, or some other kind of error?

8. What is an event?

9. Describe the role of Node-RED in an IoT application.

10. What's the role of an HTTP port number?

Make More / Explore Further

1. Follow the steps in Part 2 of this chapter, and then disconnect the Photon 2 from its power source. What happens when you plug the device into a power source again?

2. Break the code in Part 2 by changing the word `digitalWrite` to the two words `digital Write`. At what point in the process does the Particle Web IDE tell you that you've made an error?

3. With the code in Part 2, change the first occurrence of the number `1000` to a smaller number. How small can the number be before you can no longer see the LED blink off and on again?

4. In a shell application window, log in to the Particle CLI as you did in Part 3 of this chapter. Connect a Photon 2 to the same computer, and try these shell commands:

a. `particle list`

b. `particle library list`

c. `particle library search Google`

To learn more about each of these Particle CLI commands, visit
https://docs.particle.io/reference/developer-tools/cli/.

5. Find your Photon 2 among many in the same room. To do this, click the Devices icon in the Particle Web IDE. Check the Particle Devices panel for the name of your device. (For example, the panel in Figure 2.13 lists devices with the names *barry_argon01* and *Barry_boron*.)

   a. After logging on to the Particle CLI, type the following command

      `particle nyan <device-name> on`

   where `<device-name>` is the name you found in Particle's Web IDE. What happens when you issue this command?

   b. Finish this exercise by typing

      `particle nyan <device-name> off`

   in the Particle CLI.

6. Modify the code in Part 4, Step 4 so that the status LED turns colors other than green, yellow, and red. To find out how to do this, search the web for information about Particle's RGB colors.

7. In the code in Part 4, Step 4, change all three occurrences of the name `"Traffic Light"` to `"Traffic Signal"`. After making that change, do whatever you have to do to get Parts 5 and 6 working again.

8. In Part 5 of this chapter's instructions, you connect a subscriber to a debug node. When you double-click the debug node, a panel to edit the node displays three checkboxes. Put a checkmark in the *system console* checkbox. Then dismiss the panel and click *Deploy*. What happens?

9. Modify the code in Part 6, Step 7 so that the word `Go` appears for both the green and yellow lights.

10. Visit a generative AI page such as ChatGPT, Google Bard, or GitHub CoPilot. Type a request to make the page write the code that you flashed in Part 2. If the page gives you code that's different from what you flashed in Part 2, try two things:

   • Flash the code that's created by the generative AI page to find out what it does.

   • Refine your request so that the AI page's code does the same thing as the code in Part 2.

11. Repeat the previous generative AI exercise for the code in Part 4,

12. In Part 7, Step 4, change the port number 3000 to 3001. Then stop and restart Express. See if you can visit in your web browser.

13. In Part 7, Step 4, change the `res.send` line as follows:

```
res.send('Hello World<p><button>Submit</button>');
```

After stopping and restarting Express, refresh the localhost page in your web browser. What do you see? What happens when you click the button?

14. In Part 7, Step 4, change the `res.send` line as follows:

```
res.send('<button onClick="alert(\'Hello\')">Submit</button>');
```

After stopping and restarting Express, refresh the localhost page in your web browser. What do you see? What happens when you click the button?

Summing Up

An IoT project begins when you put "smarts" in a strategic place. Your "smarts" may be a microcontroller, a microprocessor, or some other kind of computing equipment. The strategic place may be a common household device such as an oven or a refrigerator, but it may also be a public setting such as a hotel lobby or a busy highway.

To take advantage of your "smarts", you create a connection to a system with more computing power. The connection is typically wireless, and the target system is called the *cloud*. In turn, the cloud might pass selected data on to entities that make use of the data.

For example, a microcontroller might count the number of people in a hotel lobby at any time of the week. The microcontroller sends this information to a central station, which relays the information to the hotel manager's computer. The hotel manager uses this information to anticipate the hotel's staffing needs and adjust the employees' schedules according to those needs.

In this book's examples, a Photon 2 senses real-world conditions. The device sends data to the Particle cloud, and the cloud relays the data to an agent such as Node-RED.

Looking Ahead

This chapter is all about nuts and bolts. You make connections and watch lights blink, but you don't do anything useful. That won't last long. In Chapter 3, you create an app that keeps your private data secret - even on the open Internet. In Chapter 4, you create an app that connects with the San Francisco transit system. In Chapter 5, you construct a smart pizza oven. In Chapter 6, you track a biker's heartbeat. And the list goes on. Keep reading to explore some exciting applications of IoT.

CHAPTER 3

Securing IoT Data

This chapter covers
    Sensing light with a microcontroller
    Client server computing
    Encrypted communication
    Shannon Entropy

© The Author(s), under exclusive license to Springer Nature Switzerland AG 2025
M. McCarthy et al., *Concise Guide to the Internet of Things*,
Undergraduate Topics in Computer Science,
https://doi.org/10.1007/978-3-031-57342-2_3

The One-time pad provides unbreakable encryption.

"Our problem right now isn't that we don't know how to secure these devices, it's that there is no economic or regulatory incentive to do so." [1]

Bruce Schneier

In a case before the Supreme Court of the United States, Justice Louis Brandeis remarked "The right to be left alone – the most comprehensive of rights, and the right most valued by a free people". In his court opinion, he warned that future technological advances may give governments a simple way to monitor the private lives of citizens. See Olmstead v. U.S. (1928).

Can we use mathematics in such a manner that our devices communicate with us and with each other securely?

In this chapter, you build a circuit on a microcontroller that is able to sense illumination levels of light. Light sensing has a wide variety of use cases. It can be used to help secure a supply chain - has this shipping container been opened? It can be used to protect items in a museum - has this work of art been exposed to light for too long? A farmer may want to know the light levels her crops are exposed to in order to reduce water consumption. The list of possibilities goes on.

In this chapter, our primary concern is the communication and encryption of the data gathered by the sensor.

You will encrypt the light level data and pass it on to the cloud for storage. You will also build the cloud storage service that records the illumination levels to a log file. The cloud storage service will be untrusted and unable to decrypt the values it stores. This exemplifies a fundamental approach, using cryptography, for storing private data on the web. The data can be decrypted and made readable only by a holder of the appropriate key.

Part 1: Building the hardware and firmware to measure light

What you need:

- Photon 2 microcontroller
- Phototransistor
- 220-ohm resistor
- Jumper wire
- Particle IDE

What to do:

1. Hold the breadboard so that row 1 is away and row 30 is near (on the bottom).

2. Place the Photon 2's bottom on row 26 of the breadboard.

3. The device's top will now cover row 7.

4. Be sure that the writing on the device is right side up.

5. Place the long leg of the phototransistor in row 5 (on the left of the device).

6. Place the short leg of the phototransistor in row 10 (3V3).

7. Place a 220-ohm resistor in row 5 and row 12 (GND).

8. Place a jumper wire in row 5 and row 13 (A0). See Figure 3.1.

9. Provide power to your device and flash the code from Figure 3.2 to your device. This code may also be found at this URL:

https://github.com/sn-code-inside/guide-to-iot/blob/main/Ch03_code/LightMonitor

10. Run the command `particle serial monitor` on the command line interface.

```
particle serial monitor
```

11. Test your system by changing your lighting and monitoring the numeric light values on the command line interface. These numeric values should change as you vary the light levels around your Particle device.

Figure 3.1 A microcontroller wired to record light levels

```
// File name: LightMonitor
// View output from the command line with
// particle serial monitor

int photoResistor = A0;
int analogValue;

unsigned long loop_timer;

void setup() {
  Serial.println("Simple setup complete");
  loop_timer = millis();
}


void loop() {
    if(millis() - loop_timer >= 1000UL) {
        loop_timer = millis();
        analogValue = analogRead(photoResistor);
        Serial.printlnf("AnalogValue == %u", analogValue);
    }
}
```

Figure 3.2 Firmware to read light levels with a phototransistor

What Did You Do, and How Did You Do It?

In the firmware of Figure 3.2, we read light levels in a loop. We will soon see why the body of the `if` statement will execute once every second. Within the `if` statement body, we read the analog value and display the result to the console.

Note that there is an alternative approach to writing this loop structure. One way we might have written the firmware is with the following program structure:

```
loop() {
  // code to read the analog signal
  // code to print the value read
  delay(1000);
}
```

This will also work and is easier to understand. We like "easy" if we can get it. We are still reading the light levels every second but we are relying on the `delay(1000)` call to stop the processor for a 1 second (1000 milliseconds) pause. This stopping of the processor, however, is not always a good idea. The operating system code in the Photon 2 has work to do and we are stopping everything for a full second.

In Figure 3.3, we focus our attention on the logic found in Fig. 3.2.

```
unsigned long loop_timer;

void setup() {
  // do setup work
  // copy the current time to the loop_timer variable
  loop_timer = millis();
}

void loop() {
    // Millis() is growing and loop_timer is not.

    if(millis() - loop_timer >= 1000UL) {
        // capture the new time in loop_timer
        loop_timer = millis();
        // do here what needs done every 1 second
        // :
    }
}
```

Figure 3.3 Providing code so that the operating systems has time to run

Initially, the variable `loop_timer` is set to the current time. This is done with a call to the `millis()` function inside the `setup` function – the `setup` function runs once.

The operating system will continually call the `loop()` function. We do not need to call it ourselves.

Inside the `loop` function, we test to see if the new current time minus the time in the `loop_timer` variable has grown greater than 1000 milliseconds. If that is true, it is time to read the light value by performing an `analogRead` on the phototransistor. We then set the `loop_timer` to the current time.

If the `if` statement is false (and it will be false far more often than not) then we will leave the `loop` function and give the operating system time to run. Take some time to study and understand this. This is a better approach and we will use this logic in the remaining examples in this text. In this case, we have to give up on "easy".

So far, we are sending light level readings to the command line console. We need to place those readings on the cloud.

Part 2. Building a cloud service to receive and log data

What you need:

- The setup from Part 1 of this Chapter
- Node.js as installed in Chapter 2
- Express as installed in Chapter 2

What to do

Our goal is for our device to store encrypted data on the cloud. We need a service that will receive the data and write the encrypted messages to a log file.

1. Create an empty directory and `cd` into it. This will be the location that you use to start up your `node.js` server and collect data in a log file:

```
mkdir Chapter03
cd Chapter03
```

2. Within the Chapter03 directory, create a file named `index.js` with the content found in the Chapter Appendix and named index.js. This code is also available at this URL:

https://github.com/sn-code-inside/guide-to-iot/blob/main/Ch03_code/index.js

3. The reader should spend some time reading over the comments in the code.

4. The program `index.js` needs to use the express framework. Within the Chapter03 directory, execute the following two commands. For the first command, it is fine to accept the defaults and just hit return when prompted.

```
npm init
npm install express
```

5. Within the Chapter03 directory, run the application by typing `node index.js` at the command line:

```
node index.js
```

6. Visit the application with a browser. In the browser, enter
http://localhost:3000/microcontrollerEvent

7. You should see the browser display "OK" and the console display "Browser visit".

What Did You Do, and How Did You Do It?

The file `index.js` is a server side web application written in JavaScript. It uses `Node` for its runtime environment. The reader should read over the code and its

documentation. Here, we will discuss some of the most important parts of this small
web server application.

The purpose of this application is to receive data and write that data to a log file. It
receives the data by way of an `HTTP post request`. It writes that data to a log file
and then responds to the caller with a status code. Consider the following code
snippet from `index.js`.

```
// Handle an HTTP POST request from a
// microcontroller.
app.post('/microcontrollerEvent', (req, res) => {

// announce a new visitor
console.log("\nNew Post request");

// Increment the visitor count
visitor++;
console.log("Visitor Number" + visitor);

// Get the time stamp of this visit.
var visitTimeStamp = Date.now();

// Access the encrypted data in JSON format from the request body
var encryptedDataInJSON = req.body;
```

At the top of this snippet, we specify that this block of code will process post
requests. More specifically, it will process post request that are addressed to
`http://localhost:3000/microcontrollerEvent`.

At the bottom of the code snippet, it extracts the data contained in the request. This
is done with the line of code:

```
var encryptedDataInJSON = req.body;
```

It takes the data, writes it to a file, and then reports a status message back to the
caller:

```
// Record this visit on the log file
stream.write("Visit: "+ visitor+ " Timestamp " + visitTimeStamp +
"," +
"Encrypted data: " + JSON.stringify(encryptedDataInJSON) + "\n");

// Send an HTTP response back to the caller.
// The encrypted message was received and stored.
// Send HTTP 200 OK.

  res.status(200).send('OK');
})
```

In the same file is code that will handle an `HTTP get` request. This code is provided as a courtesy. It does not perform any meaningful function. It is there simply to handle a browser visit (saying "OK"). Browsers visit with an HTTP get request.

```
app.get('/microcontrollerEvent', (req, res) => {
  // Our microntroller must use POST and not GET.
  // Here, we will serve up a simple OK to a browser.
  res.status(200).send('OK');
  console.log("Browser visit");
})
```

Try it out: Use a browser and visit: http://localhost:3000/microcontrollerEvent. You should see the browser display "OK".

When our microcontroller visits, it will do so with an `HTTP post` request. We will learn how to do that soon. For now, let's review some essential technologies.

World Wide Web

In this example, we are using the World Wide Web in our Agent Layer (see the model of IoT in Chapter 1).

The World Wide Web is made up of three technological components: URL's, HTTP, and standard data representations. We see all three of these components at work in this web application. Let's examine each of these.

URL's

On the web, URL's are used to address a particular service or resource and to specify a protocol. The URL used to address this service is:

http://localhost:3000/microcontrollerEvent

The protocol being used is `HTTP` and the address is:

`localhost:3000/microcontrollerEvent`.

HTTP

By examining the code in `index.js` or reading the documentation, we see that this particular service is designed to handle either `HTTP get` or `HTTP post` requests. Let's examine what this means.

HTTP is a standard `request and response` protocol. The HTTP standard defines the format of both the request message and the response message. One request message might contain the verb `get`. Another request message might contain the verb `post`. As we have seen, these may be handled differently by the same service.

As was noted, in this particular service (index.js), real processing only occurs if the service is visited with a `post` request. The client of this service will send an `HTTP` `post` message along with a JSON string, e.g., `{"encryptedData":"abcdefghijk"}`. The service, `index.js`, when visited with a post request, will simply add a time stamp to the request and store the JSON string received from the client into a log file named `MicrocontrollerLogger.txt`.

Standard Data Representations

The standard data format used by this web application is the JavaScript Object Notation (JSON). The web application assumes that the data that will arrive is in this format.

The following are four examples of possible JSON strings. The last example shows that a value in a name value pair may be numeric. One example is actually invalid. Can you find it? The reader should validate each of these strings using a JSON validator. See `https://jsonlint.com/`

```
{"id": "007"}
{"encryptedData":"bacd03saq"}
{"name": "Mike","name": "Barry"}
{"name": "Kieran","id": 862}
```

To see a formal description of JSON messages, see `http://www.json.org`.

Our web application uses the line of code:

```
console.log("Encrypted value = " +
encryptedDataInJSON.encryptedData);
```

Note the use of the name `encryptedData` in this line of code. That implies that the web application expects to receive a JSON string formatted in the following way:

```
{"encryptedData":"abcdefghijk"}.
```

In this example, the name used in the JSON message must match the name used in the code. That is, we need to use the string `encryptedData` in both the code and the message.

Proper Use of HTTP

Our use of `post` for this data storage web application rather than `get` is an important design decision. The `HTTP` `get` is meant to be used by requests that simply want to fetch a particular resource, e.g., a web page marked up in the HTML format. The `HTTP` `post` is meant to create or update a resource.

We could have easily built this web application to handle the update messages from the microcontroller with `get` requests rather than `post` requests. This would work but would be an abuse of HTTP. Violating the standard reduces interoperability and ease of use. It makes it more of a challenge in figuring out exactly how the service behaves. HTTP servers define how `get` and `post` behave and clients should be able to assume that the HTTP verbs behave correctly - as they are described in the standard.

The Web of Things

We will continue to see how a web service can be incorporated into the Internet of Things (IoT). A device as simple as a microcontroller is quite capable of making `HTTP post` requests. In this way, the "Things" in the IoT become edge components of the World Wide Web. And, by careful and consistent use of web technologies, the IoT can become a part of the web - a Web of Things (or WoT).

Part 3. Programming a microcontroller to communicate with the cloud

What you need:

- The setup from Part 1 of this Chapter
- The setup from Part 2 of this Chapter

What to do:

So far, we have a microcontroller that is able to sense light and report values on the serial interface. We also have a web server that is running on our machine - ready to receive and log post requests. Before adding encryption, let's test our web service with a simple client running on a microcontroller.

1. Make sure that your web server code from Part 2 is running.

2. Visit your account at Particle.io and create a file named `SimpleMicrocontrollerHttpClient`.

3. Click the library icon on the left side of the Particle IDE. Search for the `HttpClient` library.

4. Include the `HttpClient` library into the `SimpleMicrocontrollerHttpClient` firmware. Do this by selecting the library and then the project.

5. Copy and paste the code from the Chapter Appendix named
    `SimpleMicrocontrollerHttpClient`.

    The code is also available at this URL:

    https://github.com/sn-code-inside/guide-to-
    iot/blob/main/Ch03_code/SimpleMicrocontrollerHttpClient

6. Before flashing this code to your Photon 2, change the IP address in the code to
    your own IP address. You should not use 'localhost' here. If you do, the
    microcontroller will attempt to visit itself. You will need to find the IP address on
    your system. On a MAC, try `System Preferences/Network`. On Windows, try
    the `Start Menu`, right click `Network` and look for `properties`.

7. After flashing your firmware, note the content of the log file -
    `MicrocontrollerLogger.txt`. This is a new file created in the same directory
    as `index.js`. The file contents should be changing as messages arrive.

8. Again, take some time to read the comments within the code of
    `SimpleMicrocontrollerHttpClient`.

What Did You Do, and How Did You Do It?

In `SimpleMicrocontrollerHttpClient` we wrote a simple HTTP client for a
microcontroller. Thus, we learned that microcontrollers can act as clients of the
World Wide Web. This is similar to the way that browsers act as clients of the World
Wide Web.

Within the `loop()` function, we use the same approach as shown in Figure 3.2 but
this time, we only execute the body of the if statement once every 5 seconds.

When the `doPostRequest()` function is called, the `doPostRequest()` function
assigns a particular path and a particular body to the request object. The path is
used to complete the URL and the body is used to carry the payload data to the
service.

The actual data that leaves the microcontroller and is transmitted to the server looks
something like the following:

```
POST /microcontrollerevent HTTP/1.1
Content-Type: application/json
A blank line appears here
{\"encryptedData\":\"Simple message\"}`
```

Note the `Content-type` header. In this way, the microcontroller informs the server about the format of the data that the microcontroller is sending. In this case, we are passing a message encode in JSON.

Note that a blank line appears after the HTTP headers but before the application specific data.

In the code, we see that the `http.post` method is called. This will cause the HTTP data (HTTP headers and body) to be written to the network and the message will be routed to our server. We are using a local machine but this server might exist anywhere on the internet.

Next, we want to consider two different ways that we could encrypt the messages that we send. We will start by using a one-time pad. The one-time pad is the only encryption scheme that has been proven to be secure.

Part 4. Encrypting the application layer with a One-time pad

We want to go beyond `SimpleMicrocontrollerHttpClient` and transmit more than a simple message. We want to transmit the sensed light values as well as a unique identifier for our microcontroller. In addition, we want to encrypt the data that we send so that the recipient may store the data but is not privy to its actual content. We are assuming that the service is untrusted but provides storage that we would like to use. Moreover, we want to store the data so that it can be processed with a simple text editor.

We want to implement a pipes and filter pattern on the microcontroller. See Figure 3.4. First, we will encrypt the data. Then, we will encode the encrypted data. Finally, we will transmit the encoded and encrypted data using HTTP.

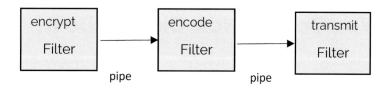

Figure 3.4 Pipes and Filter Pattern

What you need:

- The setup from Part 1 of this Chapter
- The setup from Part 2 of this Chapter

What to do:

1. Copy and paste the code of named `MicrocontrollerClientOTPEncryption` from the Chapter Appendix into the Particle IDE.

   The code is also available at this URL:

https://github.com/sn-code-inside/guide-to-iot/blob/main/Ch03_code/MicrocontrollerClientOTPEncryption

2. As you did before, add the Particle library named `HttpClient`. In addition, add the library named `Base64RK`. This library is needed for the encoding of messages into Base 64 notation.

3. Be sure to change the IP address in the code to point to your own machine.

4. Start your web service with the code from `index.js` from Part 2. That is, we are using the same server code that we created in Part 2. It simply stores JSON formatted data to a log file.

5. Flash `MicrocontrollerClientOTPEncryption` to your Photon 2.

6. Examine the file named `MicrocontrollerLogger.txt` and note the encrypted data.

7. Take a few minutes and read over the code and commentary found in `MicrocontrollerClientOTPEncryption`.

What Did You Do, and How Did You Do It?

In `MicrocontrollerClientOTPEncryption` we used a cryptographic algorithm called a one-time pad to perform the encryption. The central ideas behind the one-time pad are discussed next.

The One-time Pad

Suppose we want to encrypt the letter "A". The binary representation of "A" is 01000001. Everyone knows that. It is a common and well published coding scheme called ASCII and is found on most computers. We want to perform a mathematical operation on the bits 01000001 so that any reader will have a hard time figuring out that the content is the letter "A". The one time pad will do the trick.

First, we need a key. This key should be selected randomly. So, here, I will flip a coin 8 times. If I see a head then I will write a 1. If I see a tail, I will write a 0. After 8 flips, I got 00100111. That will be our key.

Next, we combine the key 00100111 with the "A" 01000001 in such a way that the result would be of no value to someone trying to read the letter but would be easily undone or decrypted by the holder of the key. The XOR operation fits the bill perfectly.

The XOR operation works like this. If we compute 0 XOR 0 we get a 0. Why? Because the XOR requires that, in order to get a result of 1, either of the bits must be 1 but not both. Otherwise, we get 0. So, 1 XOR 0 is 1. 1 XOR 1 is 0. And 0 XOR 1 is 1.

Let's try to do this with the letter "A" 01000001 and key 00100111.

```
"A"   01000001
key   00100111
==============
XOR   01100110
Using the XOR for one-time pad encryption
```

The value that we get after performing the XOR is called our ciphertext. You might notice that different keys will produce different ciphertexts. In fact, we could choose a key that produces any cipher text that we like.

In this example, if you do not have the randomly selected key and you are provided only with the ciphertext then you have no way to learn anything about the cleartext (the letter "A" in this example).

But can this encryption be easily undone or decrypted by someone in possession of the key? Sure, and it has to do with the way that the XOR works. Let's focus on a single bit of plaintext and a single bit of key.

```
   Plaintext    key    ciphertext        Apply key again to
                                             ciphertext
       0          0          0                    0
       1          0          1                    1
       0          1          1                    0
       1          1          0                    1
   Encrypting plaintext to ciphertext and back to plaintext with the
   same key
```

Here, we apply the XOR to the plaintext and the key to produce the ciphertext. And when we apply the XOR to the key and the ciphertext we get back the plaintext.

So, if we are given the ciphertext of 01100110 and if we know the key is 00100111, we can perform the following computation:

```
        ciphertext    01100110
        key           00100111
        ======================
        XOR           01000001
        Using the XOR for one-time pad decryption
```

The one-time pad is quite effective for the encryption of data. It has been shown to provide perfect secrecy. However, it has some significant drawbacks and these drawbacks prevent it from being widely used. For a one-time pad algorithm to work, cryptographers tell us that we need the following requirements:

1. The key must be randomly selected.

2. The key must be as long as the message itself.

3. The key may never be used again. That is why we call it a "one-time" pad.

4. The key must be kept secret.

In this chapter's example, to encrypt all of the data, we would need a random key as long as all of the data that we are sending to the server. And we would need to store that key and keep it secret somewhere. If we had that capability on our microcontroller, one wonders why we would bother storing all of the encrypted data on the cloud. Why not just store the cleartext locally and keep it secret?

The one time pad is an interesting example to study and it is used in highly sensitive scenarios. One could imagine a military ship going to sea and being equipped with a large key, perhaps on a thumb drive. The key could be used to encrypt messages back to headquarters. As long as the key is kept secret, is not reused, is randomly selected, and is as long as all of the messages it sends, we have perfect secrecy. The enemy will have no way to decrypt messages.

During the Cold War, the one-time pad was used by the Soviet Union to encrypt messages to its spies in the United States. Cryptographers working for the Venona project, part of the United States Signals Intelligence Service, were able to break many of these cyphers. The Soviet Union had made the fatal mistake of reusing some of the same keys.

Because of the four requirements surrounding the key material, the one-time pad is not in common use on the internet.

In Part 5 of this chapter, we will employ a far more practical algorithm. While we are not able to say that it provides perfect secrecy, as does the one-time pad, it does not have the same significant drawbacks and some variations of it appear to be exceptionally hard to break.

An important principle to keep in mind when studying cryptography (or, other types of security) is this: "Give the good players easy problems to solve and give the bad players hard problems to solve". We will return to data privacy in Part 5.

Base 64 Encoding

Another interesting feature found in the firmware of `MicrocontrollerClientOTPEncryption` is Base64 encoding. This is often used when we need to represent non-ASCII data in an ASCII form.

The American Standard Code for Information Interchange (ASCII) is a 7-bit code that provides binary encodings for 128 (2^7) different symbols. For example, the letter 'A' is encoded in ASCII as 1000001. In an eight bit byte (the standard byte size), the leftmost bit is set to 0 giving the letter 'A' as 01000001.

Many applications assume that their input is represented in ASCII. For example, a simple text editor will be able to read and correctly interpret 01000001 as the letter 'A'. The same text editor may not be able to interpret 8 bit bytes that begin with a 1 bit and are, therefore, outside of the range the ASCII code.

In `MicrocontrollerClientOTPEncryption`, our intention is to store the encrypted data onto a data file on the server. We would like the data to be viewable in a simple text editor. Our problem is that the encrypted data will often be in a form where the leftmost bit is 1 and is non ASCII. Base64 encoding is a way we can transform any series of 8 bit bytes to a series of legal ASCII values.

Base64 is used a great deal on the web. It may be used anywhere that textual data (ASCII) is expected but our intention is to store or transmit non-ASCII data. This non-ASCII data may require a very specific application to process correctly.

Base64 uses 6 bit chunks to represent 2^6 = 64 different symbols. These symbols include the 10 base ten digits (0,1,..9), the 26 upper case characters ('A','B',...,'Z'), the 26 lower case characters ('a','b',...'z'), the plus symbol ('+') and the forward slash ('/') symbol. A 65'th symbol, the equals sign ('='), has special significance in Base64.

Let's look at an example of the encoding of a series of bits in Base64.

Suppose our encrypted data looks like this: 100010101101010101011111

This is exactly 3 bytes or 24 bits of data.

Base 64 will treat this series of bits as four 6-bit chunks: 100010 101101 010101 011111

Base64 will represent each of these 6-bit chunks in an 8 bit byte of ASCII.

Consider the following partial table used by the base64 encoder and decoder:

```
Six bits     Base64 Encoding   ASCII interpretation of the encoded
                                              value

000000       01000001                        'A'
000001       01000010                        'B'
  :             :                             :
000100       01000101                        'E'
  :             :                             :
010000       01010001                        'Q'
  :             :                             :
010010       01010011                        'S'
  :             :                             :
010100       01010101                        'U'
010101       01010110                        'V'
  :             :                             :
011111       01100110                        'f'
  :             :                             :
100010       01101001                        'i'
  :             :                             :
101100       01110011                        's'
101101       01110100                        't'
  :             :                             :
111111       00101111                        '/'


Converting 6 bits to 8 bits of Base64 and interpreting the result in
ASCII
```

Going back to our example, how do we encode 100010 101101 010101 011111 into 4 ASCII bytes?

By consulting the table, we take the leftmost 6 bits (100010) and encode these as the 8 bit ASCII code for the letter 'i' (01101001). The next leftmost 6 bits (101101) are encoded as the 8 bit ASCII code for 't' (01110100).The next leftmost 6 bits (010101) are encode as the 8 bit ASCII code for 'V' (01010110). The next leftmost 6 bits (011111) are encode as the 8 bit ASCII code for 'f' (01100110).

So, our original bit stream 100010101101010101011111 is encoded in Base64 as 01101001011101000101011001100110. Note that this a longer series of bits. We are not being as efficient as we might like. But applications such as text editors will be able to display the string "itVf" with no problem. We are trading off some efficiency to gain interoperability. We often see this tradeoff on the World Wide Web.

Note that the length of the input data is exactly 3 bytes (24 bits) and 24 is evenly divided into 4 six-bit chunks. If the length of our input data is a multiple of 3 bytes, we will encode each of the 3 byte segments into exactly 4 bytes. Since our example maps perfectly into 4 bytes of encoded data, we do not need any Base64 padding. In general, every 3 bytes of unencoded data will map to exactly 4 bytes using Base64.

If the original data cannot be divided evenly into three byte segments, Base64 uses a padding scheme at the end of the encoded output.

For example, suppose we want to encode the letter 'A' in Base64. 'A' is represented as 01000001 and is only one byte long. Taking the leftmost 6 bits 010000 and doing a lookup on a Base64 table we find the 8 bits for the ASCII 'Q'. We are left with 01 that still needs to be encoded. We treat this as 01 and add four 0's giving 010000. A Base64 table lookup gives us another 'Q'. We add two bytes of padding at the end to tell the decoder that the original data was exactly two bytes short of a multiple of 3. Thus, The letter 'A' is encoded as QQ==. We use '==' to tell the decoder that we are 2 bytes short of a multiple of three. For another example, the two bytes "AA" would be encoded as QUE=.

Let's carry out this encoding. We begin with the two bytes "AA". On an ASCII file, these two bytes would appear this way: 0100000101000001. To process 6 bit chunks, we add two 0 bits to the end of the input and attempt to encode 010000 010100 000100.

Taking the leftmost 6 bits and using the Base64 table, we find the 8-bit encoding 01010001.This is a 'Q' in ASCII. Next, we take the next six bits from the input and get 010100. This maps to 01010101 in the table and is ASCII for the capital letter 'U'. Finishing, we perform a lookup on 000100 and get 01000101, the capital letter 'E'. We terminate the output with an ASCII byte for the single '=' because the input needs 1 additional byte to be evenly divisible by 3. The ASCII code for '=' is 00111101.

Thus, we encode 0100000101000001 as 01010001010101010100010100111101. Another way to say the same thing is that we encode "AA" as "QUE=".

Finally, note that the terms "encoding" and "decoding" should not be confused with "encryption" and "decryption". The terms "encryption" and "decryption" are concerned with data privacy. The terms "encoding" and "decoding" usually refer to simple transformations that anyone is welcome to do. There is no key material involved and the transformation is typically used to satisfy some application.

The conversion of binary data to Base 64 is clearly a mechanical process. And it would be a simple matter to write the code necessary to do this conversion. But since this is a popular activity, library routines are provided to do the work. Thus, in the case of `MicrocontrollerClientOTPEncryption`, we use the `Base64::encode()` function that is provided by a Base64 library.

Part 5. Encrypting the application layer with the Tiny Encryption Algorithm (TEA).

In Part 5, we want to perform the same general activity as in Part 4. However, in this part we will use the Tiny Encryption Algorithm (TEA) for the encryption [2]. As we will discuss below, TEA has some distinct advantages over the one time pad.

What you need:

- The setup from Part 1 of this Chapter
- The setup from Part 2 of this Chapter

What to do:

1. Copy and paste the code `MicrocontrollerClientTEAEncryption` from the Chapter Appendix into the Particle IDE.

    The code is also available at this URL:

https://github.com/sn-code-inside/guide-to-iot/blob/main/Ch03_code/MicrocontrollerClientTEAEncryption

2. Take some time to read over the code and the comments.

3. As in Part 4, you will need to add two Particle libraries: `HttpClient` and `Base64RK`.

4. Be sure to change the IP address in the code to point to your own machine.

5. Start your web service with the `index.js` code from Part 2.

6. Flash `MicrocontrollerClientTEAEncryption` to your Photon 2.

7. Watch your console and examine the file named `MicrocontrollerLogger.txt` and note the encrypted data.

What Did You Do, and How Did You Do It?

In `MicrocontrollerClientTEAEncryption` we used TEA for encryption.

TEA

The Tiny Encryption Algorithm (TEA) was created by David Wheeler and Roger Needham in 1994 at the University of Cambridge. It is fast and small in size and well suited to microcontrollers. Here we use a simple version of TEA. More advanced and more secure versions exist. See, for example, XTEA or XXTEA.

TEA is one of many symmetric key algorithms. Other important symmetric key algorithms are the Advanced Encryption Standard (AES) and the Triple Data Encryption Standard(3DES). These algorithms are called "symmetric" because they use the same key for encryption and decryption. TEA is not the only algorithm available for microcontrollers. AES, for example, is commonly found running on small devices.

Unlike the one-time pad, the TEA key need not be as large as the message and may be repeatedly used but, of course, must be kept secret.

The TEA key is 128 bits in size. In our example, the key is defined as four, 32-bit integers. Each integer is 32 bits in size and 4 X 32 bits = 128 bits.

Note that there are exactly two ways to set one bit. We can set a bit to 0 or to 1. And note that there are exactly 4 ways to set two bits. These four settings are 00, 01, 10, and 11. In fact, there are 2^n ways that we can set n bits.

This means that there are 2^{128} different TEA keys. 2^{128} is equal to 340,282,366,920,938,463,463,374,607,431,768,211,456. This is quite a large number and it would be exceptionally difficult for a bad guy to guess the correct key. Remember that a major principle in modern cryptography, and perhaps in all of security related matters, is to give the bad players hard problems to solve. Guessing the correct key in a key space of size 2^{128} is a very hard problem indeed.

The implementation details of the TEA algorithm are interesting but are well beyond the scope of this book. The interested reader can find the details in many books on cryptography.

Padding

TEA is a block cipher. This means that the clear text data is broken into blocks and each block is encrypted separately.

You may have noticed that the TEA encryption method works on two unsigned longs. These two unsigned longs represent a single block of data to be encrypted. Before we make calls to this method, we need to ensure that our clear text can be represented as complete pairs of unsigned longs. This is done in the code, prior to encryption, by adding padding to the clear text.

An unsigned long is 4 bytes of data. So, we need to pass an 8 byte block to the encryption method. But what if our clear text is less than 8 bytes or what if our clear text is not evenly divisible by 8 bytes? For this, we use padding - as described in "Applied Cryptography" by Schneier [4].

The padding scheme that is used in `MicrocontrollerClientTEAEncryption` works by adding the number of bytes used for padding to the end of clear text. Here are some examples:

Suppose that we have only 1 byte of clear text. We need 8 bytes to pass as a block to TEA. So, we add 7 bytes to the clear text. Each of these bytes (except the last) will hold a byte value of 0. The last byte will hold the number 7 – representing the number of bytes used for padding and the number of bytes that we need to remove after decryption.

Suppose we have 12 bytes of clear text. We need to pad to 16 bytes to form two 8 byte blocks. So, we add 4 bytes. The first three of which hold 0 and the last holds the value 4.

But what happens if we have exactly 16 bytes of clear text? We still need to add padding. This is because we need for the decryption logic to know exactly how much padding to remove. In this case, we will add an additional eight bytes of clear text before encrypting. Seven of those bytes will hold a 0 and the last will hold the number 8. The number 8 is the number of bytes to remove after decryption.

This scheme will work for clear text of any size. The number of padding bytes used will always be available to the receiver of the decrypted data. The reader is encouraged to study the code that adds and removes padding before and after encryption.

Symmetric Key Cryptography

There are two major types of cryptography in use today. These are symmetric key cryptography and asymmetric key cryptography. In this chapter, we have worked with two very important examples of symmetric key cryptography - the one-time pad and the Tiny Encryption Algorithm. In symmetric key cryptography, encryption and decryption use the same key.

Asymmetric Key Cryptography

In asymmetric key cryptography, two different keys are involved. One of these keys is typically made public or is available to anyone interested. This is the so called "public key". The other key is kept private and is called the "private key". If Bob wishes to send a private message to Alice, Bob would encrypt the message with Alice's public key and transmit the encrypted message to Alice. She will remove the encryption with her private key.

In asymmetric key cryptography, the message that Bob sends to Alice is often the value of a symmetric key. After the symmetric key is decrypted by Alice, Bob and her share the same key and may use symmetric key cryptography. This combining of asymmetric key cryptography with symmetric key cryptography is done for two reasons. First, symmetric key cryptography is much faster than asymmetric key cryptography and is therefore the preferred approach for large data sharing. Second, in order for Bob and Alice to use symmetric key cryptography, they must share the same key privately. This is accomplished by Bob encrypting the symmetric key to Alice's public key.

Shannon Entropy

In the one-time pad and TEA, we need the key data to be selected at random. In the examples provided, we did not use random numbers to create our keys. See the Make More/Explore further section for an exercise that asks you to include randomization in your code.

Nearly all of cryptography and, therefore, much of computer security involves the use of randomness. Each bit in a cryptographic key should be randomly generated. For example, if the bits in a one-time pad were predictable (not random and not surprising) then it might be a simple matter to learn the key and decrypt the data.

Consider the following stream of bits:

> 001001001001001001001001_

Now, if I told you that the next bit is a 0, would you be surprised? Of course not. Given this series of bits, the next bit is quite likely to be a 0.

In this case, we would say that the probability of the next bit being a 0 is close to 1. Given what we have seen of the prior bits it would be unsurprising to learn that the next bit is a 0.

Now, consider the following series of bits:

> 011010101101000000111010_

In this series of bits, there seems to be no obvious pattern. In fact, these bits were generated by flipping a coin. Honest coin flipping will produce the next bit as a 0 or a 1 with equal probability. You would be more surprised to learn that the next bit is a 0 in the second example than you would be to learn that the next bit is a 0 in the first example.

The amount of surprise has increased because the probability of the event is not close to 1 but is ½.

Let's consider another example.

Let's suppose that you are told that the United States and Canada have agreed to join and become one country. That would be quite a surprise because it is not very likely to occur. Is there a mathematical way to say that unlikely events are highly surprising?

We might make a (poor) attempt to define surprise this way:

$$S(e) = 1/p(e)$$

S(e) is the surprise associated with event e and p(e) is the probability that event e will occur. In this formula, the surprise associated with event e is inversely related to the probability of event e.

To some extent, this works. If the probability of an event is low, close to zero, then the amount of surprise is high.

But what if the probability is close to 1, the amount of surprise is also close to 1. For highly likely events, those with a probability close to 1, we want surprise to be near zero. So, this simple definition of surprise will not work.

A better approach would be to define surprise in the following way:

$$S(e) = \log_2(1/p(e))$$

How will this work? If the probability is close to zero then the surprise will be very high. Unlikely events are surprising. If the probability is close to one then the surprise will be close to zero. Events that we believe to be certain provide very little surprise.

Moreover, if we consider two independent events, we want the surprise to be additive. And this is what our formula provides:

$$S(e,f) = \log_2(1/(p(e)*1/p(f))) = \log_2(1/p(e)) + \log_2(1/p(f))$$

The logarithm function nicely converts the multiplication of probabilities (used to find the probability of two independent events) into addition.

So, if you hear of two unlikely events, the USA and Canada have agreed to a merger and the moon has just left its orbit, you are more surprised than if you heard about only one of these events. Unlike independent events in probability theory, surprise is additive.

In 1948, Claude Shannon [3], referred to by many as the "father of information theory", defined the information entropy of a data source as

$$H(x) = \Sigma\ p(x) * \log(1/p(x))$$

Which is equivalent to

$$H(x) = \Sigma\ p(x) * \log(p(x)^{-1}) = -\Sigma\ p(x) * \log(p(x))$$

The idea is to compute a sum over all possible events of the probability of the event times the amount of surprise associated with the event. If we choose the base 2 log, we get an answer in bits.

You might think of Shannon Entropy as the average amount of surprise associated with an event.

Let's do an example. Suppose we flip a fair coin. The probability of a head and the probability of a tail are both ½. So, we have p(head) = p(tail) = ½.

$$H(x) = \tfrac{1}{2} * \log_2(1/(1/2)) + \tfrac{1}{2} \log_2(1/(1/2)) = \tfrac{1}{2} * \log_2(2) + \tfrac{1}{2} \log_2(2) = \tfrac{1}{2} + \tfrac{1}{2} = 1 \text{ bit}$$

This coin flip will provide 1 bit of information. Half the time we will get a head and half the time we will get a tail. Each of these produces a surprise of 1 bit. And each of these occurs ½ of the time. The information entropy of the coin flip is thus 1 bit. So, on average, we expect 1 bit of surprise.

Now, let's suppose the coin is not fair. Suppose we know that a head has the probability of ¾ and the probability of a tail is ¼.

Before continuing, pause for a moment and ask yourself the following question. Which coin flip is less certain? It should be clear that flipping a fair coin has more uncertainty (and is more surprising) than flipping a biased coin. Let's compute the entropy of the unfair coin flip:

$$H(x) = 1/4 * \log_2(1/(1/4)) + 3/4 \log_2(1/(3/4)) = 1/4 * \log_2(4) + 3/4 \log_2(4/3) = .5 + .4147 = .9147$$

The average amount of surprise is .9147 bits.

So, flipping an unfair coin is less uncertain than flipping a fair coin. Said another way, we are more surprised when flipping a fair coin than an unfair coin.

In cryptography, when generating random numbers for keys, we want to maximize entropy. We want H(x) to be as high as possible.

Randomness is needed for security. But in a deterministic machine, true randomness may be hard to come by. We might need to reach out to the real world to capture some chaos.

It is interesting to note that an IoT based system, by providing randomness, is actively helping to secure the internet.

Suppose we took a photograph of a lava lamp with lava flowing this way and that (at random). It presents a cool looking display and looks great in a dorm room. We digitize the photograph and scramble (cryptographically hash) the result. We might use that result as a key. This key would have high entropy and each bit would have a probability of close to ½ of being a 1 and a probability of close to ½ of being a zero. Many lamps might be used and new photographs regularly taken. Such a system has been used for years to help generate random keys and help protect the internet. See, for example, the lava lamps used by CloudFlare.

In this short chapter, we are only able to touch on this fascinating and important subject. It is certainly a topic we should all be aware of. Cryptography will play an increasingly important role in the Internet of Things

Check Your Understanding

1. Modify the `LightMonitor` code in Figure 3.2 so that it only transmits messages to the serial monitor when the light level is below 10.

2. Modify the `index.js` code so that a <u>browser</u> visitor is informed about how a `POST` request from a microcontroller is designed to work. That is, inform the user about the functionality of this service for microcontrollers. This will serve as documentation for the service.

3. Modify the `index.js` code so that a `GET` request displays some HTTP headers to the console. You will need to research how to access these headers through the req object passed in on each visit.

4. Modify the `index.js` code so that a browser visitor is able to see the number of `POST` requests that have occurred.

5. Modify the `index.js` code so that a browser visitor is able to see the time of the last `POST` request.

6. Modify the `index.js` code so that a browser visitor is able to see the JSON data in the last `POST` request. This will include the Base64 encoding of the encrypted data.

7. Modify the `SimpleMicrocontrollerHttpClient` code so that the `POST` request are performed every 10 seconds rather than every 5 seconds.

8. Modify the `SimpleMicrocontrollerHttpClient` code so that it transmits a more elaborate JSON message. For example, transmit the message `{"Student":` `{"Name":"Fran","ID":1234}}`. Is this valid JSON? Use the validator discussed in the chapter to check it.

9. Modify the `MicrocontrollerClientOTPEncryption` code so that the key is much shorter. That is, change the key to "This must be truly random." Does the program still work? Explain why it does. Is this a correct usage of the one-time pad? Explain why it is not.

10. Examine the data in the log file that was generated by the one-time pad encryption (`MicrocontrollerLogger.txt`). How would this log file look if the key was as long as all of the data transferred and no parts of the key was ever reused?

11. Using the one time pad, encrypt the data 01111110 with the key 00110100.

12. Using the one time pad, decrypt the result of previous exercise using the key 00110100.

13. Consider a locked door in your home and the principle that we should "Give the good players easy problems to solve and give the bad players hard problems to solve". Does that principle apply to your locked door? Why or why not?

14. Use a full ASCII table (widely available online) and a full Base64 table (also widely available online), and show how the three ASCII characters "ABC" would be encoded in Base64.

15. Use a full ASCII table (widely available online) and a full Base64 table (also widely available online), and show how the four ASCII characters "ABCD" would be encoded in Base64.

16. Does it make good sense to encode ASCII text in Base64? Why or why not?

17. Suppose we take an image file and encode it in Base64. Can we view the image itself in a simple text editor? What would we see if we loaded the Base64 data into a text editor? Where would the '=' signs be located if they were needed by this file? What can we say about the file size of a Base64 file that has no '=' signs.

18. Modify the `MicrocontrollerClientTEAEncryption` code so that it uses the key 5,10,15,3. Does it still work? Why?

19. Which has higher Shannon entropy, a fair coin flip or a fair roll of a six sided die? Show your calculations.

20. Which has higher entropy, a fair roll of a six sided die or a roll of an unfair die – one whose probability favors a 6? A 6 on this unfair die has a probability of ½ and a roll of 1 through five each have probability of 1/10. Show your calculations.

Make More / Explore Further (Problems)

1. Modify the `LightMonitor` firmware of Figure 3.2 so that it maintains an average of the last 5 values read from the light. Initially, the last 5 light values are all zero. Only display a message to the console if a new light value arrives and this new light value differs from the average by 10.

2. Modify the `SimpleMicrocontrollerHttpClient` so that it does not make a `POST` request but makes a `GET` request instead. This is a violation of HTTP but is an interesting exercise. You will need to change the server code as well.

3. Working from the code in `MicrocontrollerClientOTPEncryption` and by using a generative AI tool, copy the one-time pad key to the server and have it perform decryption before storage. This is a JavaScript exercise.

4. In Figure 3.4 we used the pattern "Encrypt, Encode, Transmit". Would it have worked if we instead performed an "Encode, Encrypt, Transmit" approach? Why or why not?

5. Modify the `doPostRequest` function in `MicrocontrollerClientOTPEncryption` so that it generates an XML document rather than a JSON message. The server will now store a series of XML documents to the log file.

6. Do some online research. What business is CloudFlare in? What use does it make of its lava lamps?

7. Do you consider the lava lamps used by CloudFlare as an example of IoT? Why or why not? Be sure to take into account the system model from Chapter 1.

8. Use a generative AI tool (such as `ChatGPT`) to learn how to create random key data for the `MicrocontrollerClientTEAEncryption` example. Deploy this improved code to your microcontroller.

9, Ask a generative AI tool (such as `ChatGPT`) how padding works with a block cipher. Is the answer correct?

10 Working from the code in the `MicrocontrollerClientTEAEncryption` and by using a generative AI tool, copy the TEA key to the server and have it perform decryption before storage. This is a JavaScript exercise.

Summing Up

In this chapter we constructed a microcontroller circuit that senses light. We wrote the firmware needed to report illumination levels to the serial monitor.

We worked within a client server architecture using URL's, HTTP, and standard data formats. The reader should be convinced that the Internet of Things (IoT) may involve the World Wide Web and may often be thought of as a Web of Things (WoT). We also worked with two important symmetric key algorithms - the One-time pad and the Tiny Encryption Algorithm (TEA).

We learned that the One-time pad provides perfect secrecy but has significant practical limitations. We studied how the One-time pad works using the XOR operation.

We learned that algorithms like TEA are quite effective and can be run even on small devices. We discussed the how padding can be used to provide data of arbitrary size to a block cipher.

We learned the mechanics of the Base64 encoding algorithm and saw an example where its use is appropriate.

We saw how the pipes and filters pattern can be implemented on a microcontroller.

Finally, we studied some essential information theory and learned about entropy and its importance.

Looking Ahead

Security is a major issue in the IoT space and we will have occasion to visit the issue further in later chapters.

In the next chapter, we will leverage what we have learned here about the web and consider the design and usage of Application Programmer Interfaces (API's) in IoT. This is one way to make our IoT devices more intelligent and aware of their environment. For example, would it be cool to have your Particle device notify you if your train was approaching? We will do that in Chapter 4.

References

1. B. Schneier, (2020) "Schneier on Security", https://www.schneier.com/blog/archives/2020/06/analyzing_iot_s.html . Accessed June 2023
2. G. Coulouris, J. Dollimore, T. Kindberg, "Distributed Stystems Concepts and Design", 3rd ed. Addison-Wesley, 2001, pp. 276-277.
3. B. Schneier, "Applied Cryptography", 2nd ed. Wiley 1996, pp. 190-191.
4. C. E. Shannon, "A Mathematical Theory of Communication," Bell Systems Technical Journal, v. 27, n. 4, 1948, p. 393.

Chapter Appendix

```
// Guide to Internet of Things Chapter 3
// File name: index.js
// In order to execute this code, enter the CLI command
// node index.js
// Get requests from browsers will be acknowledged as a courtesy.
// A browser may visit with http://localhost:3000/microcontrollerEvent
// The main purpose is to handle HTTP POST requests to the following
URL:
// http://localhost:3000/microcontrollerEvent

// Each visit logs data to the file MicrocontrollerLogger.txt.

// Setup the express web server.
const express = require('express')
const app = express()

// The HTTP request will include JSON data.
// We need to parse JSON data.
app.use(express.json());

// Listen on TCP port 3000.
const port = 3000

// We will write data about each visit to a log file.
// So, we need access to the file system of this server.
// We will use {flags:'a'} because we want to append to the log file.
// If the file does not exist, it will be created.
// The file name is MicrocontrollerLogger.txt.
var fs = require('fs');
var stream = fs.createWriteStream("MicrocontrollerLogger.txt",
{flags:'a'});

// Set up a listener and display a note to the console.
app.listen(port, () => {
  console.log(`Logging encrypted data from POST visits to
http://localhost:${port}/microcontrollerEvent`)
})

// Used this variable to count visitors
var visitor = 0;

// Handle an HTTP POST request from a microcontroller.
app.post('/microcontrollerEvent', (req, res) => {

  // announce a new visitor
```

```
  console.log("\nNew Post request");

  // Increment the visitor count
  visitor++;
  console.log("Visitor Number" + visitor);

  // Get the time stamp of this visit.
  var visitTimeStamp = Date.now();

  // Access the encrypted data in JSON format from the request body
  var encryptedDataInJSON = req.body;

  // Show the time stamp and encrypted data on the console.
  console.log("Time:" + visitTimeStamp + " JSON Message: " +
JSON.stringify(encryptedDataInJSON));
  console.log("Encrypted value = " +
encryptedDataInJSON.encryptedData);

  // Record this visit on the log file
  stream.write("Visit: "+ visitor+ " Timestamp " + visitTimeStamp +
"," + "Encrypted data: " + JSON.stringify(encryptedDataInJSON) +
"\n");

  // Send an HTTP response back to the caller.
  // The encrypted message was received and stored.
  // Send HTTP 200 OK.

  res.status(200).send('OK');
})

app.get('/microcontrollerEvent', (req, res) => {
  // Our microntroller must use POST and not GET.
  // Here, we will serve up a simple OK to a browser.
  res.status(200).send('OK');
  console.log("Browser visit");
})
```

```
// Guide to Internet of Things Chapter 3

// File name: SimpleMicrocontrollerHttpClient


// This is a simple HTTP client that makes periodic visits on an HTTP

// server. It sends a message in JSON format using an HTTP POST
request.


// After flashing, to view the serial monitor messages enter
```

```
// particle serial monitor


// in a terminal command line interface.


// To compile this code, you must first choose Libraries

// and search for the HttpClient library in the Particle IDE.

// The library must be added to this project before flashing

// the code to the device.


// This #include statement was automatically added by the Particle IDE when

// the HttpClient library was included in this project.
#include <HttpClient.h>


// This program assumes a server is available and can receive

// HTTP Post messages such as:


// http://localhost:3000/microcontrollerEvent


// The Http headers are followed by a blank line.

// The next line (after the blank line) will contain

// a JSON string such as:


// {"encryptedData":"abcdefghijk"}



 // Define the http variable to be of type HttpClient.

 HttpClient http;


 // We always pass Http headers on each request to the Http server

 // Here, we only define a single header. The NULL, NULL pair is used
```

```
 // to terminate the list of headers.


 // The Content-Type header is used to inform the server

 // of the type of message that it will be receiving. Here,

 // we tell the server to expect to receive data marked up in

 // JSON.


 http_header_t headers[] = {

     { "Content-Type", "application/json" },

     { NULL, NULL }

 };


// Here we define structures to hold the request and the response
data.
// These are declared with types defined in the header file included
above.


 http_request_t request;

 http_response_t response;


 //A variable to hold the device unique ID

 String deviceID = "";


 // So we can avoid using sleep()

 unsigned long loop_timer;


 void setup() {


   // Specify the speed with which we will talk to the serial
interface.

   // The serial interface is associated with our shell or command
line
```

```
  // interface.

  Serial.begin(9600);


  // The IP address of the server running on our machine.
  // Do not use localhost. The microcontroller would attempt
  // to visit itself with localhost.
  request.ip = IPAddress(192,168,86,164);


  // Specify the port that our server is listening on.
  request.port = 3000;


  // get the unique id of this device as 24 hex characters
  // this value is unused in this firmware.


  deviceID = System.deviceID().c_str();


  // display the id to the command line interface
  Serial.println(deviceID);


  // find the time
  loop_timer = millis();
}


// Provided with a response, display it to the command line
interface.
void printResponse(http_response_t &response) {
  Serial.println("HTTP Response: ");
  Serial.println(response.status);
  Serial.println(response.body);
}
```

```
// Post a message to the server
void doPostRequest() {


  request.path = "/microcontrollerEvent";

  request.body = "{\"encryptedData\":\"Simple message\"}";


  http.post(request, response, headers);

  printResponse(response);
}
// Every 5 seconds, perform a POST request
void loop() {
  if(millis() - loop_timer >= 5000UL) {

      loop_timer = millis();

      doPostRequest();

  }

}
```

```
// Guide to Internet of Things Chapter 3
// MicrocontrollerClientOTPEncryption
// This microcontroller firmware demonstrates a simplified
// example of one-time pad encryption.

// The idea is to transmit messages to the server that are
// encrypted with a simplified one-time pad.

// Include header files for Base 64 and HTTP client classes.
#include <Base64RK.h>
#include <HttpClient.h>

// Define an http client object.
 HttpClient http;
```

```
 // Define a headers array holding two http_header_t objects.
 // Our request will include a JSON string. We inform the receiver
 // that it should expect to see JSON.
 http_header_t headers[] = {
     { "Content-Type", "application/json" },
     { NULL, NULL }
 };
 // Define an HTTP request object and an HTTP response object.
 // These objects hold the HTTP request and response.
 http_request_t request;
 http_response_t response;

// The photoresistor is on pin A0. Messages to the server will
// include values measured by the photoresistor.
int photoResistor = A0;

// We define a variable to hold the analog value.
int analogValue = 0;

// We define a variable to hold the device ID.
char deviceID[60];

// The analogValue and deviceID are to be transmitted over the
// network but kept private.

// Establish a loop timer to hold a value in milliseconds.
unsigned long loop_timer;

// Setup is performed once on start up.
void setup() {

    // We prepare to write to the serial port.
    Serial.begin(9600);

    // In the request object, set the IP address and port of the server
that
    // we will visit. This could be any IP address and port.
    request.ip = IPAddress(192,168,86,164);
    request.port = 3000;

    // The deviceID is found by calling System.deviceID().c_str();
    // Here, we copy the device ID into the character array named
deviceID.
    strcpy(deviceID,System.deviceID().c_str());

    // For debugging, write to the console over the serial port.
    Serial.printlnf("This device has the id %s", deviceID);

    // Set the time to the current time
    loop_timer = millis();

 }
```

```
 // Provided with a response, display it to the command line
interface.
 // This procedure is called after a post request receives a response.
 void printResponse(http_response_t &response) {
   Serial.println("HTTP Response: ");
   Serial.println(response.status);
   Serial.println(response.body);
 }

 // This procedure is called to send encrypted data to the
 // server.
 void doPostRequest(char encryptedByteArrayBase64[]) {

   // Provide the path to the service
   request.path = "/microcontrollerEvent";

   // Build the JSON request
   char json[1000] = "{\"encryptedData\":\"";
   // Add the encrypted data
   strcat(json,encryptedByteArrayBase64);
   // add the JSON ending
   strcat(json,"\"}");
   // assign the JSON string to the HTTP request body
   request.body = json;
   // post the request
   http.post(request, response, headers);
   // show response
   printResponse(response);
 }

 void loop() {

  // every 5 seconds do a post to the server
  if(millis() - loop_timer >= 5000UL) {

    // read the photoresistor
    analogValue = analogRead(photoResistor);
    // for debugging, view the value on the local console
    Serial.printlnf("AnalogValue == %u", analogValue);

    // This clear text data will be kept local to the device.
    char clearText[80];

    // Use a built in procedure to copy a formatted string to the char
array clearText.
    sprintf(clearText, "Microcontroller ID = %s Light sensor value =
%d", deviceID, analogValue);

    // For debugging, display the clear text.
    Serial.printlnf("Clear text: %s",clearText);
```

```
    // determine its length of the string holding the clear text.
    int lengthOfClearText = strlen(clearText);

    // Allocate space and move clear text into a byte array
    byte *clearTextBytes = (byte *)calloc(lengthOfClearText,
sizeof(byte));
    for(int t = 0; t < lengthOfClearText; t = t + 1) clearTextBytes[t]
= (byte) clearText[t];

    // The key is local to the device. In a real application, the key
would be random
    // and long enough to encrypt all of the data transmitted over
time. No part of the
    // key would ever be reused. In this simplified example, we reuse
the same key.

    char key[] = "This must be truly random, as long as the clear text
and used only once.";

    // determine its length
    int lengthOfKey = strlen(key);

    // Allocate space and move the key text into a byte array
    byte *keyBytes = (byte *)calloc(lengthOfKey, sizeof(byte));
    for(int t = 0; t < lengthOfKey; t = t + 1) keyBytes[t] = (byte)
key[t];

    // Encrypt the clear text bytes using a one time pad and the key.
    // The resulting bytes are the cipher text.
    byte* cipherTextBytes =
encrypt(clearTextBytes,lengthOfClearText,keyBytes,lengthOfKey);

    // Here, we check if the encryption is working.
    // Decrypt the result into an array of bytes (for testing).
    byte *decryptedClearTextBytes =
decrypt(cipherTextBytes,lengthOfClearText,keyBytes,lengthOfKey);

    // Extract the bytes from the byte array into a newly allocated
string
    char *decryptedClearText = (char *)calloc(lengthOfClearText + 1,
sizeof(byte));
    for(int k = 0; k < lengthOfClearText; k = k + 1)
decryptedClearText[k] = (char) decryptedClearTextBytes[k];

    // add the null byte back. The null byte was not part of the data
that was encrypted
    decryptedClearText[lengthOfClearText +1] = '\0';

    // Show the result for testing
    Serial.printlnf("Decrypted clear text: %s",decryptedClearText);

    // Free up the memory that was allocated for the arrays.
```

```
   free(clearTextBytes);
   free(keyBytes);
   free(cipherTextBytes);
   free(decryptedClearTextBytes);
   free(decryptedClearText);

   // We want to store the encrypted data on the server in Base 64.
   // Encode a byte array in Base64.
   // First, use a library to learn the size of the base 64 data.
   size_t sizeOfBase64 = Base64::getEncodedSize(lengthOfClearText,
true);

   // Allocate memory to hold the base 64 string.
   char * encryptedByteArrayBase64 = (char *)calloc(sizeOfBase64,
sizeof(char));

   // Use a library to perform the encoding.
   // The one-time pad uses an xor which does not change to size of
the cipher text.
   // That is, the clear text size will equal the cipher text size.
   Base64::encode(cipherTextBytes, lengthOfClearText,
encryptedByteArrayBase64, sizeOfBase64, true );

   // For debugging, view the base 64 data.
   Serial.println(encryptedByteArrayBase64);

   // Make an HTTP Post request along with JSON containing the
encrypted data.
   doPostRequest(encryptedByteArrayBase64);

   // Free memory.
   free (encryptedByteArrayBase64);

   // reset loop_timer
   loop_timer = millis();
   }
 }

// One time pad encryption.
// For each key byte and clear text byte, perform an xor operation.
// In c or c++, this is the ^ symbol.
byte* encrypt(byte clearTextBytes[], int lengthOfClearText, byte
keyBytes[], int lengthOfKey) {

    int keyIndex = 0;
    // Allocate room for the encrypted result.
    byte *cipherBytes = (byte *)calloc(lengthOfClearText,
sizeof(byte) );
    // Visit each key byte and clear text byte.
    for (int index = 0; index < (lengthOfClearText); index = index +
1) {
        // perform XOR
```

```
            cipherBytes[index] = clearTextBytes[index] ^
keyBytes[keyIndex];
        // rotate through the key
        keyIndex = (keyIndex + 1) % lengthOfKey;
    }
    // return resulting cipher bytes.
    return cipherBytes;
}


// One time pad decryption.
// Use xor again and we decrypt the cipher
byte* decrypt(byte cipherBytes[], int lengthOfClearText, byte
keyBytes[], int lengthOfKey) {

    int keyIndex = 0;
    // Allocate room for the resulting clear text data.
    byte *decryptedClearTextBytes = (byte *)calloc(lengthOfClearText,
sizeof(byte));
    // For each cipher byte and each key byte, perform an xor
operation.
    for (int index = 0; index < (lengthOfClearText); index = index +
1) {
        decryptedClearTextBytes[index] = cipherBytes[index] ^
keyBytes[keyIndex];
        // rotate through the key
        keyIndex = (keyIndex + 1) % lengthOfKey;

    }
    return decryptedClearTextBytes;
}
```

```
// Guide to Internet of Things Chapter 3
// MicrocontrollerClientTEAEncryption
// This Microcontroller firmware demonstrates TEA encryption.

// This code is for instructional and demonstration use only. In
general, it is a
// bad idea to write your own cryptography. Use open source standard
libraries.
// This code is provided for instructional purposes only and should
// not be used in a real system.

// The code for the TEA algorithm is taken from the
// textbook: Distributed Systems: Concepts and Design 3rd edition
// by  George Coulouris, Jean Dollimore, Tim Kindberg, and Gordon
Blair.

// TEA was released into the public domain by David Wheeler and Roger
Needham.
// See https://en.wikipedia.org/wiki/Tiny_Encryption_Algorithm
```

```
// Include library for Base 64
#include <Base64RK.h>

// Include libray for HTTP requests
#include <HttpClient.h>

// http is a variable of the class HttpClient
 HttpClient http;

// Define a headers array holding two http_header_t objects.
// Our request will include a JSON string. We inform the receiver
// that it should expect to see JSON.
 http_header_t headers[] = {
     { "Content-Type", "application/json" },
     { NULL, NULL }
 };

// Define an HTTP request object and an HTTP response object.
// These objects hold the HTTP request and response.
 http_request_t request;
 http_response_t response;

// Set the photResistor to A0
int photoResistor = A0;

// The analog value begins at 0.
int analogValue = 0;

// Use this char array to hold the device ID
char deviceID[60];

// Establish a loop timer to hold a value in milliseconds.
unsigned long loop_timer;

// Setup is performed once on start up.
void setup() {

    // We will communicate over the serial port.
    Serial.begin(9600);

    // In the request object, set the IP address and port of the server
that
    // we will visit.
    request.ip = IPAddress(192,168,86,216);
    request.port = 3000;

    // The deviceID is found by calling System.deviceID().c_str();
    // Here, we copy the device ID into the character array named
deviceID.
    strcpy(deviceID,System.deviceID().c_str());
    // For debugging, display the device ID on the console.
```

```
   Serial.printlnf("This device has the id of %s", deviceID);

   // Set the time to the current time
   loop_timer = millis();

}

// Provided with a response, display it to the command line console..
// &response is a reference to the HTTP response.
void printResponse(http_response_t &response) {
  Serial.println("HTTP Response: ");
  Serial.println(response.status);
  Serial.println(response.body);
}

// Perform an HTTP post request.
// The data provided, within the JSON message, is in Base 64
notation.
void doPostRequest(char encryptedByteArrayBase64[]) {

  // Provide the path to the service
  request.path = "/microcontrollerEvent";

  // Build the JSON request
  char json[1000] = "{\"encryptedData\":\"";
  // Add the encrypted data
  strcat(json,encryptedByteArrayBase64);
  // add the JSON ending
  strcat(json,"\"}");
  // assign the JSON string to the HTTP request body
  request.body = json;
  // post the request and block and wait for a response.
  http.post(request, response, headers);
  // show response once it arrives
  printResponse(response);
}
// loop() is called repeatedly by the operating system
void loop() {

   // every 5 seconds do a post to the server
  if(millis() - loop_timer >= 10000UL) {

    // read the analog value from the phototransistor
    analogValue = analogRead(photoResistor);
    Serial.printlnf("AnalogValue == %u", analogValue);

    // This clear text message will be held local to the device.
    char clearText[80];
    // Use sprintf to copy a formatted string into the clearText
array.
    // The clearText is the text we want to encrypt.
```

```
    sprintf(clearText, "Microcontroller ID = %s  Light sensor = %d",
deviceID, analogValue);

    Serial.printlnf("Clear text: %s",clearText);

     // determine the length of the string holding the clear text
    int lengthOfClearText = strlen(clearText);

    // Set a byte pointer to the clearText.
    byte *clearTextBytes = (byte *) clearText;

    // TEA needs four 32 bit ints as key. The key should be 128 bits
of random data.
    // Here, we just use four integers as our key. This approach is
not secure.
    // TEA is a symmetric cipher and so we will use the same key for
encryption
    // and decryption.
    unsigned long key[] = {12,34,56,91};

    // Do the encryption and point to the encrypted data.
    // clearTextBytes points to the data we intend to encrypt.
    // The length of this text and the encryption key is also
provided.
    // The length of the padded and encrypted data is placed in
encryptedSize.
    int encryptedSize = 0;
    byte* TEACipherBytes = padAndEncryptWithTEA(clearTextBytes,
lengthOfClearText, &encryptedSize, key) ;

    // Here, we call on decryptAndUnpad to decrypt the encrypted data
and removing the padding.
    // We do this to test that encryption is working properly.

    byte *decryptedClearTextBytes =  decryptAndUnpad(TEACipherBytes,
encryptedSize, key);

    // Compare the decrypted data with the original.
    char *decryptedString = (char *) decryptedClearTextBytes;

    Serial.printlnf("Clear text after decryption : %s",decryptedString
);

    if(strcmp(decryptedString,clearText) == 0) {
      // The decrypted data matched the original clear text.
      Serial.println("Strings matched");
    }
    else {
      // The strings did not match and so there is a problem with
      // the encryption or decryption.
      Serial.println("Error: Strings not matched");
    }
```

```
   // Encode the encrypted byte array in Base64

   // First, find the size of the base 64 data.
   size_t sizeOfBase64 = Base64::getEncodedSize(encryptedSize, true);
   // Second, allocate room for the base 64 data.
   char * encryptedByteArrayBase64 = (char *)calloc(sizeOfBase64,
sizeof(char));

   // Use a library to do the encoding from binary to base 64.
   Base64::encode(TEACipherBytes, encryptedSize,
encryptedByteArrayBase64, sizeOfBase64, true );

   // Display the encrypted data in base 64 on the console.
   Serial.printlnf("Encrypted data in Base 64
%s",encryptedByteArrayBase64);

   // Post the encrypted data in base 64 to the web server
   doPostRequest(encryptedByteArrayBase64);

   // Free up the memory that was allocated for the arrays.

    free(TEACipherBytes);
    free(decryptedClearTextBytes);
    free(encryptedByteArrayBase64);

    // reset loop_timer
   loop_timer = millis();
   }
 }

// This routine adds padding to the data to be encrypted and calls TEA
// to perform the encryption.
byte* padAndEncryptWithTEA(byte clearTextBytes[], int
lengthOfClearText, int *encryptedSize, unsigned long k[]) {

    // Set n to the number of bytes in clearTextBytes (include the
null byte).
    int n = lengthOfClearText + 1;

    // Create an array to hold the padded data
    // The array is of size (n / 8 + 1) * 8
    // The *encryptedSize is evenly divisible by 8
    *encryptedSize = (n / 8 + 1) * 8;
    byte *pa = (byte *)calloc(*encryptedSize, sizeof(byte));

    // Copy bytes to the new, padded array.
    for(int i = 0; i < n; i++) pa[i] = clearTextBytes[i];
    // Set any extra bytes to 0
    for(int i = n; i < *encryptedSize; i++) pa[i] = 0;
    // Set the rightmost byte to to the number of padding bytes
    pa[*encryptedSize - 1 ] = *encryptedSize - n;
```

```
    // set an unsigned long pointer to the padded data
    unsigned long *paddedArrayPointer = (unsigned long *)pa;

    // Call TEA for each pair of unsigned longs in the padded array.
    int numCalls = *encryptedSize / 8;
    for (int i = 0; i < numCalls; i++) {
        encryptTEA(k,paddedArrayPointer);
        // Bump the pointer by two unsigned longs
        paddedArrayPointer = paddedArrayPointer + 2;


    }
    return pa;
}

// Decrypt the TEACipherBytes using the key provided.
// Remove the padding and return a newly allocated array of clear text
bytes.

byte * decryptAndUnpad(byte * TEACipherBytes, int encryptedSize,
unsigned long key[]) {

    // First, decrypt the TEACipherBytes
    // Call TEA for each pair of unsigned longs in the padded array.

    // set an unsigned long pointer to the padded data
    unsigned long *paddedArrayPointer = (unsigned long
*)TEACipherBytes;

    // *encryptedSize is divisible by 8
    // call decrypt and each call handles 8 bytes
    int numCalls = encryptedSize / 8;
    for (int i = 0; i < numCalls; i++) {
        decryptTEA(key,paddedArrayPointer);
        // Bump the pointer by two unsigned longs
        paddedArrayPointer = paddedArrayPointer + 2;


    }
    // The data in TEACipherBytes is decrypted
    // The last byte has the number of padding bytes to remove
    int padToRemove = TEACipherBytes[encryptedSize-1];

    // Compute the number of bytes we are interested in
    int n = encryptedSize - padToRemove;

    // allocate room for n bytes
    byte *clearTextByteArray = (byte *)calloc(n, sizeof(byte));

    // Copy the bytes we are interested in into the clearTextByteArray
    for(int i = 0; i < n; i++) clearTextByteArray[i] =
TEACipherBytes[i];
```

```
    // Return the clear text bytes
    return clearTextByteArray;


}


// TEA code from Distributed Systems: Concepts and Design 3rd edition

// TEA operates on two 32-bit message blocks with a 128-bit key.
// We make use of k[0], k[1], k[2], and k[3] for the key.
// We encrypt two unsigned longs: text[0] and text[1].
// An unsigned long is 4 bytes.
// So, we are encrypting 8 bytes.
void encryptTEA(unsigned long k[], unsigned long text[]) {

    unsigned long y = text[0], z = text[1];
    unsigned long delta = 0x9e3779b9, sum = 0;
    int n;
    for(n = 0; n < 32; n++){
        sum += delta;
        y += ((z<<4)+k[0])^(z+sum)^((z>>5)+k[1]);
        z += ((y<<4)+k[2])^(y+sum)^((y>>5) + k[3]);
    }
    text[0] = y;
    text[1] = z;
}
// TEA code from Distributed Systems: Concepts and Design 3rd edition

// TEA operates on two 32-bit message blocks with a 128-bit key.
// We make use of k[0], k[1], k[2], and k[3] for the key.
// We decrypt two unsigned longs: text[0] and text[1].
// An unsigned long is 4 bytes.
// So, we are decrypting 8 bytes.
void decryptTEA(unsigned long k[], unsigned long text[]) {

    unsigned long y = text[0], z = text[1];
    unsigned long delta = 0x9e3779b9, sum = delta << 5;
    int n;
    for(n = 0; n < 32; n++){
        z -= ((y << 4) + k[2]) ^ (y + sum) ^ ((y >> 5) + k[3]);
        y -= ((z << 4) + k[0]) ^ (z + sum) ^ ((z >> 5) + k[1]);
        sum -= delta;
    }
    text[0] = y;
    text[1] = z;
}
```

CHAPTER 4

Web APIs

This chapter covers
   A Smart City Application
   Bay Area Rapid Transit
   Accessing REST APIs
   Building a REST API

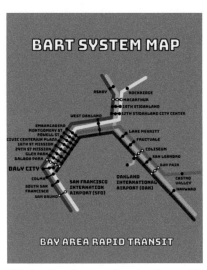

This San Francisco transit system has an API

"Mind the gap."

Electronic voice issuing a warning in the London Underground

Bay Area Rapid Transit

The construction of the Bay Area Rapid Transit (BART) system began in San Francisco in 1964 and now carries millions of passengers per year.[1]

Systems such as BART have been shown to increase the availability of jobs and improve safety. They reduce pollution, increase fuel efficiency and reduce congestion. For those unable to drive or afford an automobile, they are among the essential components of life.

BART, in particular, has been shown to reduce carbon dioxide by over 1 million metric tons per year.[2]

In this chapter, you will build an extension to the BART system. Your extension will improve on BART's convenience and thereby promote the use of green transportation.

By showing you how to make calls on the BART API, this chapter illustrates how easy it is to build a creative and useful smart city application.

This chapter is divided into three parts. In Part 1, you will experiment with the BART Application Programmer Interface (API) and learn how you can interact with BART via a stand alone JavaScript program. In Part 2, you will learn how to build a web service that makes calls on the BART API and, in turn, provides an API to a microcontroller. In Part 3, you will learn how a microcontroller can be programmed to interact with the web service that you built in Part 2 using only a Wi-Fi connection to the internet.

Figure 4.1 Making requests every 15 seconds

Part 1: Visiting the BART API

What you need:

- You will need a copy of Node.js on a computer. Installing and running Node.js was covered in Chapter 2.
- You will need an internet connection so that you can visit BART over the internet.

```
$node VisitBART.js sfia rich
Searching for schedule from
sfia to rich
Checking for train leaving
from sfia to rich
{
    destination: 'Richmond',
    abbreviation: 'RICH',

    :
    :
    minutes: '1',
```

Figure 4.2 One minute until departure

What to do:

In this Part, you will access the BART API using HTTPS requests. These requests will be made from within a program written in JavaScript for `Node.js`.

1. Copy `VisitBART.js` into an editor and save the file to an otherwise empty directory on your machine.

The program `VisitBART.js` may be found in the chapter appendix and at this URL:

https://github.com/sn-code-inside/guide-to-iot/blob/main/Ch04_code/VisitBART.js

2. In the same directory where you stored `VisitBart.js` and using the command line, enter the command

```
node VisitBART.js sfia rich
```

3. `VisitBART.js` is designed to make a new HTTPS request to BART every 15 seconds or so. The response includes real-time information on the location of BART trains. After the request goes out from your machine, the response comes back almost immediately. Here, we are asking the program to find information on trains leaving from the San Francisco International Airport (with the code 'sfia') and destined for the city of Richmond (with the code 'rich'). When running the program, use codes rather than full station names on the command line. A full list of codes for BART station names may be found at this URL:

```
https://api.bart.gov/docs/overview/abbrev.aspx
```

4. Examine the output carefully and notice how the data is structured in a regular format. Every 15 seconds, this well-formatted data is returned to the client (your machine) but often contains different values representing information about train cars that are soon to arrive at the San Francisco International Airport and are destined for Richmond.

5. Use control-c to exit the program and run it again with a slightly different command line:

```
node VisitBART.js rich daly
```

6. This time, we will view the status of trains arriving at Richmond station and destined for Daly City.

7. It is important to take some time and look over the code in VisitBART.js. Here we will examine some key parts of the code and trace the execution flow.

What Did You Do, and How Did You Do It?

A Web of Things Application

In just a few short steps, we were able to run a client-server application that exhibits the exceptional interoperability inherent in the World Wide Web.

The BART API, as shown in Figure 4.1, is an interface to a 'Web Thing'. A 'Web Thing' is an entity with a web presence. In this case, a large, expensive, and important part of a major US city is providing information about itself by leveraging standard web protocols and data formats.

The BART API client, VisitBART.js, is simple to develop and run. It can be used anywhere in the world where computers and the internet are available, and no browser is required. Don't get us wrong, we're not criticizing browsers. However, we do want to be able to access Web APIs programmatically - that is, make visits and requests from within program code. Browsers can also make use of this API and are capable of running JavaScript code

This book does not aim to teach you every feature of JavaScript. Instead, we hope that by exposing you to interesting applications of this important language, we will pique your interest and motivate you to seek a deeper understanding. We encourage you to modify and experiment with the code.

With that said, let's take a closer look at some of the key features of VisitBART.js

Using an HTTP module in Node.js

At the top of the program source code, the following line is executed:

```
const https = require('https');
```

We need this line to access the HTTPS library (an HTTPS module) in `Node.js`. An HTTPS library provides both HTTP as well as Transport Layer Security (TLS) – noted by the "S" at the end of "HTTP". HTTPS stands for Hypertext Transfer Protocol Secure.

What does this provide us? For the remainder of this program, the developer does not need to be concerned with the low-level details associated with TCP sockets (upon which HTTP runs).

In addition, the programmer is free from worrying about data encryption or decryption. That is handled by TLS.

This exemplifies the important principle of "abstraction". Low-level details are being abstracted away and the developer can focus on the application.

Using Command Line Parameters in Node.js

Next, we execute the following code:

```
var stringsFromCommandLine = process.argv.slice(2);

// We need to have the source and destination abbreviations.
if(stringsFromCommandLine[0] === undefined || stringsFromCommandLine[1]
=== undefined) {
  console.log("Usage error: node VisitBart.js SourceAbbreviation
DestinationAbbreviation");
  console.log("For example, node VisitBART.js sfia antc");
  process.exit(0);
}
```

The program needs to access the codes associated with the source station and the destination station. These data must be provided on the command line.

In this code, the process object has a property named `argv` that returns an array containing the strings entered on the command line. The program then uses the slice method to create a new array without the first two entries - the first two entries are `node` and `VisitBART.js`. From this new array, we need the first two elements. Thus, we use `[0]` to extract the station code for the start of the trip and `[1]` to access the station code for the destination station. If the user fails to enter a source or destination, they will receive an error message informing them of the proper usage and the program will terminate.

Event driven coding in Node.js

Next, the program source code contains a function definition for visitBARTAPI()

which is not executed at this time and is simply defined here. It will be executed later when we explicitly call it or when a particular clock event occurs.

We will soon see how the function `visitBARTAPI()` is executed repeatedly every 15 seconds. For now, let's look over some of the main things that this function will (eventually) do.

Visit the BART API

Whenever this function is executed, it begins by making an HTTPS GET request to the BART API:

```
const myHttpRequest =
https.get('https://api.bart.gov/api/etd.aspx?cmd=etd&orig=sfia&ke
y=MW9S-E7SL-26DU-VV8V&json=y', handleBARTResponse);
```

Understanding the request

At first glance, the code may appear cumbersome, but upon closer examination, it all makes sense.

The name `myHttpRequest` is introduced and is declared as a constant with the JavaScript keyword `const`. It takes on a value returned by a call to the `get` method of the `https` object. We have access to this particular object (that is, we can interact with it) because it was made available with the `require` statement at the start of the program.

The call to the `get` method will generate an `HTTPS get` request. This is one of the standard requests that one can make with HTTPS.

In Chapter 3, we used a post request. This was because we were sending data to the server and that data was to be stored there (posted). In this chapter, we are using a get request because we want to get a representation of a resource and process it on the client. The representation will be a JSON object describing trains arriving at a particular station.

The APIs URL Structure

The Uniform Resource Locator (URL) appears next:

```
'https://api.bart.gov/api/etd.aspx?cmd=etd&orig=sfia&key=MW9S-
E7SL-26DU-VV8V&json=y'
```

A URL has the following general format: `scheme://host:port/path?query`. Therefore, the URL for the BART API call is composed of these five components: scheme, host, port, path, and query.

The first component is the scheme. In this case, the scheme is https. As we discussed above, HTTPS provides standard HTTP but adds a layer of cryptography to perform encryption and decryption to the messages placed on the network.

The client (our Node.js program) and the server (implementing the BART API) both need to be aware that they are involved in a cryptographic protocol.

HTTPS is far preferable to HTTP if we are concerned about the security of our messages. It would be very difficult for an eavesdropper to read messages encrypted with HTTPS.

The second component is the host. In this case the host is `api.bart.gov`. This name, `api.bart.gov` will be converted to an IP address by the Domain Name System (DNS). This conversion, abstracted away and of no direct concern to the programmer, will occur before the HTTPS message is sent to BART.

The third component is the port. The port is not present and so the default HTTPS port of 443 is assumed. Other protocols will require a different port number. HTTP, for example, uses port 80. The port number is passed along with the request to api.bart.gov so that the service there can select the appropriate application to run. A server may provide many distinct services, often with different port numbers.

The fourth component is the path. The path identifies a particular resource on the host. In this case the path is `/api/etd.aspx`. This path information is included with the request and is available to the server that receives the request. Several different resources may be available at the same port. These resources may be differentiated with the path in the URL. The string `/etd` is referring to a resource that can provide an Estimated Time of Departure. The string `.aspx` is a file extension, like `.txt` or `.doc`. When combined, `etd.aspx` is the name of a particular application listening for a request coming from port 443.

The query string is the fifth component. The question mark is used to separate the path from the query string. A query string is usually a list of name and value pairs separated by ampersands. These data are passed to the `etd.aspx` application for processing. In this case, we have `cmd=etd`. This means that the client is interested in the estimated time of departures (etd). We also have `orig=sfia` which means we are interested in trains originating from the San Francisco International Airport (sfia). The string `sfia` is simply a code for this particular station. All of the codes for sources and destinations are available on the BART API web site and the URL appears above.

We also have a key field of `key=MW9S-E7SL-26DU-VV8V`. If we register for a particular key at BART then BART can track how many times we are visiting. In this case, we are using a default key provided to the general public. Note that this key is used for identification rather than encryption. It is not important for TLS but it too will be encrypted by TLS.

Finally, we have `json=y`. This tells the server that we would prefer to receive the response marked up in the standard JavaScript Object Notation (JSON) format.

Typically, Web APIs return responses in XML or JSON format. Here, we choose JSON. The resource that interests us is real-time train location data. XML and JSON are popular alternative representations of that resource. The server will provide either.

As an exercise, in order to view the XML, try opening a browser with the following URL:

```
https://api.bart.gov/api/etd.aspx?cmd=etd&orig=sfia&key=MW9S-E7SL-
26DU-VV8V&json=n
```

Be sure to note how this URL differs from our original.

Handling a callback in Node.js

Finally, after the URL is specified, you can see that the call on the https get method includes a callback function named `handleBARTResponse`. This function will be called when a response from the BART server arrives back at the client. It will be called along with a parameter containing the response. Next, we examine the `handleBARTResponse` function.

The function `handleBARTResponse` is defined but not directly invoked by the programmer. It will not actually be invoked and executed until a response arrives back from the server. The programmer who wrote `VisitBART.js` never makes an explicit call to `handleBARTResponse`. Instead, the programmer is relying on the `Node.js` system to make this call when a response arrives.

What does `handleBARTResponse` do when it is called? It accepts a response object as a parameter (from the `Node.js` system). The response object can be configured to call programmer defined functions during its life cycle. When the response object is receiving data from the server, we can provide it with a function to execute. When the response object is done receiving data, we can provide it with another function. In this program, the `handleBARTResponse` method passes two functions (both unnamed) to the response object. One unnamed function will handle the response data as it arrives:

```
response.on('data', (chunk) => {
    data += chunk;
});
```

Here, we inform the response object that as chunks of data arrive, to call the unnamed function that we define. This unnamed function simply adds the chunk to the data that has previously arrived. This function may be called several times and the final string will be included in the variable named `data`. You might think of this code as a succinct replacement for the following code:

```
function gatherDataFromResponse(chunk) {
```

```
        data += chunk;
    }
    response.on('data', gatherDataFromResponse);
```

The ambitious reader will want to give this a try. Just replace the original code with this less cryptic piece. Does it still work?

The idea is, when data arrives back from the server, we want to execute this piece of code to gather up each chunk. JavaScript allows us to handle this response in either way – as well as others.

And we also provide a function for the response object to call when it is done receiving the HTTP response. This function will handle the bulk of the application. It runs after the response has completely arrived.

```
    response.on('end', () => {
        var theResult = JSON.parse(data);
        :
        :
```

The `data` referred to here is the same `data` that received the chunks from the previous function.

It is more convenient to manipulate the response data with a JavaScript object than to have to directly process the text data arriving from BART. After all, the JSON data that the client receives is simply a well-formatted string of text. So, the first thing that this function does is parse the data that has arrived to create a new JavaScript object. This is very easy to do and is an attractive feature of the JavaScript language. The arriving JSON data maps directly into a JavaScript object. In this case, the programmer has named this object `theResult`. But what properties does this object have?

The JavaScript object referred to by the variable `theResult` will have the same properties that the JSON response message has. Let's look at the response message. By the way, you can view raw response data by opening a browser and visiting :

https://api.bart.gov/api/etd.aspx?cmd=etd&orig=sfia&key=MW9S-E7SL-26DU-VV8V&json=y

You will see the JSON response on your browser screen. Here is an example response:

```
{ "?xml": {   "@version": "1.0",
              "@encoding": "utf-8"
  },
  "root": {
            "@id": "1",
            "uri": {
              "#cdata-section":
```

```
        "http://api.bart.gov/api/etd.aspx?cmd=etd&orig=sfia&json=y"
        ],
        "date": "11/16/2024",
        "time": "08:25:46 PM PST",
        "station": [{
                "name": "San Francisco Int'l Airport",
                "abbr": "SFIA",
                "etd": [{
                        "destination": "Antioch",
                        "abbreviation": "ANTC",
                        "limited": "0",
                        "estimate": [{
                                "minutes": "36",
                                "platform": "1",
                                "direction": "North",
                                "length": "10",
                                "color": "YELLOW",
                                "hexcolor": "#ffff33",
                                "bikeflag": "1",
                                "delay": "104"
                        }]
                }]
        }],
        "message": ""
    }
}
```

In 36 minutes, a train will leave from San Francisco Airport to Antioch

After the JavaScript code `var theResult = JSON.parse(data)` is executed and the JSON string is parsed, we have a JavaScript object with the same properties as the JSON message.

The JSON message, also known as a JSON object, is a list of name-value pairs separated by commas and surrounded by curly braces.

The first name in the JSON message is `?xml`. The value associated with this name is not a simple value, such as a string or number, but is a JSON object (note that it is surrounded by curly braces). This JSON object holds the version and encoding method for this message.

The next name is `root`. Its value is also a JSON object. It contains some metadata (`id, uri, date, time, and station`). Correspondingly, inside our JavaScript program, `theResult.root` will be a JavaScript object. The value of `theResult.root.station` will be an array. Within the message and within the program, array elements are enclosed in square brackets. Thus, `theResult.root.station[0]` references the first element of the array and is a JavaScript object.

In this example, we are only looking at one station: the San Francisco International Airport station with the code name `sfia`. This station will serve as the origin for our trip. In the JavaScript code, we will use the syntax `theResult.root.station[0]` to refer to the origin station.

There may be many trains that are soon to leave from this station. Some of these trains may be heading to the same destination. As we will see, the JSON message nicely encapsulates this information and groups trains going to the same destination under the destination name, organized by time of arrival. Early trains are listed first.

Each object in the station array has a `name`, `abbreviation` and `etd`. The etd name represents all of the trains that will soon leave the origin station. Therefore, `theResult.root.station[0].etd` represents an array of objects. Each of these objects describe a list of arriving trains going to a particular destination. For example, the first element of the etd array (`theResult.root.station[0].etd[0]`) might describe all trains that are soon to leave for Antioch from the airport. The second element of the etd array (`theResult.root.station[0].etd[1]`) might describe all trains that are soon to leave for Richmond from the airport. And so on.

To verify our description of the JSON data, the reader is encouraged to use a browser and visit the URL with different station codes. For example, examine the response to a query for all trains leaving from Richmond station at the following URL:

```
https://api.bart.gov/api/etd.aspx?cmd=etd&orig=rich&key=MW9S-E7SL-
26DU-VV8V&json=y
```

Let's consider how `VisitBART.js` searches for the first train that will leave for our chosen destination.

We see the following lines of code in VisitBART.js:

```
for(j = 0; j < theResult.root.station[0].etd.length; j++) {
    if(theResult.root.station[0].etd[j].abbreviation.toUpperCase()
                === myDestination.toUpperCase()) {
```

The `for` loop will visit each object in the `etd` array. That is why we use its length to terminate the `for` loop. Each of these will hold a different station abbreviation. Within the `for` loop, the `if` statement checks to see if this is a train destination that we are interested in.

If we find such a match, we execute the following line:

```
var min =
theResult.root.station[0].etd[j].estimate[0].minutes;
```

BART provides the earliest train at `root.station[0].etd[j].estimate[0].minutes`. There also might be a value at `root.station[0].etd[j].estimate[1].minutes`. But our application is not interested in the second train. We can now use the variable `min` to inform the user about the number of minutes until the next appropriate train arrives.

As mentioned above, BART also provides messages marked up in the Extensible Markup Language (XML) data format.

Like JSON, XML formatted messages are a bit verbose but have the important advantage of being easily read by humans. If you have ever read an HTML document then you have read XML. HTML is, in fact, only one of many XML based languages.

If you want your technical idea to be successful, it is often wise to make it easily understandable. The designers of the BART API were surely aware of this principle. Both JSON and XML are fairly easy to read and understand.

To illustrate this point, not too long ago, there were no webmasters. Today, however, there are many. One of the reasons for the widespread adoption of the World Wide Web was the fact that HTML, an XML-based language, was easy for humans to read and interpret. By simply loading a web page and selecting "view source," one could easily read and learn to understand the underlying code.

The same argument applies to BART (and many other APIs). If you want to view what a BART response looks like, simply visit the site of the API with a browser. This makes it easy to become a "BART master" and write code to visit the BART API.

Let's take stock of where we are in our study of the `visitBARTAPI` function. When the function executes, it will make a request to the BART API and create an object named `myHTTPRequest`. As part of the request to the BART API, it provides a function to handle the response. That response handling will parse the arriving JSON and make decisions on what to display to the user. None of this is executed yet. After the `visitBARTAPI` function is defined (with all of this capability) we need to actually invoke it. We do that in two distinct ways.

```
visitBARTAPI();
setInterval(visitBARTAPI, 15*1000);
```

The first call is straightforward. When the program is run, it makes a call to visitBARTAPI() so that a user receives immediate feedback. After that initial call, we rely on Javascript to call the function periodically.

The call to `setInterval` is a call to a global API in `Node.js`. There is no need to include this capability with a `require` statement. This call will ask Node.js to invoke the named function, `visitBARTAPI`, after at least 15*1000 milliseconds have expired.

Concluding Part 1, one might wonder if this system is really an example of IoT. We believe that it is.

The Bay Area Rapid Transit system is sensing the speed of trains and their location with devices that we might not normally see. And it is making that data available on the internet.

Any confusion as to whether this exemplifies IoT, or not, might be due to the fact that this "Thing" is quite large and complex-and the sensing that it does has been abstracted away.

In Part 3, we will introduce a microcontroller into the system and see what creative things we might do.

Part 2: Creating a new API that uses the BART API

What you need:

- You will need Node.js
- You will need a Wi-Fi connection.

What to do:

In this Part, we will create a new web API that makes use of the BART API. We do this so that we can experiment with API development and retrieve BART information via a microcontroller in Part 3.

1. Copy `VisitBARTWebService.js` into an editor and save the file to an otherwise empty directory on your machine.

The program `VisitBARTWebService.js` may be found in the chapter appendix and at this URL:

https://github.com/sn-code-inside/guide-to-iot/blob/main/Ch04_code/VisitBARTWebService.js

2. In the same directory where you stored `VisitBartWebService.js` and using the command line, enter the following two commands. You may take the default suggestions.

```
npm init
```

```
npm install express
```

3. In the same directory where you stored `VisitBARTWebService.js` and using the command line, enter the command:

```
node VisitBARTWebService.js sfia rich
```

4. By using a browser, visit the following URL to see when the next train arrives at the San Francisco International Airport ("sfia") and destined for Richmond ("rich").

```
http://localhost:3000/minutesUntilArrival
```

What Did You Do, and How Did You Do It?

In just a few short steps, we were able to deploy a new web service using Node.js and Express. We were able to configure the web service on the command line. That is, we specified that we want to monitor trains leaving from the San Francisco International Airport ("sfia") and destined for Richmond ("rich").

This time, however, the client of the BART API (VisitBARTWebService.js) does not repeatedly visit BART every 15 seconds but, instead, only visits BART when an HTTP request arrives. We have deployed a very simple web service and tested it with a browser. We will make good use of this service in Part 3. For now, let's review the code in VisitBARTWebService.js.

Web Services can be Easy to build

At the top of the program code, we access the command line parameters as we did in Part 1. We find the source and destination codes provided by the user. These values could have been provided by the caller to our API. It was a design decision to have the user provide them at service start up. In Part 3, we will be making calls to the service from a microcontroller and the microcontroller has no keyboard. Thus, in our scenario, it makes good sense to provide these data as part of the service configuration.

A bit further down in the code, we use the Express app to establish a listener with this JavaScript:

```
app.listen(port, () => {

console.log('To cause a visit to the Bart API, use an HTTP get request
and visit http://localhost:' + port +'/minutesUntilArrival');

})
```

Later, we inform the app object that we will handle `HTTP GET` requests addressed to a particular path with an anonymous function. We never call this function directly. It is called by Node.js when an HTTP GET request arrives. The request (`req`) and response (`res`) objects are made available to us by Node.js. Typically, we read data from the request object and write data to the response object. In this application, we are only interested in writing to the response object.

```
app.get('/minutesUntilArrival', (req, res) => {

  // announce a new visitor

  console.log("\nNew Get request");

  // We will send data back with the httpResponse variable.

  httpResponse = res;

  // Call the visit BART API. When the response from BART arrives,

  // write the response data
```

```
   // to the httpResponse variable. The response will go back to the

   // client.

   visitBARTAPI();

})
```

Within the function, we associate the variable `httpResponse` with the `res` object which is provided as a parameter to the anonymous function. We will be writing to this variable after a call to the BART API completes. The httpResponse variable has scope outside of this function and will be available when the response from BART arrives. The last thing that this function does, upon each visit, is to call the `visitBARTAPI()` function.

The `visitBARTAPI()` function is based on the code from Part 1 and should be easily understood. The only new thing to mention is the code that runs after BART provides a response.

```
if (found) httpResponse.send('{"Arrival":'+'"'+min+'"}');

   // Check if there is no train leaving for this destination.

   if(!found) {

     httpResponse.send('{"Arrival":'+'"'+"-1"+'"}');

     console.log("No destination train to " + myDestination + "
found.");

   }
```

If we have found a train going to our destination, we return a JSON string with a single name-value pair. The name will be "Arrival" and the value will be the number of minutes. On the other hand, if no such train is found, we return the JSON string with a name-value pair that suggests that no train is currently scheduled to arrive for that particular destination. The JSON string would then appear as follows:

```
{"Arrival": "-1")
```

As a test, run VisitBARTWebService with a destination name that does not exist. For example, run the following command:

```
node VisitBARTWebService.js sfia rich2
```

And then visit the service with a browser:

```
http://localhost:3000/minutesUntilArrival
```

There is no station named "rich2" and so we expect to see the response:

```
{"Arrival": "-1"}.
```

Writing a Gateway

As we noted earlier, the BART API is an HTTPS API. This means that a cryptographic protocol runs prior to the HTTP request and that the application level protocol (HTTP in this example) is encrypted.

The Particle Photon 2 provides library support for HTTP and, as far as this author is aware, provides no convenient support for HTTPS. So, here we have written a simple web service in Node.js that converts the HTTP calls from a Particle Photon 2 (or browser) into HTTPS calls from Node.js to BART.

It is not uncommon for an IoT device to communicate with a more powerful device using one network protocol and have the more powerful device use another protocol for its communication. See the model in Chapter 1. The more powerful device (our computer running Node.js) bridges the two networks and is acting as a gateway.

We turn next to the firmware running on our microcontroller that communicates with the BART API (through our gateway).

Part 3: Visiting our API with a microcontroller

What you need:

- You will need Node.js
- You will need a Wi-Fi connection.
- You will need `VisitBARTWebService.js` from Part 2.
- You will need a Particle Photon 2

What to do:

1.You will need a copy of the code in `BARTLightAlert.ino`.

`BARTLightAlert.ino` may be found in the chapter appendix

and at this URL:

https://github.com/sn-code-inside/guide-to-iot/blob/main/Ch04_code/BARTLightAlert.ino

2. Within BARTLightAlert.ino, there is a line of code that sets the IP address in the request to the IP address of the server. This is the address that this microcontroller client will send messages to. Since you will run the server on your own machine, you need to change that address to the current IP address of your machine. Currently, the line of code reads as follows:

```
request.ip = IPAddress(192,168,86,216);
```

Find you IP address and change this line of code. Note that it uses commas and not periods to separate the parts of the IP address.

2. Run VisitBARTWebService.js from Part 2. This will be your server.

```
node VisitBARTWebService.js sfia rich
```

3. Using the Particle Web IDE, flash BARTLightAlert.ino to your Particle Photon 2.

What Did You Do, and How Did You Do It?

A Particle Photon 2 Communicates with BART

You have established a connection between a transportation system in San Francisco and your Particle Photon 2. See Figure 4.3. The light on your Photon 2 is responding to real world events. The movement of trains is having an impact on your device and is causing the device to change state. See Figure 4.4.This is easy to do because of the interoperability provided by the World Wide Web.

Figure 4.3 Making Requests Every 15 seconds

You downloaded and ran firmware on your microcontroller. This firmware uses HTTP to learn the time of the next train's arrival.

Figure 4.4 BART light on upper left

One way to learn to program is to study working solutions. Take some time and study `BARTLightAlert.ino`. Here we will examine some key parts of the code and trace the execution flow.

Starting at the top, we have useful comments to help the reader understand the purpose of the program. Programs are not just for computers, people have to read them too. A well-written program should be described well for human readers. What better place to include the description than right in the program itself?

The programmer may elect to set the boolean variable debug to be true or false.

```
boolean debug = true;
```

During firmware development, this variable is normally set to `true`. Some of the `if` statements found elsewhere in the code test the value of this variable. If the `if` statements see that debug is true, they generate output to the command line interface (CLI). This is in order to assist in the debugging and development process.

In preparation for deployment, after the software is tested, the programmer will normally set this variable to `false`. The `if` statements will see that debug is `false` and the associated print statements will be ignored.

Note the line of code:

```
HttpClient http;
```

The programmer is using a C++ class, `HttpClient`, and defining a variable of that class. The variable is named `http` and is used later in the program. The class `HttpClient` abstracts away many of the details associated with reading and writing data using HTTP. While this is a small application, the use of abstractions to hide details is of fundamental importance in computer science. It is even more important in larger applications.

When our application sends request messages using the http object, the request messages are sent to the server. When we receive response messages from the `http` object, we are receiving data from the server. This is the way that our program will communicate with `VisitBARTWebService.js`.

The low-level details associated with the sending and receiving of HTTP messages are largely hidden, which is what we want. Below the HTTP layer, the networking also involves the Transmission Control Protocol (TCP) and below that layer, the Internet Protocol (IP). When programming this web client application, we do not want to have to deal with those details. All this hiding of details simplifies our programming. Simple is good because it is easy to reason about (and therefore debug or prove correct) things that are simple.

But what data should we write to the `http` object? And what kind of response do we expect to receive? Using HTTP, we have a standard way to encapsulate the outgoing and incoming messages. But what about the messages themselves? These messages are at the application layer.

In our case, we provided the codes for the source and destination trains on the command line when we ran VisitBARTWebService.js. As a result, our firmware does not need to pass these codes in the HTTP request. This design decision allows us to avoid hardcoding the source and destination codes in the firmware. Our client only needs to send an HTTP GET request to the server, which will return a JSON message containing either the number of minutes until the next train arrives or an error message.

The HTTP request and response are handled by the following call in the `doGetRequest()` function:

```
http.get(request, response, headers);
```

When this function completes, the response object contains the data that we are interested in in the `response.body`. We pass the body to a function that extracts the response from the JSON data.

```
return extractResponseFromJSON(response.body)
```

The value returned by this call will either be "-1" if no such train is arriving, the number of minutes to wait, or the word "Leaving" for trains that are very close to departure.

The function `extractResponseFromJSON()` uses a built in JSON parser to simplify the process of reading a particular value from the JSON string. It uses the following line to parse the string arriving from the server:

```
JSONValue outerObj = JSONValue::parseCopy(body);
```

Since a JSON string is made up of list of name-value pairs as described on https://www.json.org, a C++ iterator can be accessed using the line

JSONObjectIterator iter(outerObj);

And we can read the name-value pairs with these access methods:

```
iter.name()
iter.value()
```

The function `extractResponseFromJSON()` returns to `doGetRequest()`, which in turn returns to `getMinutes()`. The value in the "Arrival" field of the JSON response is then returned from `getMinutes()` to `getStateUpdate()`.

The function `getStateUpdate()` is simply a nested `if` statement that returns a variable of type `State`. The new state may be one of the values defined above in its enumeration:

```
enum State {noBlink,verySlow,slow,medium,fast};
```

An interesting piece of the firmware is the `loop()` function. As we know, the `loop()` function is called repeatedly by the operating system. The application programmer tries to get work done within the `loop()` function but tries to do so quickly, to give the operating system time to do things that it needs to do, e.g., maintaining the Wi-Fi connection. See Figure 4.5.

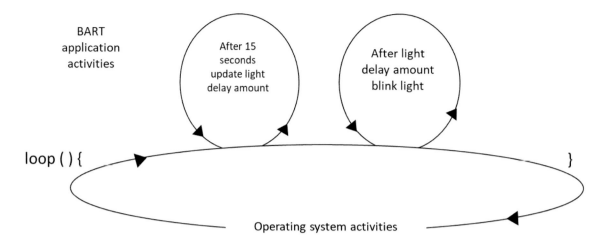

Figure 4.5 In loop(), update train status and blink light

Our `loop()` function is written so that it only calls BART every 15 seconds. This call may affect how often we blink the light. In general, the closer the train the faster we want our device to blink. We handle this with the state variable that can be in one of five different states: `noBlink`, `verySlow`, `slow`, `medium`, or `fast`. We ask BART for the number of minutes and set our state variable to one of these five values.

Each state has an associated light delay amount. If the state is `fast` then the light delay amount will be small. If the state is `verySlow` then the light delay amount is high. If the state is noBlink, we leave the light on with no blinking.

The `loop()` function then checks to see if a blink is required. It uses the light delay amount to decide this. If that amount of time has passed since the last blink, it decides to blink again.

Representational State Transfer

Representational State Transfer (REST) is an architectural style defined by Roy Fielding in his PhD thesis in 2000 [3]. Many modern APIs are based on the principles set forth in his paper. Here, we highlight a few of these principles and describe why the APIs discussed in this chapter would be considered RESTful APIs.

Fielding points out that the client-server architectural style provides for the important principle of separation of concerns. In our case, the developers at BART are able to focus on the reading of real-time train data and providing that information on a website. On the client side, we can focus on controlling lights using a microcontroller or providing a command line interaction with users.

He also promotes the idea that the interaction should be stateless. This means that the server, in order to behave properly, need not keep track of conversational state arising from prior visits. He envisions a proper REST API as having a "one and done" style conversation. Clearly, this style of conversation allows the server to scale to many visitors. By not having to maintain conversational state, the server has less work to do. In addition, the service becomes more reliable in the face of the occasional failure. If a network failure occurs, the client can simply retry the request. Both of the APIs described in this chapter were stateless APIs.

According to Fielding, some RESTful APIs will include a note in the response indicating whether or not the response is cacheable. If the data is cacheable then the client can hold the response for reuse at a later time. This may result in far fewer calls to the service. In our case, we require real-time updates on train locations. Thus, our response data is not cacheable and we do not provide cache memory to hold prior responses.

Fielding also promotes the use of a uniform interface to identify resources, represent resources with self-descriptive messages, and use hypermedia as the engine of application state.

In the example APIs in this chapter, we are using URLs (along with parameters) to identify the resources that we are interested in. For example, we are interested in the trains arriving at a particular station and we can express that with a URL. Train schedules are the resources and the representations of those resources may be retrieved in either in JSON or XML. The JSON or XML messages are self-descriptive, making them simple to understand and use.

We are using the standard HTTP GET verb to express exactly what we want to do with the resource.

With respect to "hypermedia as the engine of application state", in some application scenarios, it may be useful for the messages arriving from the server to contain additional URLs. These URLs can be dereferenced by the client to visit other services and access additional information. In the examples in this chapter, we did not use messages containing additional URLs. But see the exercise in the Make More / Explore Further section of this chapter.

Why are APIs important to IoT?

APIs are an invaluable driver for IoT. They provide information to devices that allow devices to know the state that the world is in. Where am I? What will the weather be like? What time is it? When will my train arrive? What did that person just say? Is this heartbeat normal?

APIs also provide a way for device to integrate with services that collect data from the device. These data may be used to monitor or control the device in a wide variety of ways; they may be used in machine learning applications to gather data and build machine learning models.

The possibilities seem endless.

APIs are central players in the internet of things.

Check Your Understanding

1. Describe any heterogeneity that may exist in the system that we built in Part 3 of this chapter. That is, in what way are the communicating parties different – in terms of programming languages, operating systems, networking protocols, and machines.

2. Discuss how the World Wide Web (HTTP, URL's, standard data formats) allow systems to interoperate in the presence of heterogeneity.

3. Discuss why the people at BART bothered to build an API. Do you believe that they knew, up front, exactly how it would be used?

4. Why do you think the people who designed the BART API decided to use HTTPS instead of some other protocol?

5. Modify `visitBARTAPI.js` so that, in addition to the earliest train, it reports on the number of minutes until a second train arrives. If there is no second train, be sure to report this to the user.

6. Consider a chat session with ChatGPT. Would you consider this interaction "stateless" or "stateful"? Why?

7. Would you consider an interaction with ChatGPT to be RESTful?

Make More / Explore Further

1. Explore the other APIs available at BART and modify `VisitBART.js` so that it also provides the fare price of the trip.

2. Modify `VisitBART.js` so that the source of the trip and the destination are entered at the command line. In this exercise, you may not enter codes. Hint: Build a table of station names and codes in your JavaScript.

3. Compose the BART API with another API available on the web. The only requirement is that the composition makes good sense and allows you build an interesting application. Be creative.

4. Modify `BARTLightAlert.ino` so that it switches to an even faster rate of blinking when a train is less than 4 minutes from the station.

5. Suppose you are the designer of the JSON messages returned by the BART API. What URLs might you include in the JSON messages and how might the URLs be used by the client? This question asks that you think about "hypertext as the engine of application state" with respect to the BART API.

6. Use ChatGPT and discuss exercise 5.

7. Another interesting "Thing" is the James Webb Space Telescope. Does it have an API? If so, what kind of information does the API provide and what data format is used?

Summing Up

In this chapter we have seen how a major and important part of a city can be interacted with using web technologies. The Bay Area Rapid Transit (BART) system is a web thing. We can read its real time status by way of standard web protocols.

We have worked with three small programs, two in JavaScript and one in C++, that interact with this web thing. The JavaScript programs ran on a laptop or desktop computer and the C++ code was compiled and run on an inexpensive microcontroller. This is a nice example of interoperability – a hallmark of web technologies.

This was accomplished in one chapter in a book on IoT. To see what the professional developers can do, be sure to check out "The Official BART App". It is free for Android and IOS phones and uses the same free and open API that we have used here. While we visited the API with JavaScript and a microcontroller, the Official BART App visits with a smart phone.

Looking Ahead

This chapter discussed how a very large thing, the Bay Area Rapid Transit system, can have a web presence. In the next chapter, we will examine how a small and home built item can also have a web presence. More things, like the one described in the next chapter, will be needed by humans for us to have a sustainable future.

References

1. BART Facts, 2018, "BART Ridership Quick Facts", https://www.bart.gov/sites/default/files/docs/June18FactSheet_v1.pdf. Accessed June 2023.
2. BART,(2014) "Building a better BART", https://www.bart.gov/sites/default/files/docs/BART%20Building%20a%20B etter%20BART%20Executive%20Summary_0.pdf Accessed 2023.
3. Fielding, Roy Thomas. *Architectural Styles and the Design of Network-based Software Architectures.* PhD diss., University of California, Irvine, 2000

Chapter Appendix

```
// Guide to Internet of Things Chapter 4
// VisitBART.js
```

```
// Visit the API of the Bay Area Rapid Transit system in San Francisco.
// To use a browser for trains leaving San Francisco International Airport,
// visit https://www.bart.gov/schedules/eta?stn=SFIA.
// This program uses station codes found here:
// https://api.bart.gov/docs/overview/abbrev.aspx
// A few station codes:
//    rich Richmond
//    sbrn San Bruno
//    sfia San Francisco International Airport
//    pitt Pittsburg/Bay Point
// Run with the following command:
// node VisitBART.js SourceStationCode DestinationStationCode
const https = require('https');

// Create an array of strings from the command line.
// Start from index 2 (this is the third string on the command line).
// We do not want to include "node VisitBART" - strings 0 and 1.
var stringsFromCommandLine = process.argv.slice(2);

// We need to have the source and destination abbreviations.
if(stringsFromCommandLine[0] === undefined || stringsFromCommandLine[1] ===
undefined) {
  console.log("Usage error: node VisitBart.js SourceAbbreviation
DestinationAbbreviation");
  console.log("For example, node VisitBART.js sfia antc");
  process.exit(0);
}
// Set up a string to hold the source abbreviation.
var mySource = stringsFromCommandLine[0];

// Set up a string to hold the destination abbreviation.
var myDestination = stringsFromCommandLine[1];

// Tell the user the source and destination
console.log("Searching for schedule from " + mySource + " to " + myDestination);

// This function makes a call to BART and esatblishes callback handlers.
function visitBARTAPI() {
  // Make the call to BART and provide a callback handler
  const myHttpRequest =
https.get('https://api.bart.gov/api/etd.aspx?cmd=etd&orig='+mySource+'&key=MW9S-
E7SL-26DU-VV8V&json=y', handleBARTResponse);

  // Handle error in request. For example, this method runs if the '.gov' were
removed
  // from the URL.
  myHttpRequest.on('error', (err) => {
    console.log("Error: " + err.message);
    process.exit(0);
  }); // end of myHttpRequest.on
} // end of VisitBARTAPI

// Callback handler for handling the response.
// Called by Node.js when a response arrives.
function handleBARTResponse(response) {
  // This function establishes handlers ro the http response object
```

```
  // When a response arrive, we will collect its data in the variable named
data.
  let data = '';

  // This anonymous function will be called when data is arriving.
  // Here we simply attach the anonymous function to the response object.
  response.on('data', (chunk) => {
    data += chunk;
  }); // end of on 'data'

  // This anonymous function will be called after the response has arrived.
  // Here we simply attach the anonymous function to the response object.
  response.on('end', () => {
    // We are at the end of the response.
    // Build a Javascript object from the JSON data that has arrived.
    var theResult = JSON.parse(data);

    // Check if there is an error message in the response
    // This will occur if the source is not a correct abbreviation.
    // We halt the program if the source is wrong.

     if(theResult.root.message.hasOwnProperty("error")) {
       console.log("Probable Error in source abbreviation");
       console.log(theResult.root.message.error);
       process.exit(0);
     }

    // Examine each departure (etd) and find the particular destination
    // that we expressed interest in (on the command line).
    // State when the train is expected to leave.

    // found is set to false because we have not yet found the destination
    // in the response.[0]
    var found = false;
    // before seaching for destination, make sure there is an etd for some train
    if(theResult.root.station[0].hasOwnProperty('etd')) {
        // Loop through each etd
        for(j = 0; j < theResult.root.station[0].etd.length; j++) {
          // Search for the first matching destination.
          if(theResult.root.station[0].etd[j].abbreviation.toUpperCase() ===
myDestination.toUpperCase()) {
             found = true;  // found a match
             console.log(theResult.root.station[0].etd[j]);
             // take the number of minutes until arrival or 'Leaving'
             min = theResult.root.station[0].etd[j].estimate[0].minutes;
             // Before returing to the client, echo status information to the
console
             if(min === 'Leaving') {
                console.log("Train is leaving the station");
             }
             else {
                // Describe when the train is expected to arrive
                console.log("Train leaves in " + min + " minutes.");
                if(min >= 15) console.log("You have at least 15 minutes.");
                if(min >= 10  && min < 15)console.log("You have at least ten
minutes.");
```

```
                if(min >= 5  && min < 10)console.log("You have at least five
minutes.");
                if(min < 5)console.log("You have less than five minutes. Better
hurry!");
            }
        }
    } // end of for loop
  } // end of if
  // Check if there is a train leaving for this destination.
  if(!found) console.log("No destination train to " + myDestination + "
found.");
  // Tell the user we will continue to check.
  console.log("We are checking again in 15 seconds.");
  });
  // Handle response error
  response.on('error', (err) => {
    console.log('Error in response' + err.msg);
  });
} // end of handleBARTResponse

// This code runs on startup.
console.log("Checking for train leaving from "+ mySource + " to " +
myDestination);

// Call visitBARTAPI at start and then every 15 seconds.
visitBARTAPI();
// Visit the routine visitBARTAPI every 15 seconds
setInterval(visitBARTAPI, 15*1000);
// We now have completed the program but the handlers are still running.
```

```
// Guide to Internet of Things Chapter 4
// File name: VisitBARTWebService.js
// This web service visits the BART API to collect the time
// of arrival of the next train that departs the source
// and leaves for the detination. This program is a client
// of a web service (BART) and also acts as a server - returning
// the number of minutes until the next train arrives.
// The source and destination are provided from the comand line
// at startup.
// If there is a train departing in 5 minutes from source to destination then
the
// JSON string {"Arrival" : "5"} is returned.
// If there is a train departing very soon from source to destination then the
// JSON string {"Arrival" : "Leaving"} is returned.
// If there is no train going to the destination then the JSON string
// {"Arrival" : "-1"} is returned.
// If the source station abbreviation is incorrect the program issues
// an correct usage message and halts.
// Before running this program. Be sure to have node installed and
// run 'npm init' and 'npm install express' in the same directory as this code.
// You will also need a connection to the internet.

// In order to execute this web service code, enter the CLI command
```

```
// node VisitBARTWebService.js SourceAbbreviation DestinationAbbreviation

// Create an array of strings from the command line.
// Start from index 2 (this is the third string on the command line).
// We do not want to include "node VisitBARTWebService" - strings 0 and 1.
var stringsFromCommandLine = process.argv.slice(2);

// In order to continue, we need to have both the source and destination
abbreviations.
if(stringsFromCommandLine[0] === undefined || stringsFromCommandLine[1] ===
undefined) {
  console.log("Usage error: node VisitBart.js SourceAbbreviation
DestinationAbbreviation");
  console.log("For example, node VisitBART.js sfia antc");
  process.exit(0);
}
// Set up a string to hold the source abbreviation.
var mySource = stringsFromCommandLine[0];

// Set up a string to hold the destination abbreviation.
var myDestination = stringsFromCommandLine[1];

// Tell the user the source and destination
console.log("On each http visit, we will fetch a schedule from " + mySource + "
to " + myDestination);

// Setup the express web server to handle the http requests.
const express = require('express')
const app = express()

// This code is a server but also a client of the BART API.
// Here we get access to an https client so that we can make
// calls to the BARTAPI.
const https = require('https');

// This service will listen on TCP port 3000.
const port = 3000


// Set up a listener and display a note to the console.
app.listen(port, () => {
  console.log('To cause a visit to the Bart API, use an HTTP get request and
visit http://localhost:' + port +'/minutesUntilArrival');
})

// This variable will hold the http resonse that we will send back to the
visitor.
var httpResponse;

// Handle an HTTP GET request from a microcontroller or browser.
app.get('/minutesUntilArrival', (req, res) => {

  // announce a new visitor
  console.log("\nNew Get request");
  // We will send data back with the httpResponse variable.
  httpResponse = res;
```

```
  // Call the visit BART API. When the response from BART arrives, write the
response data
  // to the httpResponse variable. The response will go back to the client.
  visitBARTAPI();

})

// This function makes a call to BART and esatblishes callback handlers.
function visitBARTAPI(res) {
  // Make the call to BART and provide a callback handler
  const myHttpRequest =
https.get('https://api.bart.gov/api/etd.aspx?cmd=etd&orig='+mySource+'&key=MW9S-
E7SL-26DU-VV8V&json=y', handleBARTResponse);

  // Handle error in request. For example, this method runs if the '.gov' were
removed
  // from the URL.
  myHttpRequest.on('error', (err) => {
     console.log("Error: " + err.message);
     process.exit(0);
  }); // end of myHttpRequest.on
} //  end of VisitBARTAPI and handlers established.

// Callback handler for handling the response.
// Called by Node.js when a response arrives.
function handleBARTResponse(response) {
  // This function establishes handlers for the http response object.
  // When a response arrive, we will collect its data in the variable named
data.
  let data = '';

  // This anonymous function will be called when data is arriving.
  // Here we simply attach the anonymous function to the response object.
  response.on('data', (chunk) => {
    data += chunk;
  });

  // This anonymous function will be called after the response has arrived.
  // Here we simply attach the anonymous function to the response object.
  response.on('end', () => {
    // We are at the end of the response.
    // Build a Javascript object from the JSON data that has arrived.
    var theResult = JSON.parse(data);

    // Check if there is an error message in the response
    // This will occur if the source is not a correct abbreviation.
    // We halt the program if the source is wrong.

     if(theResult.root.message.hasOwnProperty("error")) {
       console.log("Probable Error in source abbreviation");
       console.log(theResult.root.message.error);
       process.exit(0);
     }

     // Examine each departure (etd) and find the particular destination
     // that we expressed interest in (on the command line).
```

```
    // Respond with when the train is expected to leave.
    // This final value is placed in the httpResponse variable.

    // found is set to false because we have not yet found the destination
    // in the response.
    var found = false;
    var min = 0;
    // before seaching for destination, make sure there is an etd for some train
    if(theResult.root.station[0].hasOwnProperty('etd')) {
        // Loop through each etd
        for(j = 0; j < theResult.root.station[0].etd.length; j++) {
            // Search for the first matching destination.
            if(theResult.root.station[0].etd[j].abbreviation.toUpperCase() ===
myDestination.toUpperCase()) {
                found = true;  // found a match
                console.log(theResult.root.station[0].etd[j]);
                // take the number of minutes until arrival or 'Leaving'
                min = theResult.root.station[0].etd[j].estimate[0].minutes;
                // Before returing to the client, echo status information to the
console
                if(min === 'Leaving') {
                    console.log("Train is leaving the station");
                 }
                 else {
                    // Describe when the train is expected to arrive
                    console.log("Train leaves in " + min + " minutes.");
                    if(min >= 15) console.log("You have at least 15 minutes.");
                    if(min >= 10  && min < 15)console.log("You have at least ten
minutes.");
                    if(min >= 5  && min < 10)console.log("You have at least five
minutes.");
                    if(min < 5)console.log("You have less than five minutes. Better
hurry!");
                }
            }
        } // end of for loop
    } // end of if
  // Now, send the data back to the calling client in JSON format.
  if (found) httpResponse.send('{"Arrival":'+'"'+min+'"}');
  // Check if there is no train leaving for this destination.
  if(!found) {
    httpResponse.send('{"Arrival":'+'"'+"-1"+'"}');
    console.log("No destination train to " + myDestination + " found.");
  }
});
  // Handle response error
  response.on('error', (err) => {
    console.log('Error in response' + err.msg);
  });
} // end of handleBARTResponse
```

```
// Guide to Internet of Things Chapter 4
// BARTLightAlert monitors data from the Bay Area Rapid Transit.
// The Photon 2 blinks the light at D7 at different speeds - depending
upon how close the
// nearest train is to the station. For example, blinking slow
// signifies the train is far away. Blinking fast signifies it is near
the station.
// If there is no train scheduled to arrive or if the web service is
down, the light turns
// on but does not blink.
// You might imagine the microcontroller being embedded in a suitcase.
When you fly
// into San Francisco International, your suitcase can provide
information on how
// soon your train will arrive. Or, the microcontroller might be atached
to your bike
// and have celluar access to the web service.
// For a full view of BART, visit
// https://www.bart.gov/sites/default/files/docs/system-map-detailed-
version.pdf
// Prerequisite: This firmware makes HTTP calls to a web service named
// VisitBARTWebService.js. The IP address of the web service must be
hard coded into
// this firmware. It is VisitBARTWebService.js that actually makes https
calls to
// BART. This firmware is using http to call the web service.
// The HTTPClient library must be included in this project.
#include <HttpClient.h>

boolean DEBUG = true;

// Define the http variable to be of type HttpClient.
HttpClient http;

// We always pass Http headers on each request to the Http server
// Here, we only define a single header. The NULL, NULL pair is used
// to terminate the list of headers.

// The Accept header is used to inform the server
// of the type of message that the client understands. Here,
// we tell the server that we expect to receive data marked up in
// JSON.

http_header_t headers[] = {
    { "Accept", "application/json" },
    { NULL, NULL }
};

// Here we define structures to hold the request and the response data.
// These are declared with types defined in the header file included
above.

http_request_t request;
http_response_t response;
```

```
// Visit the BART API and, depending upon how close the train is, blink
the LED on D7.
const pin_t MY_LED = D7;


// Allow code to run before being connected to Particle.
// The light will blink before breathing cyan.
// This line is optional.
SYSTEM_THREAD(ENABLED);


// Enumerate different blinking states.
// These five identifiers are simply mapped to constants.
enum State {noBlink,verySlow,slow,medium,fast};


// The starting state is no blinking.
State state = noBlink;


// Function prototypes are declarations for the compiler.
// This is not a call to these functions.
State getStateUpdate(void);
String getMinutes(void);
String extractResponseFromJSON(String body);


// The setup() method is called once when the device boots.
void setup() {

    // We will write to the console for debugging.
    // We want to communicate over the USB connection to the computer.
    Serial.begin();

    // In the request object, set the IP address and port of the server
that
    // we will visit. This could be any IP address and port.
    request.ip = IPAddress(192,168,86,216);
    request.port = 3000;

    // We will be using the D7 pin for output
      pinMode(MY_LED, OUTPUT);
}
// A light timer is needed to control blinking speeds
unsigned long blinking_light_timer = 0;

// A state timer is needed to control calls to BART to change state
unsigned long state_timer = 0;

// blink the light
void blink(long milli) {

        if(milli == 0) {
                // no blnk condition
                // Turn on the LED
            digitalWrite(MY_LED, HIGH);
        }
        else {
                // Perform a blink
                // Turn on the LED
            digitalWrite(MY_LED, HIGH);
```

```
                    // Leave it on for milli seconds
                    delay(milli);

                    // Turn it off
                    digitalWrite(MY_LED, LOW);
        }

}

// initialize blink delay below even verySlow
long lightDelayAmt = 15000UL;

// initialize time between calls to BART
// we will only visit the web every 15 seconds
long stateDelayAmt = 15000;

// The loop() method is called frequently.
// We want to exit the loop() quickly if possible
void loop() {

    // every 15 seconds call the API and check the state of trains

    if(millis() - state_timer >= stateDelayAmt) {

        // make a call to BART
        if(DEBUG) Serial.println("Making a call to BART proxy web
service");
        if(DEBUG) Serial.println("to change the state.");
        state = getStateUpdate();

        // set the light speed based on the state
        switch(state) {
            case noBlink : lightDelayAmt = 0UL;
            break;
            case verySlow : lightDelayAmt = 3000UL;
            break;
            case slow: lightDelayAmt = 1000UL;
            break;
            case medium : lightDelayAmt = 500UL;
            break;
            case fast : lightDelayAmt = 100UL;
            break;
            default : lightDelayAmt = 15000UL;
        }

        // don't call again for 15 seconds
        state_timer = millis();
    }

    // after delayAmt, handle blinking
    if(millis() - blinking_light_timer >= lightDelayAmt) {

        blink(lightDelayAmt);

        blinking_light_timer = millis();
```

```
      }
}

State getStateUpdate(void) {
            // get the number of minutes remaining
            // String minutes = getMinutes();
            String minutes = getMinutes();

            // Check the minutes field to decide which light to display.
            // -1 means there is no train coming.
            // This may be due to a report from BART or from a failure
to contact the web
            // service. We simply know of no train arriving for this
destination.
            if(minutes.compareTo("-1") == 0) {
                // set state to no blink
                if(DEBUG)Serial.print("No current train to destination.
Halt the blinking and stay bright.");
                    return noBlink;
            }
            else
                if(minutes.compareTo("Leaving") == 0) {
                    // blink fast if the train is leaving
                    if(DEBUG)Serial.println("You had better be on the
train. It is leaving. Blink fast");
                        return fast;
                }
                else { // blink speed based on how close the train is

                    if(DEBUG)Serial.printlnf("The number of minutes until
arrival is %s", minutes.c_str());

                    int numMinutes = minutes.toInt();

                    if(numMinutes >= 15) {
                            if(DEBUG)Serial.println("very slow if the
train is at least 15 minutes away");
                            return verySlow;
                    }
                    else {
                            if(numMinutes >= 10) {
                                if(DEBUG)Serial.println("slow if the
train is at least 10 minutes but less than 15 minutes away");
                                return slow;
                    }
                    else {
                            if(numMinutes >= 5) {
                                    if(DEBUG)Serial.println("medium speed
blinking if the train is at least 5 minutes but less than 10 minutes
away");
                                    return medium;
                    }
                    else {
                            if(DEBUG)Serial.println("fast for the train
is quite close");
                                return fast;
```

```
                    }
               }

          }
        return noBlink; // The logic should never arrive here. This is
for the compiler.
    }
}
// Make a call on the web service tha, in turn, makes a call on BART.
String getMinutes() {
    String str;
    // Make call to BART proxy to get the number of minutes
    // as a string
    str = doGetRequest();
    // return the string with the number of minutes or -1 or Leaving
    return str;
}

// Provided with a response, display it to the command line interface.
 void printResponse(http_response_t &response) {
   Serial.println("HTTP Response: ");
   Serial.println(response.status);
   Serial.print("Response body:");
   Serial.println(response.body);
 }
// Get minutes from the server
String doGetRequest() {
  // set the path and clear any old response data
  request.path = "/minutesUntilArrival";
  response.status = 0;
  response.body = "";
  // perform an HTTP Get
  http.get(request, response, headers);
  // display if DEBUG is true
  if(DEBUG) printResponse(response);
  // Return the value from the Arrival key
  return (extractResponseFromJSON(response.body));
}

String extractResponseFromJSON(String body) {
    // The default is -1. This means no trains arriving.
    String message = "-1";
    // Parse the JSON
    JSONValue outerObj = JSONValue::parseCopy(body);
    // Drill in and pick up the value
    JSONObjectIterator iter(outerObj);
    if(iter.next()) {
        String name = (String)iter.name();
        if(DEBUG) Serial.println(name);
        if(strcmp(name,"Arrival") == 0) {
            // message might become -1, number of minutes, or Leaving
            message = (String)iter.value().toString();
        }
    }
    // Return -1 or Leaving or number of minutes
    return message;
}
```

CHAPTER 5

Building a Smart, Connected Product

This chapter covers
 Creating a Smart and
 Connected Product
 Sensors and I2C
 Webhooks

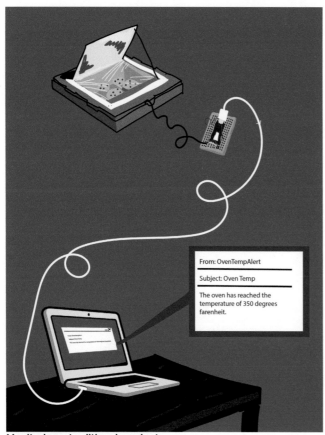

From: OvenTempAlert

Subject: Oven Temp

The oven has reached the
temperature of 350 degrees
farenheit.

Monitoring a traditional product

"The Sun, with all those planets revolving around it and dependent on it, can still ripen a bunch of grapes as if it had nothing else in the universe to do."

Galileo Galilei

Building a smart, connected pizza box oven

Carl Sagan once said, "The nitrogen in our DNA, the calcium in our teeth, the iron in our blood, the carbon in our apple pies were made in the interiors of collapsing stars. We are made of star stuff."

What if, instead of using electricity and fossil fuel, we could heat our food with the power of the stars? What if we used the sun directly? Would the food be hot enough? How would we know when the food was fully cooked?

In this chapter, you build a low-cost IoT solar oven. You'll build the oven from an old pizza box and some basic household items like cardboard, aluminum foil, food wrap, and black paper. You'll attach a temperature gauge that tells you how hot the oven gets and when the food is ready to eat. You'll use the World Wide Web to monitor the performance of your smart product.

You begin by building a traditional product – one with no smarts and no connectivity. Then, you add connectivity to the product using Wi-Fi. Next, you add decision logic by installing microcontroller firmware. And finally, you view temperature and status events on the Particle Console.

Part 1: Building the Pizza Box Oven

What you need:

- Empty pizza box
- aluminum foil
- plastic wrap
- tape
- black paper
- box cutter
- ruler
- scissors
- pie tin
- marker.

What to do:

1. On the top face of the pizza box's lid, draw four lines parallel to the four edges of the
pizza box lid. Draw these lines one inch from the edge of the box. See Figures 5.1 and 5.2.

2. Create a flap by making cuts in the pizza box lid along **three** of the four lines. Don't cut along the line that's near the hinge of the pizza box lid. See Figure 5.3.

3. Using the ruler as a brace, bend the flap's back edge upward to create a crease. See Figure 5.4.

4. Tape foil onto the inside of the flap with the shiny side of the foil facing into the oven. Keep all the tape on the *outside* of the flap. (You want to cook the food, not the tape!) See Figure 5.5.

5. When you open the flap, there's a rectangular hole in the top of the pizza box. Tape two layers of

Figure 5.1: Mark the sides of the box.

Figure 5.2: Draw four lines

Figure 5.3 Cut along three lines.

Figure 5.4 Create a crease

Figure 5.5 The shiny foil faces inside the box.

plastic wrap over the hole. Make sure to cover all the space left open by the flap. See Figure 5.6.

The plastic wrap forms a seal to allow sunshine in and prevent hot air from leaving.

6. Add a third layer of plastic wrap on the underside of the pizza box lid. Again, make sure that none of the tape is inside the box.

Figure 5.6 Apply plastic wrap.

7. Close the pizza box lid and make sure that the plastic wrap forms a tight seal.

8. Line the inside of the pizza box with foil so that the shiny side of the foil is visible. Cover the bottom of the box, and let the foil run up the box's left and right sides. That way, you can apply tape outside of the box to keep the foil in place. See Figure 5.7.

Figure 5.7 Make a seal to keep hot air in.

9. Put black construction paper on the bottom of the box so that the paper completely covers the bottom layer of foil. *Don't use any tape.* (The paper won't go anywhere on its own.) See Figure 5.8.

10. Place the pie tin on the black construction paper.

Figure 5.8 Cover the foil with black paper.

Now you're ready to cook! But ...

...Your oven has some serious drawbacks. You can't set the oven to preheat the way you can with a conventional household oven. And, since weather conditions vary from one day to another (and from one locale to another), you can't rely on cooking food for a specified amount of time.

You need a way to monitor the oven's temperature. A simple thermometer might do the trick. But, in this part of the project, you aim for something fancier.

Part 2: Sensing temperature

What you need:

- Particle Photon 2
- Breadboard
- SHT30 temperature and humidity sensor
- A personal computer with a USB port and WiFi

Figure 5.9: Photon 2 on breadboard

What to do:

1. Place the Photon 2 onto the breadboard. See Figure 5.9.

2. Note the four wires leaving the SHT30. See Figure 5.10.

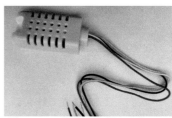

Figure 5.10: SHT30 and four wires

3. Attach the four wires to the breadboard:
   - The black wire should be attached to the Particle 2's ground pin (GND).
   - The red wire should be attached to the Photon 2's power pin (3V3).
   - The yellow wire should be attached to the Photon 2's Serial Clock pin (SCL).
   - The white wire should be attached to the Photon 2's Serial Data pin (SDA).

Figure 5.11: SHT30 connected to Photon 2

   See Figure 5.11.

4. Connect the USB cable to the Photon 2 and your computer's USB port. See Figure 5.12.

5. You will need a copy of the code in ReadTemperature_SHT30-D.ino. The file ReadTemperature_SHT30-D.ino may be found in the chapter appendix and at this URL:

https://github.com/sn-code-inside/guide-to-iot/blob/main/Ch05_code/ReadTemperature_SHT30-D.ino

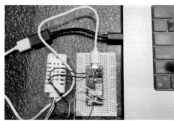

Figure 5.12: Add power to the Photon 2

6. Follow the steps in Chapter 2 to launch the Particle IDE and create a new app. By selecting the library icon and searching for adafruit-sht31, you can include the adafruit-sht31 library into your project.

7. Using Particle's Web IDE, compile and flash ReadTemperature_SHT30-D.ino to the Photon 2.

8. In a shell, execute the command

   particle serial monitor

```
particle serial monitor
Connected to SHT31
Temperature in celsius = 23.70
Temperature in fahrenheit =
74.65
Temperature in celsius = 23.66
Temperature in fahrenheit =
74.58
```

Figure 5.13: Shell with code deployed

See Figure 5.13.

9. Next, you will place the temperature sensor into your pizza box oven. Cut a small hole in the side of the oven and place the SHT30 inside of the box, near the edge, allowing the wires to run out of the hole. See Figure 5. 14. As you did in steps 3 and 4, connect the SHT30 to your Photon 2 and connect the Photon 2 to a power source.

Figure 5.14: The SHT30 placed in the pizza box oven

10. View the temperature readings in the command line shell. Experiment by opening and closing the lid of the box and modifying how much sunlight falls on the foil. The temperatures displayed on the command line should adjust to different conditions.

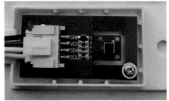

Figure 5.15: SHT30 sensor.

What Did You Do, and How Did You Do It?

What is a Sensor?

The device that you attached to your oven's Photon 2 contains a tiny component called a sensor (See Figure 5.15). As the name suggests, a sensor senses things. Just as your skin senses hot and cold, this electronic device responds to changes in temperature by measuring the properties of a small piece of polymer or ceramic material.

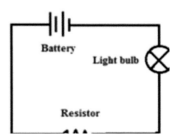

Figure 5.16: A light bulb connected to a battery with a resistor.

Think about an electric circuit like the one in Figure 5.16. You're familiar with batteries and light bulbs, but what about resistors? A resistor is a component that reduces the amount of current in the circuit. You can think of it as a drag on the flow of current. In Figure 5.16, current won't flow as quickly through the light bulb because of the resistor that's slowing down the current. In the case of the SHT30, the resistor is enclosed in the protective shell.

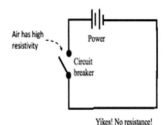

Figure 5.17: A circuit breaker provides the needed resistance.

Any material can serve as a kind of resistor because every material has a property known as its resistivity. At room temperature, materials such as silver, copper, and aluminum have very low resistivity, and other materials (glass, hard rubber, and wood, for example) have very high resistivity.

Nothing good happens when you're doing household electrical work, and you let positive and negative wires touch. (Please, don't try it!) When you do, there's almost no resistance in the circuit, so current flows too rapidly, and you get a nasty, possibly dangerous and destructive spark. If all goes well, a circuit breaker in your basement opens up, forming a gap in the circuit through which no current can flow. (See Figure 5.17). The only material in the gap is ordinary air, and air has enough resistivity to stop the current flow.

(When we say, "enough resistivity," we don't mean infinite resistivity or complete resistivity. Substances such as paraffin wax, fused quartz, and Teflon block current even more effectively than air.)

By the way, the opposite of resistivity is called conductivity. When you freeze mercury or lead to a temperature near absolute zero, you have a superconductor – a substance that offers almost no resistance to the flow of current.

For most materials, the resistivity changes when the material's temperature changes.

For some materials such as iron, steel, and copper, the material's resistance increases when the temperature increases. These materials have positive temperature coefficients.
For other materials such as carbon, the material's resistance decreases when the temperature increases. No surprise here: These materials have negative temperature coefficients.
For some materials such as quartz, the material's resistance changes almost insignificantly when the temperature changes. Yes, these materials have nearly zero temperature coefficients. (Fun fact: One reason that quartz is used in wristwatches is that quartz's temperature coefficient is near zero.)

Speaking of materials, a polymer is a kind of material made of repeating changes of molecules. Most people think of polymers as plastics, but rubber, wood, proteins, and DNA are polymers too. The sensor that you use for your pizza box oven contains a tiny bit of polymer material with a negative temperature coefficient. As the temperature near the sensor rises, the material's resistance decreases, so more current flows through the sensor. This change in current indicates a change in temperature to your Particle Photon 2, and the Photon 2 reports this change to the command line shell.

Sensors come in many varieties. Here are some ways that we classify a particular sensor:

What quantity does it sense?

Does it sense temperature, humidity, position, direction, movement, visible light, infrared light, sound, smoke, carbon monoxide, or something else? The SHT30, for example, senses both temperature and humidity.

The quantity that a sensor measures is called the sensor's input.

Does the sensor require a power source to operate?

Your pizza oven's temperature sensor requires a small amount of power because it measures the amount of current that flows through the resistive material. On the other hand, an old-fashioned mercury thermometer works with no external power. The mercury expands as the temperature rises with no electrical input of any kind.

Here's another example: Some tubular fluorescent bulbs will light up in the presence of microwave radiation. You can do a simple (but not very accurate) test of your microwave oven's leakage by holding an unpowered fluorescent bulb near the oven. (If you try this, be sure to put something in the oven before pressing Start. A cup of water will do, but don't ever turn on an empty microwave oven.

A sensor that requires power to operate, such as the sensor for your pizza box oven, is called an active sensor. A sensor that requires no power, such as a mercury thermometer, is called a passive sensor. When you use a fluorescent bulb to measure microwave radiation, the bulb requires no power other than the radiation itself, and the power that you're measuring doesn't count. So, in this example, the fluorescent bulb is a passive sensor.

Does the sensor produce analog or digital output?

In most cases, the best way to make use of a sensor's reading is to turn it into a number. For example, an accelerometer senses changes in its motion. If you drop an accelerometer from the roof of a building, the accelerometer senses increasing motion as it falls and sudden decreasing motion when it hits the ground. While the device falls, its acceleration is close to 9.8 meters per second per second. (Yes, the words "per second" appear twice.) When the device hits the ground, its acceleration is some other number whose value depends on the building's height.

An accelerometer's output voltage might increase when the acceleration increases. If so, the voltage may increase by any amount. Two voltage readings that are one second apart might be different by 2 volts, or different by only 0.0001 volts. Because the output voltages can differ by arbitrarily small amounts, we call this continuous output, and we call this an analog sensor. To make use of the sensor's output, the board that houses the sensor must (1) have a place where it can receive analog input, and (2) have some way of reporting the amount of voltage as a number.

More modern accelerometers are digital sensors. Like its analog counterpart, a digital accelerometer creates a voltage whose magnitude depends on changes in the sensor's motion. But unlike its analog counterpart, a digital sensor includes circuitry to interpret the voltage as a number. A board that houses a digital sensor must have a place where it can receive digital input. The board doesn't need a way of turning a voltage amount into a number, because the signal that the board receives is already a number.

How does a sensor represent a number? There are many ways to do it, most of them based on the binary (base-2) number system. Think about a sensor whose output can be interpreted as a sequence of eight bits, each bit being a zero or a one. When the sensor outputs 0.0101101, the board's arithmetic circuits treat this as if it's the base-10 number 0.3515625.

Wait! Why does the board interpret the base-2 number 0.0101101 to be the number 0.3515625 in base-10? See the Check Your Understanding section.

Now let's change just one bit. What if the sensor outputs 0.0101100 instead of 0.0101101? The base-10 representation of 0.0101100 is 0.34375. The difference between 0.0101101 and 0.0101100 is a whopping 0.0078125 in base-10, and we got this difference by changing only the last of the eight bits! This means that the smallest difference between two of the sensor's outputs is 0.0078125. It might not seem to be a big difference, but the values that the sensor can output look like this:

    0.0000000
    0.0078125
    0.0156250
    0.0234375
    0.0312500
    ... etc.

There's a gap of size 0.0078125 between any two values that the sensor can output. Because of these gaps, we don't say that the sensor's output is continuous. Instead, we describe this output as being discrete.

The SHT30 is a digital sensor and interprets temperature readings as numbers, producing discrete values.

If you want to measure a particular quantity, and you have a choice of sensors to use, how do you decide which one to use? Here are some criteria:

Which sensors are compatible with the board that you're using?

Some sensors can't be connected to a Particle Photon 2 or, if they are connected to a Particle Photon 2, they simply won't work. If you're using the Photon 2, you can eliminate these sensors immediately.

Which sensors are compatible with the physical limitations of your project?

Imagine having a pedometer that weighs 50 pounds. How useful would that be?

Which sensors have adequate range?

A typical bathroom scale measures weights between 0 and 400 pounds (about 180 kilograms). What would happen if you tried to weigh an elephant with one of these things?

Which sensors have enough resolution?

A sensor's resolution is the extent to which it can distinguish small differences in input values. A high resolution distinguishes very small differences, and a low resolution distinguishes only large differences. Another term to describe high resolution is fine resolution, and the opposite of fine resolution is coarse resolution.

In the United States, a letter weighing one ounce or less (up to roughly 28.35 grams) costs $0.50 to send in the mail. But a letter weighing an ounce and a half costs $0.65. You can't check the weight of your letter on a bathroom scale. The scale doesn't have sufficiently high resolution.

Think again about the digital device that outputs eight binary bits. It can report the difference between the values 0.0000000 and 0.0078125, but it can't distinguish between 0.0000000 and 0.00390625. The fact is, 0.00390625 is halfway between 0.0000000 and 0.0078125. So, if an input's value is 0.00390625, the sensor has to output an approximation (either 0.0000000, which is lower than the real value, or 0.0078125, which is higher than the real value).

Which sensors are accurate enough?

You wear a fitness band to track your heartbeat and the number of steps that you walk each day. How accurate are the band's readings? Does the tightness of the band around your wrist affect the band's heartbeat count? Does the band think you're walking when you're just swinging your arms? Accuracy matters. Sometimes it matters a little bit, and sometimes it matters a lot.

Which sensors can you afford?

Sensors with a wide range, very fine resolution, or a high degree of accuracy generally cost more than those with lesser features. You might not think twice about spending an extra $5.00 for a sensor with a bit more range than what you need, but what if you're planning to put sensors in each of 10,000 units that you'll sell to the public? In that case, a difference of $5.00 or even $0.05 might make a big difference for your bottom line.

How does the sensor communicate?

In your pizza box oven project, you are using an SHT30 temperature sensor that communicates with the Photon 2 using a protocol called I2C. I2C stands for Inter-Integrated Circuit. Developed by Philips Semiconductor in 1982, it is a very popular protocol. It's used by a great number of sensors and actuators.

You provided power to the sensor by connecting the red wire to 3Vc and the black wire to ground (GND). Thus, this sensor is an active sensor, as defined above. The two remaining wires are bidirectional and are used to signal clock pulses with the Serial Clock (SCL) wire and to transmit data bits with the Serial Data (SDA) wire.

Unlike HTTP, an asynchronous protocol, I2C is synchronous. The controller and the peripheral share the same series of clock pulses (generated by the controller) and everything happens in a lock step fashion. There may be more than one peripheral and each has a unique address.

The basic idea is this: the controller sends clock pulses along the SCL wire. At particular moments in time, the controller sends out a device address along the data wire. This transmission also includes a command, e.g., "read" or "write". The address is recognized by the device that is assigned that address and if the command is "read", the peripheral sends data back to the controller along the data line. If the command is "write" then the peripheral expects to receive additional data on the data line. All I2C devices follow this general plan. For more details on how I2C works, see [1].

Note that there are a wide variety of I2C peripherals, our SHT30 sensor is only one type, and different ones may transmit or receive different data depending on what they are designed to do. So, individual controllers must know the application associated with particular peripherals.

In the case of the pizza box oven, the microcontroller firmware uses an address to identify the peripheral. The SHT30 uses the address 0x44 and this is specified in the code. And since we are dealing with a SHT30, we know what middleware library to include.

If we were to use a different peripheral, we would need to change the address and the middleware library. But the basic I2C protocol would remain the same.

Review the code

The code in ReadTemperature_SHT30-D.ino is fairly simple. The simplicity is due to the nice abstractions provided by the adafruit-sht31 library.

Periodically, once every six seconds or so, we make a call on the readTemperature() method of the sht31 object.

float celsius = sht31.readTemperature();

As application developers, we do not need to be concerned with low level details such as the clock speed, acknowledgements from peripherals, or reading the data line. The middleware library makes our lives simpler.

Next, the program converts the Celsius value to Fahrenheit and displays the result on the command line shell.

Part 3: Viewing temperature data in a browser

In Part 2, we worked locally. We added some smarts to a traditional product and we were able to display the temperature of a pizza box oven on a command line console. In Part 3, we will transmit the temperature values to the cloud. In addition, we want to watch those values change in a browser.

What you need:

- Particle Photon 2
- Breadboard

- SHT30 temperature and humidity sensor
- A personal computer with a USB port and WiFi
- A Particle account and access to a browser

What to do:

1. You will need a copy of the code in
`WriteTemperatureToParticle.ino`.The file
`WriteTemperatureToParticle.ino` may be found in the chapter
appendix and at this URL:

https://github.com/sn-code-inside/guide-to-
iot/blob/main/Ch05_code/WriteTemperatureToParticle.ino

2. Using Particle's Web IDE, compile and flash
`WriteTemperatureToParticle.ino` to the Photon 2.

3. View the temperature readings on the Particle Console by
selecting `Events`. When you do, you should see a table like the one
in Figure 5.18. The Photon 2 reports its temperature to the Particle
cloud every six seconds or so. Notice that the event name is
temperature and the data is the value of the temperature.

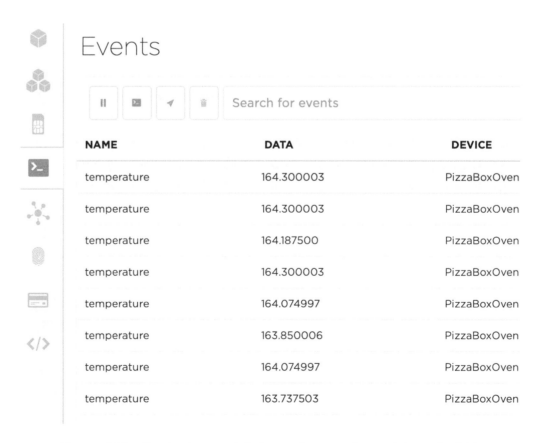

NAME	DATA	DEVICE
temperature	164.300003	PizzaBoxOven
temperature	164.300003	PizzaBoxOven
temperature	164.187500	PizzaBoxOven
temperature	164.300003	PizzaBoxOven
temperature	164.074997	PizzaBoxOven
temperature	163.850006	PizzaBoxOven
temperature	164.074997	PizzaBoxOven
temperature	163.737503	PizzaBoxOven

Figure 5.18: View the pizza box reports its temperature every 6 seconds (approximately).

What Did You Do, and How Did You Do It?

The code in Part 3 is only a slight variation from the code in Part 2. The only addition is some logic to publish the temperature reading to the Particle Console. This is done with the line:

```
Particle.publish("temperature", String(fahrenheit));
```

Again, we see the power of abstraction. The `Particle.publish()` call is causing the transfer of a name-value pair over the internet to Particle. The actual details of how that transfer takes place are handled by the developers of the middleware – not by the application programmer.

At this point, we are simply transmitting the oven temperature to the cloud. Our next step is to add smarts to the controller.

Part 4: Monitoring the pizza box Oven

It's one thing to display an oven's temperatures on a computer screen. It's another thing for the system to be smart about cooking. For example, we want to know if the oven is hot enough and we would like to know when our food is cooked.

In this part of the project, you add logic to selectively display status information to Particle's console in the cloud. This exemplifies edge computing.

Edge computing is an architecture style that leverages computing power to processes data near the edge of the network. In our case, we will use this style to determine if our oven temperature is sufficient to cook a meal and whether or not the cooking is done.

What you need:

- Particle Photon 2
- Breadboard
- SHT30 temperature and humidity sensor
- A personal computer with a USB port and WiFi
- A Particle account and access to a browser

What to do:

1. You will need a copy of the code in `WriteCookingStatusToParticle.ino`.The file

`WriteCookingStatusToParticle.ino` may be found in the chapter appendix and at this URL:

https://github.com/sn-code-inside/guide-to-iot/blob/main/Ch05_code/WriteCookingStatusToParticle.ino

2. Using Particle's Web IDE, compile and flash `WriteCookingStatusToParticle.ino` to the Photon 2.

What Did You Do, and How Did You Do It?

Review the code

The file `WriteCookingStatusToParticle` contains two global variables near the top: a floating-point variable named `cookingTemperature` and an integer variable named `numMinutes`. These must be set by the developer before flashing the firmware to the device. You will want to modify these values before cooking food in your pizza box oven. The current values are for testing the logic.

It also has a `loop()` function that makes a call to `writeCookingStatus()` every six seconds or so. The idea is to sample the cooking temperature every six seconds.

The code defines 1 cooking interval to be six seconds. Therefore, 1 cooking interval divided by six seconds equals 1. If we want to cook our meal for 5 minutes, we need

5 * 60 sec * (1 cooking interval / 6 sec) = 50 cooking intervals.

This is the way that `writeCookingStatus()` determines if the meal is done. If the temperature has been high enough for more than the correct number of intervals, the event `your_food_is_done` is published to Particle.

If the temperature has been high enough but the cooking time is not sufficient then the event `cooking_in_progress` is published to Particle.

If the temperature is too low then the event `temperature_below_threshold` is published and the interval counter is set to zero.

There is no attempt to handle over cooking conditions and if there is a brief drop in temperature (and if that drop is noticed at the end of a six second interval) then the program assumes that interval counting must begin from scratch. These are problems that you might want to explore along with the exercises.

Firmware

Firmware is a specific kind of software. It's software that's stored in *non-volatile memory*. Whatever you store in non-volatile memory stays in the memory when you power down the device. When you power up again, the firmware is able to execute again. The code discussed in this chapter is C++ code that is compiled and then installed as firmware on your device.

Part 5: Using Webhooks[2]

Suppose that you would like to receive an email message when your food is cooked. You can do this by informing Particle that when a particular event arrives, to make an HTTP request to a service (outside of Particle) that responds by sending an email notification to a pre-arranged address. Two popular services that will do this for you are If This Then That (IFTTT) and Zapier (there are several others). Here, we will build such a system using IFTTT.

What to do:

You will first configure IFTTT and then configure Particle.

IFTT uses a *trigger* that, when true, causes an *action* to run.

1. Visit https://ifttt.com/home and sign up for IFTTT.
2. Choose `Create` to create a new Applet.
3. On the `If This` select `Add` and choose a service as Webhook.
4. Click the Webhook icon.
5. The trigger will be "Receive a web request with JSON payload".
6. The event name field will be your_food_is_done (without quotes). This is the same name we are using inside our firmware.
7. Select `Create Trigger`.
8. On `Then That` select `Add`.
9. Enter `email`. Select the email button and click `Send me an email`.
10. Complete the subject field with: Pizza Box Oven Notification.
11. Complete the body field with: Your food is done cooking!
12. Select Create Action.
13. Select Continue and then Finish.
14. You will need and API key. Visit https://ifttt.com/maker_webhooks/settings
15. Copy the API key that follows /use/.

Configure Particle by using the Web IDE.

1. Select the Console icon on the left of the screen. It appears as a bar graph.
2. On the Events page, select the integrations icon on the left. It appears as a star network.
3. On the top right, click the Add New Integration button.
4. Choose Webhook.
5. The name field is: Cooking complete. This is just a description.
6. The Event Name is your_food_is_done. This is the particle event name.
7. The URL is: https://maker.ifttt.com/trigger/your_food_is_done/with/key/YOUR_IFTTT_API _KEY
8. Take the remaining defaults and select Create Webhook.
9. Before flashing the firmware, it is suggested that you first modify the code in `WriteCookingStatusToParticle` so that the `your_food_is_done` event is only generated once. Otherwise, you may receive too many emails (and go beyond the daily limit of 30 set by IFTTT). Hint: add a boolean variable to your code and test it before generating the event to Particle.

What Did You Do, and How Did You Do It?

The importance of the World Wide Web to IoT

One of the central themes of this book is to view the Internet of Things as an extension of the World Wide Web. The principles found in the design of the Web provide guidance for the creation of an interoperable Internet of Things.

Some of the protocols described here are not web protocols. The I2C conversation between the sensor and the microcontroller is not based on the World Wide Web. But much of the backend conversation that allows your oven to interoperate with your email server is based on the Web.

The Web-based IFTTT site lets you connect two systems (the Particle cloud and Email messaging from IFTTT) even though neither was designed to work with the other. This is an example of *system integration*. It's an important software engineering activity from the enterprise level down to our simple experiment with a pizza box oven.

How was this system integration accomplished? It was accomplished because the system designers at Particle and IFTTT provide an *application programming interface* (API).

Parties that aren't associated with IFTTT can make *standard* HTTP requests to a particular URL. For each request, IFTTT sends back a *standard* HTTP response with *standard* JSON text. Upon receiving the request, IFTTT can carry out its mission – in this case, by sending email

Notice how we use the word "standard" three times in the previous paragraph. We do this to emphasize the fact that the use of standard data formats (JSON) and standard protocols (HTTP) and standard URL's make this degree of interoperability commonplace.

The use of standard interfaces is, of course, not restricted to the design of the Web. For example, if you purchase a new microwave oven, then you're not normally concerned with the shape of its electrical plug. The plug is designed according to a standard, and your kitchen's electrical outlets abide by that standard. Your kitchen may have been built well before the invention of microwave ovens. Even so, the kitchen's electrical outlets interoperate with the microwave oven just fine. This may not be true, of course, if you take your new microwave oven to a different country. The other country's standards for plugs and outlets may be quite different.

In Figure 5.19, we show the architecture of the IoT system built in this chapter. In Figure 5.20 we add some details showing the communication protocols.

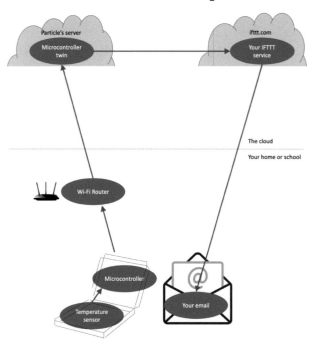

Figure 5.19: An architectural description of the system built in this chapter..

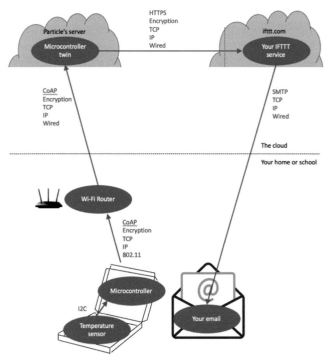

Figure 5.20: A view of the system built with some protocol details.

Check Your Understanding

1. Describe the steps needed to convert a product into a connected product.

2. Describe how smarts can be added to a product without being connected.

3. Describe how the system that we have built is using the microcontroller as a gateway device.

4. Describe the greenhouse effect in terms of the pizza box oven.

5. Use a calculator (or a web site) to convert the base-2 number 0.0101101 to base 10.

7. How does network layering contribute to the important property of separation of concerns?

9. Modify `WriteCookingStatusToParticle.ino` so that only one email is sent. Currently, it will cause an email to be sent every six seconds.

11. Describe the importance of standards and what role they play in connecting the pizza box to your email server.

Make More / Explore Further

1. **Moving Average.** Modify your microcontroller firmware so that it transmits to the Particle cloud only an average of the last five temperatures arriving from the sensor. With every new temperature reading, your code recomputes this *moving average*. A moving average smooths out momentary variations in temperature. You will still transmit a message every 6 seconds or so.

2. **Cumulative Average.** Modify your microcontroller firmware so that it generates a *cumulative average* -- an average of all temperature values from when the microcontroller starts running (not just the five most recent values).

Hint: To do this, you don't have to store all previous temperature values.

3. **Dead band Filtering.** Modify your microcontroller firmware so that it reports only temperatures outside of a particular range. For example, if you establish your range as 100 to 120 degrees, the `DATA` column in Figure 5.18 contains rows only for any values below 100 or above 120.

4. **Transforms.** Modify your microcontroller firmware so that all reports are in degrees Celsius rather than degrees Fahrenheit.

5. **Mash-Up.** Using the Open Weather API (`https://api.openweathermap.org`), build a system that notifies the user if rain is in the local forecast. (Bring the pizza box oven indoors before it gets wet!) The detailed design of this system is in your hands.

6. **Safety.** The World Health Organization reports that bacteria is killed at a cooking temperature of 149 degrees Fahrenheit. Modify your microcontroller firmware so that it generates events to the `Particle` console when and if this threshold is crossed (in either direction). One event would be called `safe_cooking` and the other would be called `unsafe_cooking`. The events are only generated when the threshold is crossed.

7. Use generative AI to search for a list of five different sensors that use I2C to communicate.

8. Use generative AI to search for a list of five different actuators that use I2C to communicate.

9. How does our smart and connected pizza box oven implement the IoT model found in Chapter 1?

10. Rather than using email, we would like a Slack message to be sent to the user when the food is cooked. Use IFTTT to implement a Slack solution.

11. Zapier competes with IFTTT. Use Zapier to notify the user when the cooking is done. You may use email, SMS, or Slack.

Summing Up

Who knew that a pizza box oven could be so intricate? You started with a physical oven - nothing fancy, but certainly functional. By adding the Particle Photon 2, you made the oven smart. But being smart isn't useful unless information reaches the outside world. So, you connected your Particle Photon 2 to the cloud and viewed the oven's temperatures on a web page. At that point, you didn't need to be anywhere near the oven. You could have been in Paris while the oven was in New York.

But what if you weren't keeping an eye on the web page? For the oven to notify you of its interesting events, you connected the Particle web page with IFTTT and IFTTT with your email server. When the pizza was cooked, you received an email.

You did all this with only a few inexpensive parts - some cardboard, aluminum foil, cellophane, a small microcontroller, and free access to the cloud and two web services. But what if we want to scale up an IoT solution? What if we need thousands of devices communicating in real time with many users? Perhaps our IoT devices are embedded in a factory or a truck and are mobile.

Looking Ahead

IoT devices should blend in with their surroundings. They should be small and unobtrusive. There can be thousands of identical devices, so each device should be inexpensive. IoT devices are built into common, everyday items - items that may move from place to place. Each of these devices must communicate with users or other systems in real time. On occasion, they will be disconnected and fail. How do we keep these thousands of devices well organized? How do we tolerate the failures in the devices and the networks?

In 1999, two engineers published the first version of a standard called *Message Queue Telemetry Transport*. It's a standard for communicating over channels that may be slow or easily interrupted. The standard works with large and small devices (with limited storage, faulty networks, and limited processing power). MQTT (as the acronym goes) is perfect for device-to-device communication in an IoT application. That's why, in the next chapter, you learn how MQTT works, why it works so well, and what kinds of things you can do with it.

References

1. Leens, Frederic. *An introduction to I2C and SPI protocols.* IEEE Instrumentation & Measurement Magazine 12, no. 1 (2009): 8-13. https://doi.org/10.1109/MIM.2009.4762946
2. Particle, *Webhooks*, Particle Documentation, accessed July, 2023, https://docs.particle.io/getting-started/integrations/webhooks/."

Chapter Appendix

```
// Guide to Internet of Things
// Chapter 5
// ReadTemperature_SHT30-D.ino monitors temperature data from
// SHT30-D temperature sensor.
// Be sure to include the adafruit-sht31 library in this project.
// Include the header file for this library.

#include <adafruit-sht31.h>

// Get access to an Adafruit_SHT31 object.
Adafruit_SHT31 sht31 = Adafruit_SHT31();

// Initialize timer
unsigned long timer = 0;
// Delay amount is set to six seconds
unsigned long delayAmount = 6000;

void setup() {
   // The variable connected will be true or false depending on the
  connection to SHT31-D.
   bool connected;
   // We may use the USB connection as well.
```

```
    Serial.begin();
    // Establish a connection to temperature sensor.
    connected = sht31.begin(0x44);
    // Inform the user if the connection was established.
    if (connected) {
      Serial.println("Connected to SHT31");
    }
    else {
      Serial.println("Error: Not connected to SHT31");
    }
    // initialize timer
    timer = millis();
} // end of setup

void loop() {

    // The variable goodTemp will be true when the temperature is a
number.
    bool goodTemp;
    // Get the temperature every 6 seconds or so.
    if(millis() - timer >= delayAmount) {

        // The device reports temperatures in celsius.
        float celsius = sht31.readTemperature();

        // Is the value a number? If so then not a number (isnan) is
false and !isnan is true.
        goodTemp = !isnan(celsius);

        if (goodTemp) {

            Serial.print("Temperature in celsius = ");
            Serial.println(celsius);

            // Convert to fahrenheit.
            float fahrenheit = (celsius* 9.0) /5.0 + 32.0;

            Serial.print("Temperature in fahrenheit = ");
            Serial.println(fahrenheit);
        } else { // not a good temp
            Serial.println("The temperature is not a number.");
        }
        // reset the timer
        timer = millis();
    }
}
```

```
// Guide to Internet of Things
// Chapter 5
// WriteTemperatureToParticle.ino reads data from a SHT30-D
 temperature sensor
```

```
// and writes temperature data to the Particle Console.
// Be sure to include the adafruit-sht31 library in this project.
// Include the header file for this library.

/* Example usage:
   Publish a name-value pair to the Particle Console
   int temp = 19;
   Particle.publish("temperature", String(temp));
*/

#include <adafruit-sht31.h>

// Get access to an Adafruit_SHT31 object.
Adafruit_SHT31 sht31 = Adafruit_SHT31();

// Initialize timer
unsigned long timer = 0;
// Delay amount is set to six seconds
unsigned long delayAmount = 6000;

void setup() {
  // The variable connected will be true or false depending on the
 connection to SHT31-D.
  bool connected;
  // We may use the USB connection as well.
  Serial.begin();

  // Establish a connection to temperature sensor.
  // The SHT30-D's address is 0x44. Other I2C sensors will
  // have other addresses. These addreeses are specified in the
datasheet
  // for the device.
  connected = sht31.begin(0x44);
  // Inform the user if the connection was established.
  if (connected) {
    Serial.println("Connected to SHT31");
  }
  else {
    Serial.println("Error: Not connected to SHT31");
  }
  // initialize timer
  timer = millis();
} // end of setup

void loop() {

  // The variable goodTemp will be true when the temperature is a
number.
  bool goodTemp;
  // Get the temperature every 6 seconds or so.
  if(millis() - timer >= delayAmount) {

      // The device reports temperatures in celsius.
      float celsius = sht31.readTemperature();
```

```
        // Is the value a number? If so then not a number (isnan) is
    false and !isnan is true.
        goodTemp = !isnan(celsius);

        if (goodTemp) {

            Serial.print("Temperature in celsius = ");
            Serial.println(celsius);

            // Convert to fahrenheit.
            float fahrenheit = (celsius* 9.0) /5.0 + 32.0;

            // If not connected do not try to publish
            if(Particle.connected()) {
                Particle.publish("temperature", String(fahrenheit));
            }
            Serial.print("Temperature in fahrenheit = ");
            Serial.println(fahrenheit);
        } else { // not a good temp
            Serial.println("The temperature is not a number.");
        }
        // reset the timer
        timer = millis();
    }
}
```

```
// Guide to Internet of Things
// Chapter 5
// WriteCookingStatusToParticle.ino reads data from a SHT30-D
 temperature sensor
// and uses decision logic to write cooking status information to
 the Particle
// Console.

// Be sure to include the adafruit-sht31 library in this project.
// Include the header file for this library.

#include <adafruit-sht31.h>

// Get access to an Adafruit_SHT31 object.
Adafruit_SHT31 sht31 = Adafruit_SHT31();

// Initialize timer
unsigned long timer = 0;
// Delay amount is set to six seconds
unsigned long delayAmount = 6000;

void setup() {
  // The variable connected will be true or false depending on the
 connection to SHT31-D.
```

```
  bool connected;
  // We may use the USB connection as well.
  Serial.begin();
  // Establish a connection to temperature sensor.
  // The SHT30-D's address is 0x44. Other I2C sensors will
  // have other addresses. These addreeses are specified in the
datasheet
  // for the device.
  connected = sht31.begin(0x44);
  // Inform the user if the connection was established.
  if (connected) {
    Serial.println("Connected to SHT31");
  }
  else {
    Serial.println("Error: Not connected to SHT31");
  }
  // initialize timer
  timer = millis();
} // end of setup

// Cooking values
float cookingTemperature = 78.0;
int numMinutes = 1;

void loop() {

  // The variable goodTemp will be true when the temperature is a
number.
  bool goodTemp;
  // Get the temperature every 6 seconds or so.
  if(millis() - timer >= delayAmount) {

      // The device reports temperatures in celsius.
      float celsius = sht31.readTemperature();

      // Is the value a number? If so then not a number (isnan) is
false and !isnan is true.
      goodTemp = !isnan(celsius);

      if (goodTemp) {

          Serial.print("Temperature in celsius = ");
          Serial.println(celsius);

          // Convert to fahrenheit.
          float fahrenheit = (celsius* 9.0) /5.0 + 32.0;
          // Write ststus evey 6 seconds or so
          writeCookingStatus(fahrenheit, cookingTemperature,
numMinutes);

          Serial.print("Temperature in fahrenheit = ");
          Serial.println(fahrenheit);
      } else { // not a good temp
        Serial.println("The temperature is not a number.");
      }
      // reset the timer
```

```
                    timer = millis();
        }
}
// If we rise above the cooking temperature we are in an interval.
bool inInterval = false;
// We count how many times we are in that interval.
int intervalCounter = 0;

// Send the current temperauture and the cooking status to the
 Particle Console.
void writeCookingStatus(float currentTemperature, float
 cookingTemperature, int minutes) {

  // 1 cookingInterval == 6 seconds
  // 1 cookingInterval/(6 seconds) == 1
  // For one minute of cooking, we need 10 cookingIntervals.
  // cookingIntervals == minutes * 60 / 6
  int cookingIntervals = minutes * 60 / 6;
  // store current temperature  in "temperature" string
  String temperature = String(currentTemperature);
  // Publish a name-value pair to Particle
  Particle.publish("temperature", temperature, PRIVATE);

  if(currentTemperature > cookingTemperature) {
    // We are cooking at the proper temperature
    inInterval = true;
    // Count the number of times that we are in a cooking interval.
    intervalCounter = (intervalCounter + 1);

    // In the interval for long enough?
    if(intervalCounter >= cookingIntervals) {
      // publish to cloud that the cooking is done
      Particle.publish("your_food_is_done");
    }
    else {
      // publish to cloud that cooking is in progress
      Particle.publish("cooking_in_progress");
    }
  }
  else {
    // Publish to cloud that the current temperature is not
 sufficient.
    // We are not in a cooking interval.
    inInterval = false;
    intervalCounter = 0;
    Particle.publish("temperature_below_threshold");
  }
}
```

CHAPTER 6

Publish Subscribe Using MQTT

This chapter covers
> **Publish Subscribe with MQTT**
> **Microcontroller Publications**
> **Browser Subscriptions**
> **Visualization**

Bicycling in France

"You can't reason with your heart; it has its own laws, and thumps about things which the intellect scorns."

Mark Twain
A Connecticut Yankee
in King Arthur's Court

Failure detection with heartbeats at scale

Johan Museeuw, the former world champion bike rider, once said that "Crashing is part of cycling as crying is part of love".

Sometimes it seems that crashing is part of everything!

In this chapter, we explore the ramifications to IoT of this fact. How do we detect that a rider has crashed or that her system has failed or that she has temporarily disconnected from her network?

Just think of all of the useful data that can be generated, transmitted, and visualized by bike riders in a great bike race such as the Tour de France. A web user will want to view the current winner, the map of the race, the speed and GPS location of individual racers and, of course, whether a particular rider is still actively producing data. This last bit of data is more fundamental, without it, the others are not possible.

The focus of this chapter will be on simple failure detection, web visualization, and scaling.

You begin by setting up an MQTT broker that can handle incoming data from many microcontrollers and, at the same time, produce data for many browsers.

Then, you will add firmware to your microcontroller that produces heartbeats to the MQTT broker. And finally, you build a web application that uses Google Charts to visualize the data in a graphical display. We will see that this architecture might work quite well in the Tour de France.

Part 1: Set Up and interact with an MQTT Broker

What you need:

- Access to the Web
- An Apple or Windows computer

What to do:

1. With a browser, visit `https://mosquitto.org/`
2. Select the `Download` tab.
3. You want to select the binary installation.
4. Follow the directions on `https://mosquitto.org/` to install Mosquitto on your local machine. There are directions for Windows, Mac, and Linux machines.
5. Run mosquito from the command line by typing:

    ```
    mosquito
    ```

6. Notice that it starts up and is waiting for connections. Leave this command shell running. Watch this window as you perform the following two steps.
7. Open a new command shell and execute a command to subscribe to a topic. Suppose we are interested in any messages published to the `heartbeat` topic. The `-h` stands for host and the `-t` stands for topic. Enter the command

    ```
    mosquitto_sub -h localhost -t heartbeat/#
    ```

8. Open another command shell (you need to have three command shells open at this point). Enter the following command (using `-m` for message) to publish the message `thump` to the heartbeat topic:

    ```
    mosquitto_pub -h localhost -t heartbeat -m "thump"
    ```

9. Execute this publishing command several times and watch the subscription window. It should change every time that you publish a "thump".

What Did You Do, and How Did You Do It?

In Part 1, you downloaded the mosquitto program and ran it on your machine. You interacted with mosquitto with two MQTT clients – a subscribing client and a publishing client. The subscribing client sent a message to mosquitto and told it that it (the subscribing client) was interested in any message published to a topic named `heartbeat`. When a message was sent to the `heartbeat` topic by the publishing client, mosquitto forwarded the message to the subscriber. See Figure 6.1.

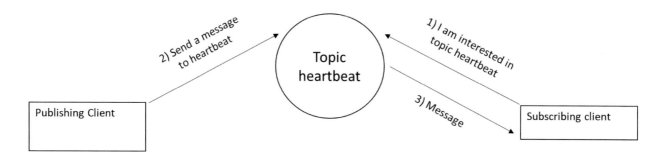

Figure 6.1 The steps of publish subscribe. 1) subscribe to topic 2) publish to topic 3) receive message.

Wildcards in Topics

The reader may have noticed that our subscriber did not subscribe to the topic `heartbeat` but to the topic `heartbeat` followed by an octothorp character. That is, the subscribing client subscribed to:

        heartbeat/#

The symbols `/#` allow the client to subscribe to `heartbeat` as well as any sub-topic under `heartbeat`. It acts as a wild card. That is, by subscribing to `heartbeat/#` the client is also subscribing to the following topics:

        heartbeat
        heartbeat/rate
        heartbeat/rate/bps
        heartbeat/is/nice/to/have

If the publisher client publishes a message to the topic `heartbeat/is/nice/to/have` then a subscribing client that subscribes to `heartbeat/#` will receive the message. Give this a try. The octothorp character is optional. If used, it must appear as the last character in the topic.

Subscribers may also use the plus character as a single-level wild card. For example, a subscriber might subscribe to the following topic:

        home/+/motion

A publication to any of the following topics will be forwarded by the broker to the subscriber:

```
home/kitchen/motion
home/basement/motion
home/livingroom/motion
```

Note that only subscribers and not publishers may use wild cards.

In general, it is good practice to refrain from using space characters in topics. And note that topics are case sensitive. A subscription to `vehicle/electrical/recharge` is not the same as a `Vehicle/Electrical/Recharge` subscription.

The publish-subscribe design pattern

The publish-subscribe pattern used here is an old and important one.

People have been publishing and subscribing to newspapers since at least the 1500s. Today, we subscribe to web-based information feeds for news updates in politics, sports, and entertainment.

Machines may also act as publishers of messages. For example, a machine may publish reports on its status or what it has recently sensed. A human may then view the data on a static report or a dynamic real-time dashboard.

Machines may also play the role of subscribers. The messages that they subscribe to may contain commands that they are built to carry out. The publisher of the order may be a human or another machine.

For reasons we explore below, the publish subscribe pattern is typically done by adding a third party, a broker, that sits between the source of the message and its destination.

The idea is actually quite simple. Some broker keeps track of subscribers and topics. That is, the broker keeps track of who is interested in what. When a publication to the broker arrives, it contains a message associated with a particular topic. If any subscribers have expressed an interest in that specific topic, the broker forwards the message to the subscribing clients.

Let's consider a single broker and two clients – one that subscribes and one that publishes. First, the broker is established. Second, a subscribing client sends a message to the broker stating that it is interested in a particular topic. The subscribing client also provides the broker address information so that the broker can send messages to the subscribing client. This address is referred to as the callback address or simply a callback. Third, a publishing client sends a message to the broker, specifying the topic of the message. Fourth, the broker passes along the message to any subscribing client who has expressed interest in the topic. It can do this because it knows the callback addresses of the subscribing clients.

This communication between the two clients uses the broker as a third party. Why not just have the publisher send information directly to the subscriber? Why is the third party necessary?

The answer is that the involvement of a third party has some very nice properties.

Scaling

The reader may have noticed that a system architected in this way scales very well to many subscribers and many publishers. Suppose we have 10 or 100 subscribers and a single publisher. The publisher simply sends one message (to the broker), and the broker handles the rest – sending the message out to each subscriber that has expressed interest in the topic. Suppose we have many subscribers and many topics, and many publishers. As long as the broker is fast enough and has memory available, the broker will select those interested in the topic and forward the message to them. See Figure 6.2.

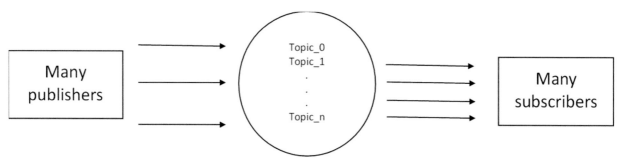

Figure 6.2 Scaling to many subscribers, publishers, and topics

Loose Coupling

Karl Weick[1] was the first to coin the term "loose coupling" when describing organizations. The term is also widely used in software engineering. In short, an organization or computer system is considered loosely coupled if one part of the system is only lightly associated with or dependent upon the other parts.

Consider a hospital emergency room for an example of a loosely coupled organization. If the emergency room were to shut down, the other parts of the hospital could continue to work, for the most part, as usual. There may be some disruption, but it would not be catastrophic. The emergency room is only loosely coupled to the rest of the organization.

For a tightly coupled system, consider the traditional conveyor belt. Raw materials are placed on the belt, and as they move along, work on the material is performed in fixed stages. Each stage requires that the prior stage be correctly executed and complete. If, however, the raw materials fail to arrive or early work is performed poorly, the entire system may be disrupted. Later stages are tightly coupled to the timely performance of earlier stages.

In communication systems design, MQTT brokers (or, more generally, the publish subscribe architectures) provide us with the ability to design loosely coupled communicating systems. In general, we want to reduce the amount of information that one party needs to know about the other and reduce the dependency of one party on the other.

There is always some dependency or coupling. For example, the publisher and subscriber need to know the location (URL) of the broker. Both players do depend upon the broker being available and at a specific location.

However, the publisher does not need to know where any of its subscribers are located. Nor does the publisher need to know how many subscribers are interested in its publications. The subscribers may be many or few or non-existent. Only the broker needs to know those details. The publisher is not at all disrupted by changes on the subscriber side. Only the broker needs to be aware of changes in the number of subscribers, their locations, and their interests.

In addition, a subscriber need not be concerned with the location of publishers and may not even be aware of who or what is publishing. It simply informs the broker of its interest in a particular topic. The subscriber may receive messages from many publishers.

Subscribers may even come and go. If a subscriber decides to leave the system, it simply informs the broker that it is no longer available to receive publications. The broker can simply discard that subscriber from its list of subscribers. The publisher is not impacted by a change in the number of subscribers.

Publishers may come and go as well. If a publisher decides to leave the system, it can simply stop sending publications. There is no additional work for the broker to do. Subscribers may receive fewer messages but are otherwise not disrupted.

As was mentioned, every system has some degree of coupling. If an emergency room goes down, other parts of the hospital will not be able to direct patients needing emergency care to that location. Likewise, if the messages being published to an MQTT broker are being sent by a faulty or compromised device, bad data may be sent, and poor decision making on the part of subscribers may result.

Separation of Concerns

The design principle of "separation of concerns" also applies to organizations and computer systems. The idea is to break a system into components or modules where each component or module does one thing well. By following this principle, we may more easily reason about the systems we are building.

Organizations are usually broken into modules where each module has certain well-defined responsibilities. A university, for example, may have a module devoted to advising and another devoted to human resources. Hopefully, each module does what it does well and is separated from the other modules. The separation of concerns that we find in organizations reduces complexity and confusion.

The use of a publish subscribe broker, such as mosquitto, also exemplifies this design principle. The publishing and subscribing clients do what they do well – subscribing and publishing application-level messages. The broker handles all of the many details associated with matching publishers with subscribers through topics. Using this third-party approach, the overall effect is to increase modularity and reduce confusion and complexity.

Creators of MQTT

MQ Telemetry Transport (MQTT) was created at IBM by Andy Stanford-Clark and Arlen Nipper in 1999. It was open sourced and became an OASIS standard [2] in 2014. It was originally used for remote pipeline monitoring via satellites.

Both Stanford-Clark and Nipper have had interesting carreers.

Andy Stanford-Clark, currently the Chief Technology Officer for IBM in the United Kingdom and Ireland, installed sensors in his home to monitor energy use. Insights gained allowed Andy to reduce his electricity bills by one third. IBM refers to Andy as "Master Inventor" and he has been active on the Isle of Wright – an island whose community is intent on building a sustainable future. By using solar, wind, tidal, and geothermal energy sources, the hope is to convert the Isle of Wright into a self-sufficient and energy efficient community.

Arlen Nipper, currently President and Chief Technology Officer of Cirrus Link, argues that just as HTTP drove the success of the Internet of People, MQTT will drive the success of the Internet of Things.

Drawbacks

There are drawbacks to using a loosely coupled publish subscribe system. All messages must travel through the third party, the broker, before being delivered. This is slower than if we were to connect the communicating parties directly. If you need lightning speed in a hard real time system, MQTT may not be appropriate. In addition, the broker represents a single point of failure. If the broker crashes, all of the communication in the system comes to a halt.

Despite these drawbacks, and due to its loosely coupled nature, IoT systems designers typically separate concerns and leverage the publish subscribe communication pattern. You will find MQTT or other publish subscribe brokers being used in many IoT systems – large and small.

For the reasons outlined here, the publish subscribe pattern has become very important in everyday life, in the world of IoT, and even in the world of enterprise computing. See the sidebar on publish subscribe in the enterprise.

Publish Subscribe in the Enterprise

Suppose you work in a large company and different parts of the enterprise have their own database. Records about you might be held in your own department as well as in human resources, financial management, and security.

If you were to change your address, how could all of these systems, held by different stakeholders, be cleanly brought up to date?

The Enterprise Integration Patterns site[3], maintained by Gregor Hohpe and Bobby Woolf, provides us with a solution based on publish-subscribe messaging.

The publisher publishes a new address and the subscribers all receive the update. See Figure 6.3.

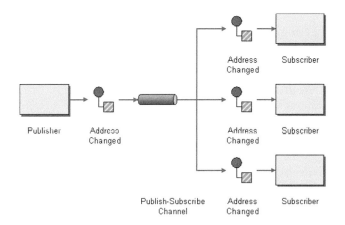

Figure 6.3 Publish subscribe in the enterprise (with permission)

Part 2: Publish to MQTT with a microcontroller

What you need:

- An MQTT broker, such as mosquitto, running on a computer
- A Particle Photon 2
- WiFi

What to do:

1. Prior to running Mosquito, edit its configuration file.

    a. On a Mac, depending on the setup, the configuration file may be found at:

        ```
        /usr/local/etc/mosquitto/mosquitto.conf
        ```

    b. Also on a Mac, the configuration may be found at:

        ```
        /opt/homebrew/etc/mosquitto/mosquitto.conf
        ```

    c. On a Windows machine, the configuration file is typically found at:

        ```
        C:\Program Files\mosquitto\mosquitto.conf
        ```

    d. At the very bottom of the `mosquitto.conf configuration file`, add the following five lines:

        ```
        listener 1883
        protocol mqtt
        listener 9002
        protocol websockets
        allow_anonymous true
        ```

2. On a MAC, run a command shell and start mosquitto (picking up the new configuration file) with the following command. See Figure 6.4.

    ```
    mosquitto -c /opt/homebrew/etc/mosquitto/mosquitto.conf -v
    ```

3. On a Windows machine, run a command shell and start mosquito (picking up the new configuration file) with the following command:

    ```
    mosquitto -c "C:\Program Files\mosquitto\mosquitto.conf"
    ```

```
mosquitto -c /opt/homebrew/etc/mosquitto/mosquitto.conf -v
1689267264: mosquitto version 2.0.14 starting
1689267264: Config loaded from /opt/homebrew/etc/mosquitto/mosquitto.conf.
1689267264: Opening ipv6 listen socket on port 1883.
1689267264: Opening ipv4 listen socket on port 1883.
1689267264: Opening websockets listen socket on port 9002.
1689267264: mosquitto version 2.0.14 running
```

Figure 6.4 Running Mosquitto from the command line on a MAC

4. Visit Particle.io at `https://www.particle.io/`

5. Login with your credentials at Particle (as described in Chapter 2) and select the `Web IDE`.

6. Select the `<> Code` icon on the left and under Particle Apps, name the current app `Photon2_Heartbeat_To_MQTT`. Hit return and save this file by clicking the folder icon on the left.

7. Select the Libraries icon on the left. In the text box, under Community Libraries, search for MQTT. Click on the library named `MQTT`.

8. Select `Include in Project`. Select `Photon2_Heartbeat_To_MQTT` and select `Confirm`.

9. Within the file `Photon2_Heartbeat_To_MQTT`, copy and paste the code found at this URL:

   https://github.com/sn-code-inside/guide-to-iot/blob/main/Ch06_code/Photon2-heartbeat-to-MQTT.ino

   The code is also available in the chapter appendix.

10. Within the code of `Photon2_Heartbeat_To_MQTT`, change the IP address to your IP address. Currently, the lines reads:

    ```
    byte IPAddressOfBroker[] = { 192,168,86,29};
    ```

    You should be able to locate the IP address of your machine. The address associated with the name `localhost` will not work. Using the `localhost` address will cause the Photon 2 to visit itself. And we have no MQTT broker running on the Photon 2.

11. Plug your microcontroller device into the USB port. Wait until it is breathing cyan.

12. Before flashing the code, click on the `Devices` icon and click on the small star next to your device.

13. Flash your firmware `Photon2_Heartbeat_To_MQTT` to the Photon 2.

14. The `Photon 2 client` will send heartbeats to the mosquitto broker. The broker will announce the connection.

15. Watch the heartbeat messages arrive on your broker. Every 10 seconds, a new message should arrive. See Figure 6.5.

```
New connection from 192.168.86.236:53789 on port 1883.
1638666715: New client connected from 192.168.86.236:53789 as
Photon2Client1
(p2, c1, k15).
    1638666715: No will message specified.
    1638666715: Sending CONNACK to Photon2Client1 (0, 0)
    1638666716: Received PUBLISH from Photon2Client1 (d0, q0, r0, m0,
    'heartbeat', ... (39 bytes))
    1638666726: Received PUBLISH from Photon2Client1 (d0, q0, r0, m0,
    'heartbeat', ... (39 bytes))
    1638666736: Received PUBLISH from Photon2Client1 (d0, q0, r0, m0,
    'heartbeat', ... (39 bytes))
```

Figure 6.5 Heartbeats arriving at the broker from the Photon2

16. Subscribe to publications using the MQTT command line tool and see Figure 6.6.

```
mosquitto_sub -h localhost -t heartbeat/#
```

```
$mosquitto_sub -t localhost -t heartbeat/#
{"deviceID":"e00fce6834ad070f2346a26a"}
{"deviceID":"e00fce6834ad070f2346a26a"}
```

Figure 6.6 Messages arriving at the subscriber from the broker

17. Unplug your Photon 2 from your computer. Do this with the USB port that is near to the computer and not the connection near to the Photon 2. This will cut power to the Photon 2. Note the behavior of your subscription client and note the behavior of Mosquitto. You may have to wait a bit for Mosquitto to realize that the connection is down. See figure 6.7.

```
1638667872: Client Photon2Client1 has exceeded timeout, disconnecting.
```

Figure 6.7 Report on broker console

18. Plug the Photon 2 back in. Note the behavior of you subscription client and note the behavior of Mosquitto. Do things return to normal or has the communication been totally disrupted? We will return to this issue shortly.

What Did You Do, and How Did You Do It?

Configuration file changes

In the configuration file, we have chosen two different ports for mosquito to listen on. Different ports are used for different protocols. We want mosquito to listen on port 1883 (for standard MQTT) and 9002 (for standard MQTT over websockets).

In addition, we have specified an authentication setting. Authentication is all about proving the identity of a person or thing. Here, we specify that we will allow anonymous visitors – those providing no password. In other words, in this example, we are not authenticating our users. In the next chapter, we will set the value of anonymous visitors to false and check each visitor's user ID and password.

We have also specified that we want Mosquitto to interact with clients via the standard MQTT protocol and the websockets protocol. In order to speak to the broker, the Particle Photon 2 will use standard MQTT messages written to a TCP socket. In order for a browser to speak to the broker, it will use standard MQTT messages but over websockets. The websocket protocol allows browsers to interact with other peers over a bidirectional channel. This is not the normal way you might think of using a browser. We will make use of this protocol in Part 3 below.

Abstraction

The reader should take some time and read over the comments and the code in the `Photon2_Heartbeat_To_MQTT` file. The following discussion assumes that you have done so,

The code in the `Photon2_Heartbeat_To_MQTT` firmware is able to speak to the broker that you ran on your laptop. The code utilizes the principle of abstraction to make the programming effort fairly simple and understandable.

Note that we included the `mqtt.h` header file. This C++ header file contains descriptions of classes and types that are available in the mqtt library that we imported using the Particle Web IDE. This header file is used by the compiler to ensure that any calls we make to the library code are done properly. That is, the compiler ensures that we have included the appropriate number of arguments in our calls and the arguments are of the appropriate type.

We construct an MQTT object, i.e., an object that knows precisely how to speak to an MQTT broker, with the following simple line of code;

```
MQTT broker(IPAddressOfBroker, 1883, callback);
```

In this call to a C++ constructor, we instantiate an object named `broker` and provide it with three values. The first is the IP address of where the broker is running. Note that this might be anywhere on the internet and anywhere in the world. Next, we provide the port that the broker will be listening on. The IP address plus the port is a way we can specify a particular application running on a particular machine. The third parameter is the name of a function (running on the Photon 2) that will be called if the Photon 2 receives a publication from the broker. In this example, we are only using the Photon 2 to publish messages and so this last parameter will not be used.

The next line of MQTT related code appears in the setup() method:

```
broker.connect(clientName);
```

Here, we call the connect method on the broker object. We pass along a client name and Mosquitto will use this name to keep track of this particular client. In MQTT, client names must be unique.

The final two lines of MQTT related code appear in the loop method. Periodically, we executed the following two instructions:

```
if (broker.isConnected()) {
            :
             broker.publish(topic,message);
}
```

The `isConnected()` call checks to see if we are currently communicating with a broker. If so, we publish a particular message to a particular topic. Note that the ultimate destination of these messages is unknown. That is, the Photon 2 publishing client has no easy way to learn what messages (if any) actually arrive at what subscriber. There may be many subscribers or none. That is not of concern to us. That is entirely in the hands of the broker itself.

As was noted, this code makes good use of the *principle of abstraction*. This principle encourages us to consider what needs done, not how. There are many low level details involved with communicating with an MQTT broker. Every bit, every 0 and 1, coming and going from the Photon 2, must be correct. And yet, this firmware was written without struggling with that level of detail.

Abstraction is truly one of the great ideas of computer system design. It allows the software designer and hardware designer to be productive. Rather than worrying about the precise series of bits that need to be transmitted over a communication channel, for example, we can write code at a higher level - such as that illustrated here. It says, essentially, that if we are connected then publish a message to a topic..

Fault Tolerance

An especially tricky issue when designing systems involving more than one computer communicating over a network, is the handling of partial failures.

When the Photon 2 was disconnected from its power source, it became unable to communicate via WiFi. This is an example of a partial failure. Only one component in our system, the Photon 2, failed. Mosquitto kept running and so did our subscribing client.

MQTT was designed to be a fault tolerant publish and subscribe protocol. Note how gracefully it handled the plugging and unplugging of the Photon 2 client.

First, after the unplugging event, Mosquitto was able to detect the fact that it was no longer hearing from the other component.

Second, the subscribing client was completely unaffected. It did not mind that the Photon 2 was down. It was not receiving heartbeats during the downtime but was ready to receive messages if and when they were sent.

During the downtime, Mosquitto was fine and so was the subscriber.

When the Photon 2 was brought back to life, it made a connection request from the setup() function in the firmware. Mosquitto granted that request and the heartbeats began to arrive at the subscriber as though the failure never occurred.

Fault tolerance is an important topic in the design of distributed systems. Here, we have seen how MQTT can be resilient in the face of partial failures.

Citizen Science

There is a new way to map out the condition of your city's streets.

Road surface monitoring is crucial in providing smooth and safe road infrastructure for automobiles, bicyclists, and even pedestrians. An accurate picture of road surface conditions such as potholes, cracks, bumps, and litter could change how government agencies monitor and respond to the need for road maintenance and clean-up. Citizen science using IoT could communicate with local authorities to repair potholes.

Google Maps already uses your phone's position to help plan journeys for you, notify you about other drivers, and tell you about the number of visitors to restaurants and bars. Unfortunately, current smartphone sensors operate at too low a sampling frequency to provide accurate data for road hazard detection. Low-cost standalone sensors installed on cars, bicycles, and baby strollers could be used to communicate these data to local authorities. These devices could communicate with smartphones via Bluetooth or Wifi and map road conditions as they travel. Problems like potholes could then be detected long before becoming costly liabilities for local authorities to repair.

Using Citizen Science, road users could provide cities with free, instant information about their roads' maintenance needs. Cars, bike riders, and walkers could capture real-time data on road conditions, and share this data to OpenStreetMaps and open databases, making the data accessible to anyone.

Using citizen science to help local governments make better planning decisions to improve their street conditions could also help other cities and countries understand how to build safer bike lanes and sustainable transportation networks. And, yes, it's not just bicycles that can benefit from such mapping initiatives. Self-driving cars, too, will be reliant on these kinds of data sets. Consider the case of Tactile-Mobility `http://tactilemobility.com`, utilizing in-car systems to "bring the missing sense of tactility" to autonomous vehicles. Their work into vehicle-road dynamics hopes to feed actionable insights to self-driving cars and inform driving decisions in real-time.

Laws in New York require that landlords provide a certain level of heat. Heat Seek `http://heatseek.org`, a tiny nonprofit, has created a low-cost temperature sensor that uploads temperature data to the cloud. The sensor's hourly temperature readings can be viewed online by tenants, downloaded, and presented in court as evidence if the law has been violated.

Every day our technology collects massive amounts of data in every sphere of human activity. The question should not be limited to all of the exciting uses it can be put to, but more importantly, who gets to own and use this data. Citizen science communities can help local governments make better planning decisions as they look to improve their street conditions and help create networks of mutual care and collaboration.

The Future Is Here.

Part 3: Subscribe to Photon 2 Heartbeats with a Browser

What you need:

- Node.js
- An MQTT broker, such as Mosquitto, running on a computer. See Part 2 and uses Part 2's configuration file.
- A Particle Photon 2 running the same firmware as Part 2.
- WiFi

What to do:

1. Start Mosquitto as you did in Part 2. Be sure to include the configuration file.

2. Plug in your Photon 2. Be sure that it is running the `Photon2_Heartbeat_To_MQTT` firmware from Part 2.

3. Now that the Photon 2 is publishing heartbeats to MQTT. We want to subscribe to those heartbeats with a browser.

4. Build a web site using Node.js

    a. Create an empty directory named `Chapter6_Part3`.

```
mkdir Chapter6_Part3
```

    b. Use `cd` to change directory into `Chapter6_Part3`.

```
cd Chapter6_Part3
```

    c. Create a file named `index.js` and save the content found here:

        https://github.com/sn-code-inside/guide-to-iot/blob/main/Ch06_code/Ch06_Photon2_publish-to-mqtt/Chapter6_Part3/index.js
(This file is also available in the chapter appendix).

    d. Within the directory, `Chapter6_Part3`, create a sub directory named public.

```
mkdir public
```

    e. Use `cd` to hange directory into the public directory.

```
cd public
```

    f. Save this file in the public directory with the name `index.html`.

        https://github.com/sn-code-inside/guide-to-iot/blob/main/Ch06_code/Ch06_Photon2_publish-to-mqtt/Chapter6_Part3/public/index.html
(This file is also available in the chapter appendix).

    g. Change directory into `Chap6_Part3` (the parent of public).

```
cd ..
```

    h. Within the `Chap6_Part3` directory, run the following two commands (accept the defaults) :

```
npm init
npm install express
```

    i. And, to start our web server serving a web page, run the following command:

```
node index.js
```

j.   Visit the web page at `http://localhost:3000/index.html`.

5. After 10 seconds or so, your browser should begin displaying the heartbeats of the microcontroller. See Figure 6.8

6. Be sure to run a second browser and visit the same web site. An MQTT broker may have many clients.

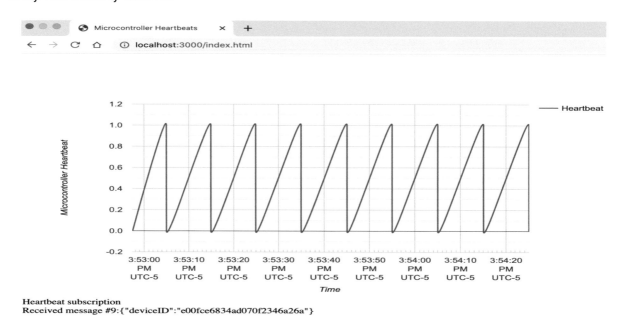

Heartbeat subscription
Received message #9:{"deviceID":"e00fce6834ad070f2346a26a"}

Figure 6.8 Heartbeats arriving on the web

MQTT Qualities of Service

MQTT has three qualities of service (QoS) named QoS 0, QoS 1, and QoS 2. These qualities of service determine how hard two players work to ensure that a message that is sent is actually delivered to the receiver. A particular quality of service pertains to a particular client and a broker.

QoS 0 is the simplest to understand. Suppose that we have a fairly reliable connection and our application does not mind if there is an occasional lost message. We might decide to use QoS 0. This is a fire and forget protocol. The sender (perhaps a publishing client or a broker sending a publication to a subscribing client) simply fires off the message and forgets about it. It may arrive at the receiver or it may get lost. As long as the underlying network is fairly reliable, we may be able to get by with this simple design. Our heartbeat example is a case in point. Remember, simple is good and this will do fine in many applications.

QoS 1 would be more appropriate if your application cannot easily tolerate an occasional lost message. The essential idea is that the client will send the message repeatedly until it receives an acknowledgement from the receiver. With respect to the sender. this is not quite as simple to implement as QoS 0. The sender must retain the message in memory. It needs to do that so that it is able to perform retries. Retries will occur after a period of time has lapsed with no acknowledgement from the receiver.

QoS 1 will also be more complex for the receiver. The main issue is that the receiver may receive the same message more than once. How could this occur? Suppose the sender sends a message and the message arrives at the receiver. The receiver acknowledges the message (the server knows that it is working with QoS 1) but the acknowledgement itself is lost. The sender will time out and send the same message again. Thus, we may have one or more duplicate messages arriving at the server. This will not be so bad if the message is making a request on an idempotent service. For example, suppose the request asks the service to set an oven to 176 degrees Celsius. If this request arrives once or twice or several times, everything is fine. The oven is set to 176 degrees.

If, however, the services is not idempotent, things are not so simple. Suppose the message asks that the server turn up the temperature in the oven by 10 degrees Cesius. This message, arriving several times because of lost aknowledgements, may cause a fire. If our service is not idempotent, that is, one request is not the same as many duplicate requests, then we will likely choose QoS 2. QoS 2 will require more messages and more complexity in the sender and the receiver.

QoS 2 includes a message identifier with each message. The receiver, therefore, will be able to recognize any duplicate messages and discard them. Note that this requires the receiver to retain the message identifier. The sender tries and tries until it receives an acknowledgement. In QoS 2 this acknowledgement is called a "publication received" or PUBREC message. However, the receiver will not know for certain that the sender has received the PUBREC and so the protocol requires that the receiver continue to send PUBREC until the sender acknowledge the PUBREC with a "publication release" or PUBREL message. This too will be tried and tried until the sender receives a "publication complete" or PUBCOMP message from the receiver. When this occurs, both the sender and receiver may discard the state that each had to maintain in memory.

What Did You Do, and How Did You Do It?

Node.js

The reader should take some time and read over the comments and the code of the two files: `index.js` and `index.html`. The discussion here assumes that you have done so.

The code in `index.js` remains on the server and is executed when we enter the command: `node index.js`. The JavaScript code uses the Express framework. This framework provides abstractions that make it fairly easy to build a web application. The `index.js` code causes Node to listen on the port 3000 for HTTP requests. It will allow visitors to access the content in the directory named `public`.

Within the public directory, we have placed the file named `index.html`.

The `index.html` contains some HTML for describing a document that will be rendered by a browser. It also contains JavaScript code that subscribes to heartbeat messages from an MQTT broker, draws the heartbeat arrivals with a Google Chart line graph, and detects failures of the network or the microcontroller.

Subscribing to MQTT from the browser

The JavaScript code that allows the browser to behave as a subscribing client of an MQTT broker begins with the inclusion of an MQTT library. This library provides the necessary abstractions and hides the low level details associated with the MQTT protocol.

Review the code and note the two essential MQTT activities. First, we need to subscribe to an MQTT topic. We do that with the line:

```
client.subscribe("heartbeat");
```

The client object was constructed earlier and knows how to interact with MQTT.

Second, we need to receive messages from MQTT. We do that by providing a function that will be called when a message arrives:

```
function onMessageArrived(message) {
    :
}
```

Who calls this function? The library code will call it when messages from MQTT arrive.

Our application level code makes direct calls to the library, e.g., the call to the subscribe function. But note that we also provide functions that will be called by the library. The `onMessageArrived()` function is such a function.

Google Charts

Another important piece of `index.html` is the code we use to visualize the heartbeat data. Here, we chose the Google Chart library but many such JavaScript libraries exist.

In this example, we populate a Google Chart supplied object with data. This object is a Google Chart `DataTable`. We also create an object named `options` to establish various configuration parameters, e.g., `titles` for the x and y axes of a graph.

We create a LineChart object and associate it with a location in the HTML document:

```
chart = new
google.visualization.LineChart(document.getElementById('chart_div
'));
```

We then pass the `DataTable` and the options objects to a Google Chart `LineChart` by calling the `draw` method of the `LineChart` object:

```
chart.draw(dataTable, options);
```

Our application code is able to generate an engaging graphical display simply by calling the library methods appropriately. This is another illustration of the power of abstraction.

Failure Detection in JavaScript

We can talk to an MQTT broker and we can draw a line graph. But what is the application?

Our application waits for 13 seconds. If we fail to hear a heartbeat, what do we know? There are several possibilities. Perhaps the microcontroller has crashed and is no longer executing its code and generating heartbeats. Or, perhaps the microcontroller is fine but the network between the microcontroller and the broker has failed. Or, perhaps the broker is down. These are all quite possible. We suspect a failure of the device but are not sure that that is the cause.

The key line of code that helps us to build this application is the line:

```
interval = setInterval(reportSuspectedFailure, 13000);
```

This line ensures that the browser will call a function named `reportSuspectedFailure()` after 13000 milliseconds (13 seconds) have elapsed. We can cancel this timer by calling the `Node.js` provided function:

```
clearInterval(interval);
```

The functions `setInterval()` and `clearInterval()` are provided to the application developer by JavaScript. We can carefully use these functions to detect failures in devices or communications. The reader should read the code to see how this can be done.

Bicycles and the IoT

Bike riding is an essential feature of modern transportation. It has huge benefits to the individual rider as well as to the environment.

Contributing to their attractiveness and usefulness, modern bicycles are both smart and connected products.

In this chapter, we built a simple application, a protype, that illustrates how failure detection might be visualized on the web. We also implemented the publish subscribe model using MQTT. The publish subscribe model provides scalability. We may need to build a system where many microcontrollers are monitored and visualized by many web users.

While it is true that our system is simplified, it is also the case that it provides many of the core ideas behind real systems. We gathered status information, communicated that status information to a browser and did so using a publish subscribe pattern. For a real biking application, we would need to replace the Wi-Fi connectivity with cellular (likely using BLE and a phone as a gateway) or more directly by using Low Power Wide Area Networking (LPWAN).

Aside from simple heartbeat generation, modern bike riding generates a lot of data. These data have a wide variety of uses. Here, we list a few:

- A smart city safety application wants to know what road conditions are poor and in need of repair. Accelerometers attached to bikes and communicating over cellular or Low Power Wide Area Networking could report on potholes and damaged pavement.
- The safety of individual riders is improved by the addition of an alert button. By communicating over cellular or Low Power Wide Area Networking, alert notifications are sent to authorities or friends.
- Riders engage in fitness competitions with friends. Each rider's GPS data is available on a web display or map for all to see. People love to compete and this makes the ride more fun.
- The lights on the bike display differently depending upon the particular circumstances of the ride. If the breaks were hit hard the light might begin to blink red. If the ride is stable and without breaking or swerving, the light might glow with a softer white.
- Bike sharing programs are in full swing. GPS sensors can be used to sense the location of bikes for pickup and storage by their owner or for retrieval by a person needing a ride.
- City government can measure the amount and location of bike riding and learn which bike riding programs and incentives work best.
- Private enterprise can measure individual employee bike riding and provide incentives for employees who bike. This saves on space for parking lots and the savings might be passed on to the riders.
- Health insurance providers might reduce premiums for those who are active bikers. Trip reports might be provided as verification.
- Scooters can leverage many of the innovative IoT solutions that have already been applied to bikes.

Check Your Understanding

1. How is a broker different from a dealer? Give three real world examples.

2. Describe how you use callbacks in your everyday life.

3. Describe a loosely coupled organization other than the one described in the text.

4. Describe a tightly coupled organization other than the one described in the text.

5. Is the architecture of World Wide Web loosely coupled or tightly coupled?

6. Describe how you use the "separation of concerns" principle in your own life.

7. Describe what needs to go on inside an MQTT broker such as Mosquitto.

8. Modify the firmware to generate a heartbeat every second. Is the MQTT broker able to work at that speed? How about the browser?

Make More / Explore Further

1. Run Mosquitto. Use the command line subscription command to subscribe to `heartbeat/#`. Use the command line publishing command to publish `thump` to `heartbeat/rhythm/value`. Does `thump` arrive at the subscriber?

2. Run Mosquitto. Use the command line subscription command to subscribe to `heartbeat`. Use the command line publishing command to publish `thump` to `heartbeat/rhythm/value`. Does `thump` arrive at the subscriber?

3. Run Mosquitto. Use the command line subscription command to subscribe to `heartbeat/+/value`. Use the command line publishing command to publish `thump` to `heartbeat/rhythm/value`. Does `thump` arrive at the subscriber?

4. In Part 2, when we disconnected the Photon 2, how was the command line subscription affected?

5. In Part 2, when we reconnected the Photon 2, how was Mosquitto affected?

6. Suppose all of the bicyclists in a bicycle race are carrying microcontrollers that are able to communicate over cellular connections. The microcontrollers are sending sensed data (speed, humidity, temperature, etc.) to an MQTT broker. Suppose a bicyclist enters a tunnel and her communication halts for a few minutes. Will this event be handled well by MQTT? What will be seen by the hundreds of spectators watching the race data on their browsers?

7. In Part 3, were you able to visit the heartbeat web application with several browsers at the same time? Explain how this is done.

8. In Part 3, would it be possible to use several microcontrollers or is the system restricted to one. Explain your answer.

9. Currently, our microcontroller sends messages over WiFi. WiFi would not work for bikes in the Tour de France. Purchase a microcontroller that is able to transmit messages over a cellular connection (the Particle Boron, perhaps). Make any required modifications to the firmware, attached it to your bike, provide the same heartbeat signals to MQTT and to the web. You will also need a battery.

10.   Modify the web application so that it has two working buttons that allow users to subscribe or unsubscribe to messages from MQTT. When subscribed, the output will appear as in Figure 6.8. When unsubscribed, no new heartbeats are shown.

11. In what industries is MQTT used? Ask ChatGPT.

12. What is AQMP and how does it compare to MQTT? Ask ChatGPT.

Summing Up

In this chapter we introduced the reader to the publish and subscribe paradigm and to MQTT. We learned that we could quickly build a web application that receives signals from a microcontroller. The signals that we were interested in were of a fundamental type, answering the question "are you alive and able to communicate?". In wireless networks, communication may be intermittent and heartbeat messages may be of high importance.

Looking Ahead

In the next chapter, we use MQTT and the World Wide Web again. We will learn how we can control a device via the web.

In other words, the next chapter turns this chapter on its head. Our web application will publish commands to the broker. Our microcontroller firmware will subscribe to MQTT to receive instructions.

We will also imagine how our system might contribute to saving birds.

References
1. Weick, Karl E. "Educational Organizations as Loosely Coupled Systems." *Administrative Science Quarterly* 21, no. 1 (1976): 1–19. https://doi.org/10.2307/2391875.
2. OASIS. 2019. "MQTT Version 5.0." OASIS Standard. https://docs.oasis-open.org/mqtt/mqtt/v5.0/os/mqtt-v5.0-os.html.
3. Hohpe, Gregor, and Bobby Woolf. Enterprise Integration Patterns. Accessed July 2023. https://www.enterpriseintegrationpatterns.com/.

Chapter Appendix

```
// Photon2-heartbeat-to-MQTT
// Firmware to run on an Photon 2 microcontroller
// This program runs on a microcontroller and
// sends a heartbeat message to an MQTT broker
// every 10 seconds.

// The local broker is run with the following command:
// mosquitto -c /usr/local/etc/mosquitto/mosquitto.conf -v
// The broker uses a modified configuration file.

// The MQTT library must be included in the project.
// Here, we only include the header file.
#include "MQTT.h"

// This is the function prototype for a callback function.
// A callback function will be used when we subscribe
// to a topic and expect to receive calls from the broker.
// In this program, we are only publishing to the broker
// and we do not expect to receive calls from the broker.
// Still, we provide the prototype and the function body.
void callback(char* topic, byte* payload, unsigned int length);

// Here, we include the IP address of a running MQTT broker.
// We do not use localhost because localhost would refer to
// the microcontroller itself. Be sure to change this to
// your own IP address.
byte IPAddressOfBroker[] = { 192,168,86,29};

// Create an MQTT object by calling its contructor.
// MQTT brokers have an IP address.
// MQTT brokers listen on port 1883.
// And MQTT brokers may need to call back if the microcontroller
// is a subscriber.
MQTT broker(IPAddressOfBroker, 1883, callback);

// The callback is called by the broker if the microcontroller
// has subscribed to a topic and there are publications to that
// topic. In this publishing program, we do not expect this callback
// to be used.
void callback(char* topic, byte* payload, unsigned int length) {
   Serial.println("An unexpeted message received from broker");
}

// This is the MQTT topic name to publish under.
String topic = "heartbeat";

// This is the name of this Photon 2 client.
// The broker will require unique client names.
String clientName = "Photon2Client1";

// When DEBUG is true we will write output to the serial console.
boolean DEBUG = true;

// Establish the number of seconds to wait until we publish a message.
```

```
int NUMSECONDS = 10;

// The variable timeCtr will be used to hold the current time in milliseconds.
int timeCtr = 0;

// Device ID will be stored here after being retrieved from the device.
// This is a unique, 96 bit identifier.
// This looks like the following hex string: 0x3d002d000cf7353536383631.

String deviceID = "";

// The message array will hold a JSON string.
// This is the message we are sending to the topic.
char message[80];

// This class makes handling JSON data easy.
// Associate it with the message array of char.
JSONBufferWriter writer(message, sizeof(message));

// This method is run once on startup.
void setup() {
    // We plan on writing debug messages to the command line interface (CLI).
    // To see these debug messages, eneter particle serial monitor on the command line.
    Serial.begin(9600);

    // Here we get the unique id of this device as 24 hex characters.
    deviceID = System.deviceID().c_str();

    // Display the id to the command line interface.
    if (DEBUG) Serial.println(deviceID);

    // Establish the JSON string that we will send.

    writer.beginObject();
    writer.name("deviceID").value(deviceID);
    writer.endObject();

    // The JSON is now available through the message array.

    // Connect to the broker with a unique device name.
    // Start the broker before running this client.
    broker.connect(clientName);

}

// Start the broker before starting the Photon 2.
// Subscribe from the command line with:
// mosquitto_sub -t localhost -t heartbeat

void loop() {
    // If timeCtr is above the current time wait until the current time catches up.
    // Initially, timeCtr is 0. It is then set to the current time plus 10 seconds.
    // millis() returns an updated time.
    if (timeCtr <= millis()) {
```

```
        // If we are connected publish the message to the topic
      if (broker.isConnected()) {
        if (DEBUG) Serial.println("Connection to MQTT established");

        broker.publish(topic,message);


        if(DEBUG) Serial.println("Message sent");
      }


      // set timeCtr to current time plus NUMSECONDS seconds
      timeCtr = millis() + (NUMSECONDS * 1000);
    }
}
```

```
// Guide to Internet of Things
// Chapter 6 Node.js server code

// This file is named index.js.
// This code is used to serve up the single file in the public directory.
// The file being served is named index.html.

// A directory named "public" is available in the current directory.
// The public directory holds index.html containing HTML and Javascript.
// A browser will visit with http://localhost:3000/index.html.
// The file index.html will be fetched by HTTP and loaded into the browser.
// The browser is able to render the HTML and execute the Javascript.

const express = require('express')
const port = 3000
app = express();
// allow access to the files in public
app.use(express.static('public'));

app.listen(port, () => {
  console.log(`Photon 2 heartbeats available at  http://localhost:${port}/index.html`)
})
```

```
<!--
Guide to Internet of Things

Chapter 6 code

This web application will cause the browser to connect to a
running instance of an MQTT broker and subscribe to messages
published to the heartBeat topic.

The broker was started with:
```

```
mosquitto -c /usr/local/etc/mosquitto/mosquitto.conf -v

A Google Chart line graph is used to display the hearbeats.
After every 10 heartbeats are received and drawn, the drawing begins
again from a fresh graph.

The Google Chart related code fills a DataTable object an Options object.
The DataTable and Options objects are passed to the LineChart object when
the draw method is called.

In general, DataTable methods are setValue, addRow, addColumn, etc.

A Chart is passed a DataTable when draw is called.

-->

<html>
<head>
 <!-- Include Google Charts. -->
 <script type="text/javascript" src="https://www.gstatic.com/charts/loader.js"></script>

 <!-- Include MQTT. -->
 <script src="https://cdnjs.cloudflare.com/ajax/libs/paho-mqtt/1.0.1/mqttws31.min.js"
type="text/javascript"></script>

 <!-- Begin Javascript. -->
 <script type="text/javascript">

 <!-- Load the linechart. -->
 google.charts.load('current', {packages: ['corechart', 'line']});
 <!-- After the load is complete, call the drawGraph() function. -->
 google.charts.setOnLoadCallback(drawGraph);

 <!-- Establish some global variables -->
 var dataTable = null;  // For holding the DataTable data.
 var options = null;    // For holding the options that a line graph needs.
 var chart = null;      // For holding the DataTable and Options objects.
            // After a heartbeat, we will draw the chart with an
            // updated dataTable.
 var heartBeats = 0;    // This variable tracks the number of heartbeat
            // messages that arrive.

 // Call reportSuspected failure function in 13 seconds
 // if no message arrives. When a message arrives, we will reset the
 // timer to 13 seconds. The veraible "interval" is used later
 // to clear or reset the timer.
 var interval = setInterval(reportSuspectedFailure, 13000);

 // This function runs when the browser loads this document.
 // It also runs after every 10 heartbeats. After every 10
 // heartbeats, we want a new, fresh, graph to be drawn.
 function drawGraph() {

    // create an empty data table
```

```
    dataTable = new google.visualization.DataTable();
    // X is of type date and Heartbeat is of type Number.
    // Types are important here.
    dataTable.addColumn('date', 'X');
    dataTable.addColumn('number', 'Heartbeat');
    // Start with point on the plane.
    // The x-value will be a date and the y value 0.
    dataTable.addRow([new Date(), 0]);

    // Describe how we want our graph to appear.
    options = {
      curveType : 'function',   // given x, compute y
      hAxis: {
        title: 'Time'          // title on x axis
      },
      vAxis: {
        title: 'Microcontroller Heartbeat'  // title on y axis
      }
    };

    // Create a new line chart and associate it with a location
    // in the html document.
    chart = new google.visualization.LineChart(document.getElementById('chart_div'));

    // Draw the chart with this data and with these options.
    // The only point will be a single date, 0 pair.
    chart.draw(dataTable, options);
}

// This function is called for each message that arrives.
function displayResults(heartBeatJSON) {

    // The data arrives in JSON format. We parse it to a
    // Javascript object.
    var heartBeatMsg = JSON.parse(heartBeatJSON);

    // Create a point and draw a line for this heartbeat.
    // A line will be drawn from the last point drawn
    // to this new point.
    dataTable.addRow([new Date(), 1]);

    // Draw another point back to zero.
    dataTable.addRow([new Date(), 0]);
    // Draw the new chart with updated data.
    chart.draw(dataTable, options);
    // On the next call to displayResults, we will add more
    // rows to the same DataTable.

} // end of displayResults

// This function runs if we have not heard a heartbeat in the past
// 13 seconds
function reportSuspectedFailure() {
    // Place a note in the html document of this suspected failure.
```

```
    document.getElementById("messageDisplay").innerHTML = "Missing heartbeat(s).
Suspected failure of device.";
    // And color the note red.
    document.getElementById("messageDisplay").style = "color:red";
    // Clear the timer.
    clearInterval(interval);
    // Start it up again with a new delay of 13 seconds.
    interval = setInterval(reportSuspectedFailure, 13000);
}


    // The MQTT related code runs when the page loads.
    // For a remote broker, we might use
    // var loc = {'hostname' : 'iot.eclipse.org', 'port' : '80' };
    var loc = {'hostname' : 'localhost', 'port' : '9002' };


    // Create a client instance with a unique ID.
    // We use the "new Date" to make sure we provide a new, unique, ID.

    client = new Paho.MQTT.Client(loc.hostname, Number(loc.port),
'HeartbeatSubscriber'+new Date());


    // Set two callback handlers.
    // One if the connection is lost.
    client.onConnectionLost = onConnectionLost;
    // Another when a message arrives.
    client.onMessageArrived = onMessageArrived;


    // Connect the client and after successful, call the onConnect function.
    // This function will only be called if the connection has been established.
    // The call to connect is asynchronous and will return right away. So, we provide
    // a callback to perform the subscribe.

    client.connect({onSuccess:onConnect});


    // called afer the the client sucessfuly connects to the broker

    function onConnect() {
      // Once we have a connection, we subscribe to the
      // topic 'heartbeat'.
      client.subscribe("heartbeat");
    }


    // Called if the client loses its connection.
    function onConnectionLost(responseObject) {
      alert("Lost the connection to the broker");
      if (responseObject.errorCode !== 0) {
        console.log("onConnectionLost:"+responseObject.errorMessage);
      }
    }


    // This function is called each time a message arrives from the broker.
    // We will pass the content to displayResults.
    function onMessageArrived(message) {
      // Clear the interval timer. We have a new heartBeat
```

```
    // and so we should begin counting from now.
    clearInterval(interval);
    // Associate the new interval with the function named
    // reportSelectedFailure. This will run reportSuspectedFailure
    // in 13 seconds - unless it is cleared by a new heartbeat.
    interval = setInterval(reportSuspectedFailure,13000);

    // count the beats
    heartBeats = heartBeats + 1;
    // Draw a brand new graph after every 10 heartbeats.
    if(heartBeats % 10 === 0) { drawGraph(); }
    // Place a note in the HTML document that shows this heartbeat message.
    document.getElementById("messageDisplay").innerHTML = "Received message #"+
(heartBeats) + ":" + message.payloadString;
    // And color the note black.
    document.getElementById("messageDisplay").style = "color:black";
    // Update the graph with the new data.
    displayResults(message.payloadString);
  }

</script>

<!-- This HTML is where the chart and messages are displayed. -->
<title>Microcontroller Heartbeats</title>
</head>
<body>
<!-- container for the chart -->
<div id="chart_div" style="width: 900px; height: 500px"></div>
<!-- Some text -->
Heartbeat subscription
<!-- container for the messages -->
<div id = "messageDisplay"></div>
</body>
</html>
```

CHAPTER 7

Actuation Using MQTT

This chapter covers
  Actuation
  Subscribing with MQTT
  Publishing with a browser

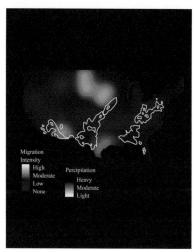

Saving birds with BirdCast [1]

"I hope you love birds too. It is economical. It saves going to heaven."

Emily Dickinson

Saving birds with BirdCast

Approximately 80% of North American birds that migrate, do so at night. The number of birds that die by colliding with buildings each year is estimated to be in the hundreds of millions. Light pollution is an important cause of these accidents. Light attracts the birds, placing them nearer to human activity and buildings.

Birds are important to our environment. If only we could tell when the birds are flying by. If only we knew, we could dim our lights and save millions of birds.

Radar was developed during World II to track enemy planes and the technical problem was to remove the noise, that is, the birds. Today, we can use radar to track bird migration and, hopefully, not worry so much about enemy planes.

Weather radar stations are abundant and the data sensed can be leveraged to detect not only weather but bird migrations in real time.

In this chapter, we explore the idea of remote control over the web. Given that we know the birds are coming, how do we switch off the lights – remotely and with authentication?

We begin by deploying firmware to our microcontroller that subscribes to commands from an MQTT broker. These commands will instruct the microcontroller to turn a light on or off.

Part 1: Controlling a light using MQTT

What you need:

- Access to the Web
- An Apple or Windows computer
- MQTT running on your laptop (see Chapter 6)
- A Particle Photon 2 Microcontroller

What to do:

1. From a command line. run your MQTT broker (Mosquitto) as described in Chapter 6 Part 2. Be sure to pick up the modified configuration file.
2. Run the firmware named `Photon2-Command-from-MQTT`, which can be found at this URL:
   `https://github.com/sn-code-inside/guide-to-iot/blob/main/Ch07_code/Photon2-Command-From-MQTT.ino`.
   This code is also available in the chapter appendix. Using the Particle IDE, modify the IP address in the code, include the MQTT library, compile, and flash the code to a Photon 2.
3. To monitor the Photon 2, use a second command line shell and run the serial monitor:

   ```
   particle serial monitor
   ```

4. Watch the MQTT console for connections from the microcontroller.
5. From a third command line, publish a message to MQTT to turn the light on.

   ```
   mosquitto_pub -h localhost -t microcontrollerCommand -i
   commander -m "{\"light\":\"on\"}"
   ```

6. Again, using the third command line, publish a message to MQTT to turn the light off.

   ```
   mosquitto_pub -h localhost -t microcontrollerCommand -i
   commander -m "{\"light\":\"off\"}"
   ```

What Did You Do, and How Did You Do It?

The reader should take some time and read over the comments and the code in the `Photon2_Heartbeat_To_MQTT` file.

In Chapter 6, the Photon 2 made direct calls to the MQTT broker. It did so because the Photon 2 was the publisher and was informing subscribers that it was alive and well. In this chapter, your Photon 2 is only making direct calls to the broker for the initial set up. After that, it sits back and waits for publications. The publications represent commands that instruct the Photon 2 to behave in certain ways – turn your light on or off. It is acting not as a publisher but as a subscriber. How is this done?

The Callback Function

The programmer needs to provide a mechanism for the broker to pass information to the microcontroller. This is done with a callback function.

The callback function has the following signature:

```
void receiveCommand(char* topic, byte* payload, unsigned int
length);
```

This function takes three arguments. Through these arguments information will be passed from the broker to the application program on the Photon 2. The first argument has the type `char *`. This means that the first argument will be a null terminated sequence of characters. By "null-terminated" we mean that eight zero bits will appear at the end of the sequence of characters – clearly marking its end. This sequence of characters will be the topic that has been published to and to which we have subscribed. The second argument has type "byte*". This means that the message being transmitted will be a sequence of bytes (MQTT allows for a binary or textual payloads). A sequence of bytes may contain important data bytes holding eight zero bits and so we cannot use null termination to mark the end of this sequence. We must directly specify the length of this sequence. We do that with the third parameter of type `unsigned int`.

The signature of this function is specified by the MQTT library. It is part of the MQTT Application Programmer Interface (API). If we want to receive messages from the broker in C++, we must conform to this signature.

Note that this function is never directly called by any application code in the firmware. Instead, it is called by the middleware.

Middleware

The term "middleware" is sometimes used too broadly and this can lead to confusion. Here are two definitions of "middleware" that, hopefully, will make the meaning clear.

According to Coulouris, Dollimore, Kindberg, and Blair [2], "The term middleware applies to a software layer that provides a programming abstraction as well as masking the heterogeneity of the underlying networks, operating systems and programming languages".

Since middleware "masks heterogeneity", the programmer need not be concerned with the variety of different environments that the program is run on.

According to Tanenbaum and Steen [3], "all middleware, one way or another, attempts to implement access transparency, by offering high-level communications facilities that hide the low level message passing through computer networks."

Since middleware implements *access transparency,* the programmer writes code as if all activities were performed locally, when in fact, some of the activities require a network and processes running on other machines.

The MQTT library that we are using in the `Photon2-Command-from-MQTT` firmware is an example of middleware as defined by these authors. It provides a software layer that hides details associated with low level MQTT messages.

The middleware allows us to create an object that represents the broker, passing along its address, port, and the name of the callback function:

```
MQTT broker(IPAddressOfBroker, 1883, receiveCommand);
```

We are able to make direct calls on this object with such commands as `broker.connect()`,`broker.isConnected()`,and `broker.subscribe()`.

Note that the middleware is able to make direct calls to the callback handler, `receiveCommand()`, that we provide. It does this after receiving messages over the network. See Figure 7.1.

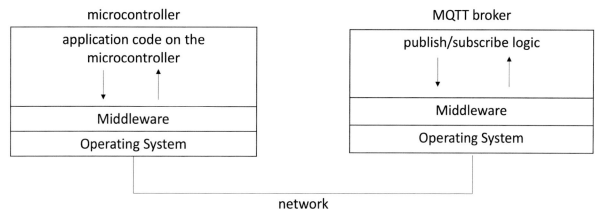

Figure 7.1 Middleware making calls and receiving calls

This is a commonly used technique. The programmer makes calls to the middleware, and the middleware is able to make calls to functions provided by the programmer.

The broker itself is not middleware. While it is true that the broker is "in the middle" between the publisher and the subscriber, this is not what is meant by "middleware." Instead, middleware is the software layer running on the client and also on the broker that hides the many low-level details associated with a particular communication protocol over a network. This separation of concerns is hugely important for developing code on distributed systems.

The End-To-End Principle

In a famous paper by Saltzer, Reed, and Clark [4], the end-to-end argument is presented. The paper points out that the internet itself is dumb – efficiently shuffling packets to their correct destination and not doing much else. The real smarts of an application are, and should be, at the endpoints. They argue that this design has resulted in much of the innovation that we have seen on the internet.

In our remote-control application, the network itself is not very bright. In other words, the network and the computers that make it up are not aware that we are turning lights on and off, saving birds, or even that we are using MQTT. It simply routes IP packets from point A to point B. The meaning of those packets is determined at the endpoints of the communication. This is one important aspect of the end-to-end principle. See Figure 7.2.

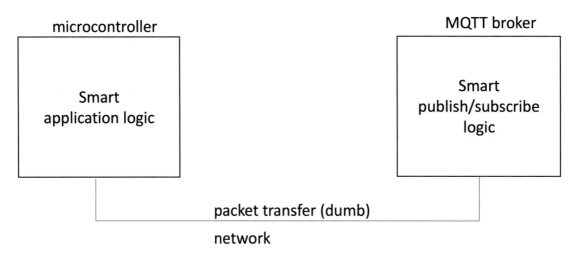

Figure 7.2 Smarts are at the endpoints

Application-level concerns are only apparent at the endpoints. The broker is matching topics to subscriptions and publications, and the microcontroller is adjusting the LED. This is all being done, but the network is only shuffling packets from point A to point B.

Many believe that the end-to-end principle is a central one and needs to be preserved.

Net Neutrality

In the United States, regulations were put in place in 2015 that prevent Internet Service Providers (ISPs) from prioritizing some packets over others. These regulations were put in place to enforce what has come to be called "net neutrality." Since that time, net neutrality has become a political football, and these rules may have a major impact on the internet of things.

An argument in favor of allowing prioritization, and opposed to Net Neutrality, is that some data is simply more essential than other data. For example, life-saving medical devices or automobile safety devices may have hard real time constraints, and these data should be prioritized and placed on a fast track.

An argument in favor of Net Neutrality is that these regulations preserve the end-to-end principle upon which the internet is based. Many small companies have been successful by leveraging the level playing field provided by the internet. Placing more smarts in the network itself may hinder innovation by allowing only well-funded players to enjoy the fast lanes.

Part 2: Remote Control from a browser

What you need:

- MQTT running on your laptop (see Chapter 6)
- A Particle Photon 2 running the firmware from Chapter 7 Part 1.
- Access to the web
- An Apple or Windows computer
- Node.js installed as described in Chapter 2.

What to do:

1. Build a web site using `Node.js`:

    a. Create an empty directory named `Chapter7_Part2`.

    ```
    mkdir Chapter7_Part2
    ```

    b. Use the `cd` command to change directory into `Chapter7_Part2`.

    ```
    cd Chapter7_Part2
    ```

    c. Create a file named `index.js` and include the content found here: https://github.com/sn-code-inside/guide-to-iot/blob/main/Ch07_code/Ch07_Actuators/Chapter7_Part2/index.js

    This code is also available in the chapter appendix.

    d. Within the directory, `Chapter7_Part2`, create a sub-directory named `public`.

    ```
    mkdir public
    ```

    e. Use the `cd` command to change into the `public` directory.

    ```
    cd public
    ```

f. Save this file in the public directory with the name `index.html`. It is also available in the chapter appendix.

https://github.com/sn-code-inside/guide-to-iot/blob/main/Ch07_code/Ch07_Actuators/Chapter7_Part2/public/index.html

g. Change the IP address in the index.html file to be your computer's IP address. Currently, the line reads:

var loc = {'hostname' : '192.168.86.29','port':'9002'};

h. Use `cd` to change directory into `Chap7_Part2` (the parent of public).

```
cd ..
```

i. Within the `Chap7_Part2` directory, run the following two commands:

```
npm init
npm install express
```

j. And, to start our web server serving a web page, run the following command:

```
node index.js
```

k. Visit the web page at `http://localhost:3000/index.html`

2. Experiment! Turn the light on your microcontroller on and off using a browser.

What Did You Do, and How Did You Do It?

The reader should take some time and read over the comments and the code in the `index.html` file provided.

Middleware Revisited

Here too we see the abstractions provided by a middleware layer. In this case, the middleware is provided in JavaScript. When the HTML document is loaded into the browser, the JavaScript library is fetched by the browser when it encounters the following script tag:

```
<script src="https://cdnjs.cloudflare.com/ajax/libs/paho-
mqtt/1.0.1/mqttws31.min.js" type="text/javascript"></script>
```

We are able to create an object that knows exactly how to speak to the broker:

```
broker = new Paho.MQTT.Client(loc.hostname, Number(loc.port),
'CommandPublisher'+new Date());
```

And we can connect to the broker with:

```
broker.connect({onSuccess:onConnect});
```

This connection command can also take an object with several name-value pairs. For example, if our broker is configured to require a user ID and password, we can provide it this way:

```
broker.connect({onSuccess:onConnect,username:"someName",password:
"somePassword"});
```

BirdCast and Lights Out Texas

BirdCast is sponsored by Cornell University, Colorado State University, and the University of Massachusetts. The overall goal is to reduce the number of bird injuries and death due to flying into man-made structures. By leveraging existing weather radar systems, big data, and machine learning technologies, BirdCast, perhaps for the first time, is able to predict bird migration as it is occurring.

The migration patterns are displayed on very cool maps, see https://birdcast.info/news/a-primer-for-using-weather-surveillance-radar-to-study-bird-migration/.

Your help is needed. With current technologies, it is still difficult to determine the species of the birds that are flying by. Human observers – acting as citizen scientists can help with this process.

Working with BirdCast, "Lights Out Texas" is an effort to aid the estimated two billion birds that pass through Texas each year. Businesses and individuals are encouraged to dim lights between the hours of 11:00 PM and 6:00 AM each night. Major companies, such as the Bank of America Tower (Fort Worth) and Marathon Petroleum (San Antonio) have made commitments. Alerts are issued when migrating birds are headed your way.

Part 3: Adding authentication

We only want certain users to be able to turn our lights on and off. Here, we will require that clients that use our broker provide a user name and a password. First, we need to establish authorized user names and passwords on the broker. Second, we need to place the user name and passwords in the client code. Only properly credentialed clients will be allowed to adjust our lights.

What you need:

- MQTT running on your laptop (see Chapter 6)
- A Particle Photon 2 running the firmware from Chapter 7 Part 1.
- Access to the web

- An Apple or Windows computer
- Node.js installed as described in Chapter 2

What to do:

1. Modify your `mosquitto.conf` file.

    a. Edit your `mosquitto.conf` configuration file. Currently, it holds the following lines:

    ```
    listener 1883
    protocol mqtt
    listener 9002
    protocol websockets
    allow_anonymous true
    ```

    b. Change the content of this file so that we now have:

    ```
    listener 1883
    protocol mqtt
    listener 9002
    protocol websockets
    allow_anonymous false
    password_file mycoolpasswordfile.txt
    ```

2. Create a password file holding user IDs and cryptographic hashes.

    a. In the same directory that holds your `mosquitto.conf` file, create a new file named `mycoolpasswordfile.txt`.
    b. We need a file holding user ID and password pairs. Place the following lines at the very start of the `mycoolpasswordfile.txt` file:

    ```
    Alice:sesame
    Bob:changeMe
    ```

    c. Save this file. And, within the same directory, at the command line, enter the command:

    ```
    mosquitto_passwd -U mycoolpasswordfile.txt
    ```

    d. View the file again. Note that the password has been replaced with a cryptographic hash.
    e. You only want to run the `mosquito passwd -U` command once. If you run it a second time, it will replace the hash with a hash of the hash. This is not what we want.
    f. Restart your broker, picking up the new configuration file and the new password file (note how the password file is named in `mosquitto.conf`):

    ```
    mosquitto -c /usr/local/etc/mosquitto/mosquitto.conf -v
    ```

3. The Photon 2 would like to make use of the broker. Modify the firmware to include a user name and password in the connect method.

```
broker.connect(clientName,"Alice","sesame");
```

4. Modify the command line calls to include a user name and password.

```
mosquitto_pub -h localhost -t microcontrollerCommand -i
commander
-m "{\"light\":\"on\"}" -u Bob -P changeMe
```

5. Modify the JavaScript in the browser to include a user name and password.

```
broker.connect({onSuccess:onConnect,username:"Bob",password:
"changeMe"});
```

6. Experiment. Notice that Bob is able to change the lights on the Photon 2 with the name `Bob` and password `changeMe`. And note that the Photon 2 is able to subscribe to MQTT using the name `Alice` and password `sesame`. Other names and passwords don't work.

What Did You Do, and How Did You Do It?

In Part 3, we provided Mosquitto with a configuration file that instructed the broker to only permit two users (Alice and Bob) to connect. These are the only players that we have decided are authorized to use the broker. Presumably, Alice and Bob both know their own passwords. We can assume that they were provided with their passwords during a secure registration step. Alice and Bob will know to present their passwords when requesting a service from the broker. Alice and Bob may or may not be people.

We fitted a microcontroller with an identifying ID (`Alice`) and a password (`sesame`). The microcontroller, by providing these credentials, was permitted to connect and subscribe to commands from the broker. We used a command line shell and a browser to issue commands to the microcontroller. These commands were issued by an authenticated user, his ID was `Bob` and his password was `changeMe`.

Note that we used short, easily understandable passwords in this example system. This is a very bad idea. It would be far more secure if Alice were to use a password over 9 characters in length and with random symbols. Rather than `sesame`, Alice would be far better off using `8hJy3s12ppmx!?`. Below, to keep the reading clear and simple, we use `sesame`. In a real system, we would use something like `8hJy3s12ppmx!?`.

It is interesting to consider how the password file could be stored on the broker. After all, this file is an important one. It helps to control who or what is authorized to use our system and how proper authentication (proving that one is in fact who or what one claims to be) is achieved.

Storing a password file on the broker - Attempt 1

One approach might be to simply store the ID and password pairs in the password file. For example, we might simply store the following data on the file:

```
Alice:sesame
Bob:changeMe
```

When Alice connects to the broker, she can simply provide her ID and password. The server performs a lookup for Alice and checks to see if the two passwords (one provided at run time and one stored in the password file) match. If they do match, it must be Alice and Alice is authorized to connect.

This scheme will work but we have serious concerns. One problem is that the passwords are easily viewable by anyone with access to the password file.

Suppose a malicious player, let's name him Mallet, has either authorized or unauthorized access to this file. He may be a systems administrator with authorized access or an intruder who breaks into the computer holding the file. Mallet can now masquerade as Alice or Bob. He simply presents the name `Alice` and the password `sesame` and he has access. We need a better approach.

Storing a password file on the broker - Attempt 2

OK, let's assume that Mallet has access to the password file. Is there any way to prevent him from pulling off a masquerade attack?

Recall the Tiny Encryption Algorithm (TEA) from Chapter 3. This is a symmetric key cipher that we can use to encrypt data. Perhaps we can use TEA to encrypt the passwords. Our password file might now look like the following:

```
Alice:TEAEncrypted(sesame)
Bob:TEAEncrypted(changeMe)
```

Mallet may have access to this file but he will not be able to read the encrypted data. The passwords `sesame` and `changeMe` will appear as strings of gibberish.

But how, exactly, will this work?

Alice will try to connect with her ID (`Alice`) and her password (`sesame`). Upon receipt of the password from the network, the receiver simply encrypts it with the same key that is used to encrypt the passwords on the password file. If the encrypted data from the network matches the encrypted data on the file, she passes the test. It must be Alice and Alice is authorized.

This too seems to work. But again, we have concerns. TEA is a symmetric cipher and uses a key that needs to be kept private. Where, exactly, is the key stored and who or what has access to that key? Anyone who has administrative privileges or who breaks into this machine may be able to capture the key and decrypt the passwords on the password file. He or she will then be able to impersonate any of the authorized users. It seems that we have moved the problem of hiding the passwords to the problem of hiding the key. If Mallet gains access to the key and the password file, we are in trouble.

Let's try another approach.

Storing a password file on the broker - Attempt 3

Let's try to store the password file in the following format:

```
Alice:SHA-512Hash(sesame)
Bob:SHA-512Hash(changeMe)
```

In this case, we are using a cryptographic hash function to compute a hash of the password. Cryptographic hash functions are used in a wide variety of applications and have the following characteristics:

- The input to the function, in this case a password, is of any length.
- The output of the function is of fixed size. In this case, using SHA-512, the output is always 512 bits in length.
- It is computationally infeasible to invert the function. In other words, if we know the hash value, it is computationally very hard to find the password.
- The function is deterministic. Every time the same input is provided to the function, the same output is produced.

Here is an example. Suppose we want to find the SHA-512 hash of the string `sesame`. We can use one of the widely available online calculators and compute:

```
SHA-512("sesame") =
bb947e9c96a5620c696bd175a1b28eea6337fa8ca6c3dd19efb65e2cb1a4dfee0
256cc87c21589354f1a9f5887af5d23ce05d72a143ae2f1efea9c455bf3d056
```

Try it out. Visit this URL and compute the hash of sesame.
`https://emn178.github.io/online-tools/sha512.html`

The result is 512 bits of what appears to be random data. How can this be used to authenticate Alice and Bob?

As before, when Alice tries to establish a connection with the broker, she provides her ID and password. The server, Mosquito in this case, will hash the password that it receives from the network and compare that hash value with the hash value that is stored in the password file. If they match then Alice is allowed to connect. If they do not match then the two inputs to the same function are different. If Mallet tries to connect as `Alice` with a password of `NotSesame` the server will reject the connection. The server will see that SHA-512("NotSesame") does not equal SHA-512("sesame").

Note that a cryptographic hash (or digest) is not the same as encryption. Encrypted data can be undone or decrypted. All that you need is the correct key. There is no easy way to undo what has been done with a cryptographic hash. Given a SHA-512 digest, it is computationally hard to find the input data used to produce that digest.

Are there concerns with this approach? Unfortunately the answer is "yes". While it is unpractical for a malicious player to find `sesame` given the hash, there is a way to attack this system.

Mallet might start by creating a very large file containing many commonly used passwords along with the hashes of those passwords. It is a simple matter to compute the hash given a password. If the password file becomes available (perhaps by a leak from a systems administrator or an attack on the system) Mallet can simply search all of the hashes in the password file for a match with a hash in the file that was pre-computed. If anyone in the organization has registered a password that happens to be in the set of commonly used passwords, Mallet will learn that ID password pair. He can then present that pair to the system and can masquerade as that user. This is called a dictionary attack.

Is there a way to prevent this type of attack?

Storing a password file on the broker - Attempt 4

Let's store the password file in the following format:

```
Alice: salt, SHA-512Hash(salt+sesame)
Bob: salt, SHA-512Hash(salt+changeMe)
```

In Chapter 3, we mentioned that we often employ randomness when protecting systems. The value called `salt` is simply a random number. Typically 32 bits in size, it is created when the user registers and it is stored in the clear along with the hash of the random number concatenated with the password. How does this work?

As before, when Alice attempts to establish a connection, she presents her ID (`Alice`) and her password (`sesame`). The system looks in the password file and does a lookup for Alice. It finds the random number (`salt`) that was assigned to Alice. It takes the password that has arrived over the channel, prepends the salt to that password, and computes a SHA-512 hash. If that hash matches the one in the password file, Alice is permitted to connect to the service.

The password file might appear as follows:

```
Alice: 3654387, SHA-512Hash(3654387+sesame)
```

In this way, a malicious player will have a much harder time masquerading as Alice. Even with full access to the password file, the file of commonly used hashed passwords is of little use. The problem is that the file of commonly used passwords contains the hash of `sesame` but does not contain the hash of `3654387sesame`.

Is there a way to attack this system? Perhaps. Since the attacker has access to each user's salt (remember, we are assuming that Mallet has access to the password file) and since computing SHA-512 can be done quickly, an attacker may concatenate the salt with each of the commonly used passwords and compute the hash, looking for a match with a particular user's entry in the password file.

How can we prevent this attack?

Storing a password file on the broker - Attempt 5

In Chapter 3 we learned a fundamental principle of cryptography. The principle that we learned was "give the good guys easy problems to solve and give the bad guys hard problems to solve". How can we do this in our password table example?

One way to do this is to slow down the hash algorithm. What? Shoot for poor performance? Yes. As was pointed out, SHA-256 is fast. An attacker can compute millions of these hashes every second. If, instead of requiring a single hash, we require a full second worth of hashes, this becomes a tolerable delay for the authorized user but a major time sink for the attacker. This can be done by repeatedly having the output of one hash serving as the input to the next. Only the final hash is stored in the password file.

With the single command:

```
mosquitto_passwd -U mycoolpasswordfile.txt
```

we are provided with all of these features. The command `mosquito_passwd` uses the standard "Password Based Key Derivation Function 2 - Secure Hash Algorithm 512 (PBKDF2-SHA512)". This is a state of the art password protection scheme.

Unfortunately, we still have a major problem. When Bob issues a command to the microcontroller through MQTT, he does so on an open channel. Anyone with the appropriate tools can see Bob's password as it travels from Bob to the MQTT server.

Packet sniffing is simple and the tools are widely available. Given our set up so far, Mallet will have and easy time masquerading as Alice or Bob.

Which brings us to TLS.

Transport Layer Security (TLS)

Transport Layer Security (TLS) is a layer of software lying just above the TCP layer. See Figure 7.3.

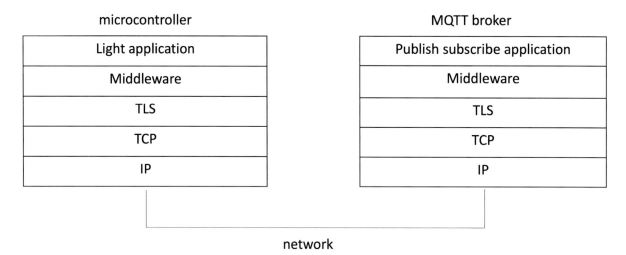

Figure 7.3 Transport Layer for secure communications

Any message that we send through the TLS layer will be encrypted and will only be understandable by the recipient. This is an end-to-end solution. The machines on the network will not be able to decipher the contents of the messages. If we are sending an ID and a password through TLS, we need not worry about malicious player viewing the password. If anyone or any computer on the network tampers with the message, that tampering will be detected by the TLS layer on the receiving end.

Note that we still might use IDs and passwords to authenticate and authorize users. But we would do so over TLS.

The fascinating cryptography used in TLS is beyond the scope of this book. Suffice it to say that TLS has been exceptionally good at encryption – providing a private channel between two ends of the conversation. We turn now to an important threesome: confidentiality, integrity, and availability. TLS is very good at providing the first two.

Confidentiality, Integrity, and Availability

A central concern of information security professionals is the maintenance of confidentiality, integrity, and availability (CIA).

When transferring information from point A to point B, we often want the transfer to be **confidential**, that is, we may not want others to be able to understand what information is being transferred. In order to perform a confidential transfer of data over an open channel (like the internet), we would use an encryption algorithm. We reviewed two of the many encryption algorithms in Chapter 3. We saw the need to encrypt passwords when transmitted over a network in Part 3.

During the transfer of information, we also often want to be able to verify that the data has not been manipulated or accidentally modified. In other words, we want to verify the **integrity** of the data. A cryptographic digest or Message Authentication Code (MAC) is commonly employed to ensure that the data was not changed in transit. A shared key may be included in the hash so that the receiver also knows who (or what) sent the message. The message and its digest are sent in the clear. When the message arrives at the receiver the digest is computed again. If the received digest is the same as the one computed by the receiver, the message has not been tampered with. See Figure 7.4.

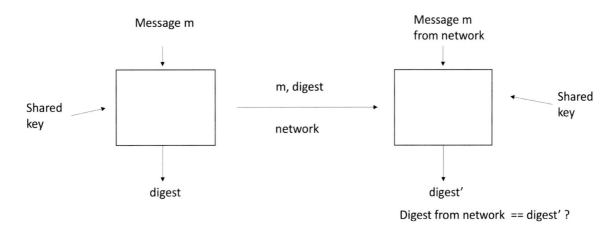

Figure 7.4 Including a digest with message

And, of course, we need our systems to be **available** for use. Systems need to be designed to detect and respond to system failure and denial of service attacks.

Information security is a broad and exciting topic. We hope that our introduction to password file security motivates the reader to explore the topic further.

Check Your Understanding

1. Why did we use JSON to send command messages?

2. How is middleware related to the end-to-end principle?

3. How is net-neutrality related to middleware?

4. Given a cryptographic hash, is it computationally easy or hard to find the value that was hashed?

5. Given a value, is it easy or hard to compute a cryptographic hash?

6. What is the SHA-512 hash of the string `3654387sesame` ?

7. Why are hashes, rather than encrypted passwords, stored in a password file?

8. Why is password protection not enough? Why must we also include TLS?

9. Does "computationally hard" mean the same thing as "impossible"? Ask ChatGPT.

Make More / Explore Further

1. In this exercise, let's explore what happens if we fail to run mosquito first. Set DEBUG to true in your firmware. Flash the firmware to your Photon 2. Run the serial monitor. Explain what you see on the console. Now, start mosquito. Do you connect? Why or why not?

2. Start mosquito and flash the firmware. What quality of service is being used by the firmware in its subscription request? You will be able to see this by viewing the MQTT console.

3. Notice the `PINGREQ` and `PINGRES` messages being exchanged. Why is MQTT doing this? What happens if the Photon 2 is unplugged?

4. In the firmware, change the subscription quality of service to 1. Is this change recognized by mosquito?

5. For those with an interest in programming the web, modify the web site so that it prompts the user for a user name and password before attempting to connect to Mosquitto.

6. Suppose a password is made up of the 26 lower case letters and that the password length is 8. How many possible unique passwords are there?

7. Suppose a password is made up of the 26 lower case letters and that the password length is 12. How many possible unique passwords are there?

8. Give a reason (not covered in the text) why net-neutrality is a good idea.

9. Give a reason (not covered in the text) why net-neutrality is a bad idea.

10.   Add a TLS layer to the system that we built in this chapter.

11. Explain the difference between identification, authentication, and authorization and how each is exemplified in the system we built.

12. Mallet is up to no good. Suppose he decides to compute a SHA-512 hash for every possible 9 character passwords that are made up of the 52 lower and upper case letters in English. On average, how much time will it take for him to compute the hash if the computation takes 1/1,000,000 seconds per hash? How much time will it take for him to compute the hash if the hashing take 1 second per hash?

13. Use SHA-512 and compute the hash of some arbitrary text that you make up. Provide ChatGPT with the hash and ask it to find the original text. Is it able to do so? Why or why not?

Summing Up

As a motivating example, we learned about the efforts to save migrating birds. We reviewed the work of the BirdCast team and its efforts in the Lights Out Texas program.

In the technical parts of this chapter, we used the World Wide Web and MQTT to build a system that turns on or off a light remotely. Remote control has many potential applications. We took security into consideration – recognizing the fact that we would only want authenticated and authorized users to have this capability.

This chapter was a continuation of Chapter 6. In these two chapters we discussed some important ideas from computer science: publish/subscribe, callback functions, the use of abstractions, middleware, the end-to-end principle, net-neutrality, password protection and cryptographic hashing.

Looking Ahead

In the next chapter, we look at Identification Technologies. In particular, to improve hygiene, we will build a system that uses QR-codes to provide contactless menus in restaurants. This idea took root during the outbreak of Covid-19. Other innovations based on identification technologies are very likely to emerge.

References
1. Van Doren, B. M. and Horton, K. G. Year/s of migration forecast map image. BirdCast, migration forecast map; date and time (July, 2023). Cornell Lab of Ornithology, Colorado State University and Oxford University. birdcast.info.July, 2023.
2. Coulouris, George, Jean Dollimore, Tim Kindberg, and Gordon Blair. *Distributed Systems: Concepts and Design*. 5th ed. Addison-Wesley, 2011.
3. Tanenbaum, Andrew S., and Maarten van Steen. *Distributed Systems: Principles and Paradigms*. Prentice Hall, 2002. 39.
4. Saltzer, Jerome H., David P. Reed, and David D. Clark. "End-to-End Arguments in System Design." *ACM Transactions on Computer Systems* 2, no. 4 (November 1984): 277-288.

Chapter Appendix

```
// Photon2-Command-From-MQTT
// This firmware runs on a Photon 2 microcontroller.
// It receives commands from MQTT.

// The local broker is run with the following command:
// mosquitto -c /usr/local/etc/mosquitto/mosquitto.conf -v
// The broker uses a modified configuration file.

// The MQTT library must be included in the project.
// Here, we only include the header file.
#include "MQTT.h"

// When DEBUG is true we will write output to the serial console.
boolean DEBUG = true;

// This is the function prototype for a callback function.
// We do not need a prototype unless we reference the function
// by name before actually defining the function.
// This code refe=rences the function when the MQTT broker object
// is constructed. So, we include this prototype.

void receiveCommand(char* topic, byte* payload, unsigned int length);

// Here, we include the IP address of a running MQTT broker.
// We do not use localhost because localhost would refer to
// the microcontroller itself. Be sure to change this to
// your own IP address - the address where the broker is running.
// The broker might be running anywhere on the internet. But
// we need to have its IP address.
byte IPAddressOfBroker[] = { 192,168,86,29};

// Here, we create an MQTT object by calling its contructor.
// MQTT brokers have an IP address.
// MQTT brokers listen on port 1883.
// The middleware need to know the name of the callback
// handler. In this case, the name of the callback function
// is "receiveCommand".
// The compiler is able to check that the function
// has the appropriate signature. The prototype has already
// been encountered.
MQTT broker(IPAddressOfBroker, 1883, receiveCommand);

// For our light, we will use the LED on D7.
const pin_t MY_LED = D7;


// A callback function will be used when we subscribe
// to a topic and expect to receive calls from the broker.
// In this program, we are receiving command messages
// from MQTT. This code will be called from within the MQTT library
// code. The MQTT library is acting as a middleware layer and
// is handling the communication details.


void receiveCommand(char* topic, byte* payload, unsigned int length)
{
```

```
    if(DEBUG) Serial.println("A message was received from the broker.
The message is from a publication to ");
    if(DEBUG) Serial.println(topic);

    // Copy the message into an array of char.
    char message[length + 1];
    memcpy(message, payload, length);
    message[length] = NULL;

    // Parse the JSON message
    JSONValue commandJSONValue = JSONValue::parseCopy(message);

    // Wrap the object with an iterator.
    JSONObjectIterator iter(commandJSONValue);

    // If there is a value of "on" or "off" turn the light "on" or
"off"
    if(iter.next()) {

        if(DEBUG) Serial.print("Found the name: ");
        if(DEBUG) Serial.println(iter.name().data());
        if(DEBUG) Serial.print("Found the value: ");
        if(DEBUG) Serial.println(iter.value().toString().data());

        // If the command is "ON" set the light on.

        if(strcmp(iter.value().toString().data(),"on") == 0) {

            digitalWrite(MY_LED, HIGH);

        }
        // if the command is "off" then turn the light off
        else if (strcmp(iter.value().toString().data(),"off") == 0) {

            digitalWrite(MY_LED, LOW);
        }

    }
    else if(DEBUG) {
        Serial.println("iter.next() returned 0");
    }

}

// This is the MQTT topic name that we are subscribing to.
String topic = "microcontrollerCommand";

// This is the name of this client.
// The broker will require unique client names.
String clientName = "CommandReceiver1";



// This method is run once on startup.
void setup() {
```

```
        // We plan on writing debug messages to the command line
    interface (CLI).
        // To see these debug messages, eneter particle serial monitor on
    the command line.
        Serial.begin(9600);
        // Connect to the broker with a unique device name.
        // Start the broker before running this client.
        broker.connect(clientName);
        if (broker.isConnected()) {
            if (DEBUG) Serial.println("Connection to MQTT established");
            // Subscribe to a topic. Messages published to that topic
            // will result in the callback receiveCommand being called.
            broker.subscribe(topic,MQTT::QOS0);
        }
        else {
            if (DEBUG) Serial.println("Connection to MQTT not
    established in setup().");
        }
        // We will be using the D7 pin for output
        pinMode(MY_LED, OUTPUT);
        digitalWrite(MY_LED, LOW);

}


// To publish a command from the command line, we can use:
//   mosquitto_pub -h localhost -t microcontrollerCommand -i commander
-m "{\"light\":\"on\"}"
// The broker is on localhost (-h).
// The topic is microcontrollerCommand (-t).
// The name of the client is commander (-i).
// We are sending a JSON message {"light" : "on" }
// Start mosquitto:
// mosquitto -c /usr/local/etc/mosquitto/mosquitto.conf -v
// Flash this firmware.



void loop() {
    // Call loop on the broker so that it can process network data.
    // If there is data to process, it will make a call on the
callback
    // function.
    // If we do not call loop(), there is no chance that the
callback will get called.

    if (broker.isConnected())  broker.loop();
}
```

```
// Guide to Internet of Things
// Chapter 7 Node.js server code

// This file is named index.js.
// This code is used to serve up the single file in the public
directory.
// The file being served is named index.html.
```

```
// A directory named "public" is available in the current directory.
// The public directory holds index.html containing HTML and
Javascript.
// A browser will visit with http://localhost:3000/index.html.
// The file index.html will be fetched by HTTP and loaded into the
browser.
// The browser is able to render the HTML and execute the Javascript.

const express = require('express')
const port = 3000
app = express();
// allow access to the files in public
app.use(express.static('public'));

app.listen(port, () => {
  console.log(`Remote control of a Photon 2 light
http://localhost:${port}/index.html`)
})
```

```
<!--
   Guide to Internet of Things
   Chapter 7 code
   Index.html
   This web application will cause the browser to connect to a
   running instance of an MQTT broker and publish commands to
   a microcontroller.

   Two buttons are displayed. One to turn a light on and the
   other to turn a light off.

   The broker is started first with:
   mosquitto -c /usr/local/etc/mosquitto/mosquitto.conf -v

-->

<html>
<head>

  <!-- Include MQTT. -->
  <script src="https://cdnjs.cloudflare.com/ajax/libs/paho-
mqtt/1.0.1/mqttws31.min.js" type="text/javascript"></script>

  <!-- Begin Javascript. -->
  <script type="text/javascript">

      // The MQTT related code runs when the page loads.
      // For a remote broker, we might use
      // var loc = {'hostname' : 'iot.eclipse.org', 'port' : '80' };
      // var loc = {'hostname' : 'localhost', 'port' : '9002' };
      var loc = {'hostname' : '192.168.86.29','port':'9002'};
      // Create a broker instance with a unique ID.
```

```
      // We use the "new Date" to make sure we provide a new, unique,
ID.

      broker = new Paho.MQTT.Client(loc.hostname, Number(loc.port),
'CommandPublisher'+new Date());

      // Set two callback handlers.
      // One if the connection is lost.
      broker.onConnectionLost = onConnectionLost;
      // Another when a message arrives.
      broker.onMessageArrived = onMessageArrived;

      // Connect the broker and after successful, call the onConnect
function.
      // This function will only be called if the connection has been
established.
      // The call to connect is asynchronous and will return right
away. So, we provide
      // a callback to perform the subscribe.

      broker.connect({onSuccess:onConnect});

      // called afer the the broker sucessfuly connects to the broker

      function onConnect() {
        alert("MQTT Connection established")
      }

      // Called if the broker loses its connection.
      function onConnectionLost(responseObject) {
        alert("Lost the connection to the broker");
      }

      // This function is called each time a message arrives from the
broker.
      function onMessageArrived(message) {
        alert("We do not expect messages from the broker");
      }

      function sendCommand(command) {
        commandObject = new Object();
        commandObject.light = command;
        commandJSON = JSON.stringify(commandObject);
        message = new Paho.MQTT.Message(commandJSON);
        message.destinationName = "microcontrollerCommand"
        broker.send(message);
      }

</script>

<!-- This HTML is where the chart and messages are displayed. -->
<title>Controlling Lights Remotely</title>
</head>
<body>

Remote control
```

```
<!-- container for the messages -->
 <button onclick="sendCommand('on')">Turn on light</button>
 <button onclick="sendCommand('off')">Turn off light</button>
</body>
</html>
```

CHAPTER 8

Identification Technologies

This chapter covers
      QR Codes
      HTML and CSS
      GitHub Pages
      QR Code Generation
      NFC and Beacons

A restaurant booth with a QR code

Adapting to change using QR codes

"If you do not change direction, you may end up where you are heading"

Lao Tzu

In 2020, COVID-19 necessitated the quick adoption of new technologies, in order to maintain safety and productivity during the pandemic. An example of this is the widespread adoption of Identification Technologies like QR codes. QR stands for "quick response", and these codes provide a way for everyday objects to have a web presence.

By using a smartphone, users can scan QR codes and receive more information about an object, place, or event. In the context of COVID-19, this allows for contactless interaction. Customers can view a menu, sign up for an appointment, and more, using only their smartphone. This reduced the amount of potential virus exposure between people.

In this chapter, we'll explore a practical application of QR codes. We'll take on the role of a restaurant owner who wants to substitute a contactless, digital menu for a typical paper menu. The following pages will outline the entire process, from building the website, to generating and using the QR code.

First, we'll begin by building a simple yet effective website for our restaurant. Next, we'll go through the process of hosting our new website on GitHub Pages. This will provide us with a URL. After that, we'll use an online tool to generate the QR code. Lastly, we'll walk through the process of scanning the QR code and navigating to the online menu.

Part 1: Build the Restaurant Website

What you need:

- A computer with access to the Web
- A code editor (Visual Studio, Atom, etc.)

What to do:

1. Create an empty directory named `Chapter8_Part1`.

2. Change directory into `Chapter8_Part1`.

3. In this directory, add four files:

   a. Create the file `index.html` and save the content found at this URL. The file is also available in the chapter appendix.

      https://github.com/sn-code-inside/guide-to-iot/blob/main/Ch08_code/index.html

   b. Create the file `menu.html` and save the content found at this URL. The file is also available in the chapter appendix.

      https://github.com/sn-code-inside/guide-to-iot/blob/main/Ch08_code/menu.html

   c. Create a file named `contact.html` and save the content found at this URL. The file is also available in the chapter appendix.

      https://github.com/sn-code-inside/guide-to-iot/blob/main/Ch08_code/contact.html

   d. Create the file `styles.css` and save the content found at this URL. The file is also available in the chapter appendix.

https://github.com/sn-code-inside/guide-to-iot/blob/main/Ch08_code/styles.css

4. After adding all these files, open `index.html` in a Web browser. (This should be possible by double-clicking the HTML file in a file explorer.)

5. Explore the website! You'll find a home page, a contact page with a form, and a page with the digital menu. Take note of the different information on each page, as well as the visual design.

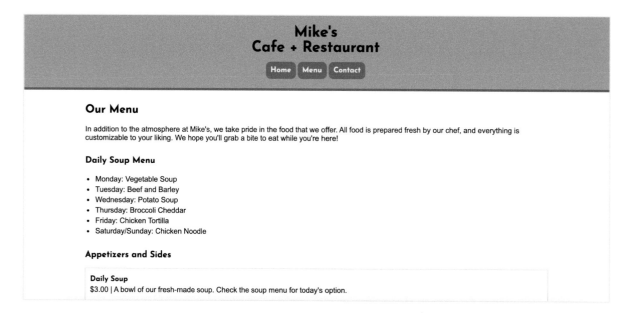

Figure 8.1 Mike's Cafe menu (desktop)

Figure 8.2 Mike's Cafe menu (mobile)

What Did You Do, and How Did You Do It?

The reader should take some time to review the website's HTML and CSS code, including comments. These files are available in the chapter appendix and by following the links above.

The Structure of the Website

The website's code is separated into four files: `index.html`, `menu.html`, `contact.html`, and `styles.css`. The HTML files hold the actual content for each page. These files are made up of elements (or tags) and attributes (name, value pairs within tags.) For example, the following `<div>` element (or tag) has an `id` attribute whose value is "1234".

```
<div id = "1234">...</div>
```

The CSS file holds the formatting and style rules for the pages. (Note that we aren't using Node.js for this site; this is explained further in "Why Aren't We Using Node.js?".)

When designing a website like this, it's important to consider the best way to present each type of information. When users navigate to a website, they have a mental model of how the website should be structured. For example, when trying to find the restaurant's hours, they'd probably check the home page. When trying to find the daily specials, they'd probably check a page called `Menu` first. Coding the website is only one aspect of success; the website should be user friendly and intuitive as well.

If you look through the HTML files, you will see a series of comments that highlight certain aspects of each page's structure and code. Three concepts worth explaining further are `meta` tags, semantic markup, and attributes. First, `meta` tags are an important part of any webpage. They are not normally seen by users, but are there to tell the browser and search engines important information about the page and the site, like the charset, description, and keywords.

```
<meta charset="utf-8"/>
    <meta name="description" content="Mike's Cafe"/>
    <meta name="viewport" content="width=device-width, initial-
    scale=1.0"/>
```

Second, you'll notice that there is a lot of semantic markup used in the HTML code. These are special tags that provide meaning to what they enclose. HTML5 provides a lot of new tags like `<header>`, `<nav>`, and `<section>`, and these new tags create a more informative structure to the webpage. They are also thought to be more accessible and useful to assistive technologies. It's typically a good practice to use semantic markup, rather than using `div` and `span` repeatedly.

```
<nav>
    <a class="button">Home</a>
    <a class="button">Menu</a>
    <a class="button">Contact</a>
</nav>
<main>
    ...
</main>
```

Lastly, attributes given to HTML elements help increase the robustness and complexity of websites and web applications. Any given HTML element can have several attributes, including `id`, `class`, `name`, `type`, and more. The available attributes depend on the element. In our code, the `class` attribute helps us apply CSS rules to certain elements.

```
<div class="item">
    <h4>Daily Soup</h4>
    <p>$3.00 | A bowl of our fresh made soup.</p>
</div>
```

Formatting and Design

HTML by itself will give us all the necessary content for a page, but the page might still be very hard to use. Modern websites are visually complex and appealing, and they are easy to navigate. By using CSS, we can improve the user interface and user experience (UI/UX) of our website, and we can make it conform to users' mental models.

As with the HTML code, there are some important aspects of the CSS code that are worth discussing further. First, we are using Google Fonts and we are importing the font Josefin Sans into our website. Google Fonts (`https://fonts.google.com`) is a great tool for exploring different font options and adding them into a website or web app.

Second, even with simple layouts, we always need to make sure that our website designs are *responsive*. This means that the layout and formatting on the page will adapt to the size of the screen on which we're viewing it. By making our page responsive, we ensure that users can easily view our page, whether they are viewing on a computer, smartphone, or other device. This is especially important when using Identification Technologies like QR codes. When the QR code directs our smartphone to our digital menu, we must be able to easily view the menu on a mobile screen. Having the menu available only on a desktop computer would be far less useful.

When using responsive layouts, we need to include the following `meta` tag in our HTML files:

```
<meta name="viewport" content="width=device-width, initial-scale=1"/>
```

This tells the browser that the width of the viewport (the browser screen size) will depend on the width of the device. This also says to have the browser's initial zoom at 100%.

In our CSS file, here are our responsive style rules:

```
@media screen and (max-width: 600px) {
    input:not(#submit), select, textarea {
        width: 90%;
    }
    main {
        width: 90%;
    }
}
```

The first line tells us that these style rules will apply on devices where the screen size is 600px or less. On these devices, we want the main content container to take up 90% of the page width, and we want to do the same thing for the different aspects of our contact form. This way, the site's layout remains consistent on smartphones and other small devices.

Why Aren't We Using Node.js?

Unlike the web applications in Chapters 6 and 7, we are not using Node.js as a foundation for our website. There are two reasons for this.

First, Node.js would simply be overkill for this website. In this example, we want our restaurant menu to be up and running as fast as possible. Thinking in the context of COVID-19, restaurants needed to adapt quickly to new safety policies. Getting static HTML and CSS online is relatively easy, while setting up a Node.js-based application requires more steps and technical know-how. We want this to be easy to set up.

Second, we will use GitHub Pages to host our website in Part 2, and GitHub Pages can only host static content (HTML and CSS, in this case). Server-side technologies like Node.js are not supported on this platform.

If we wanted to continue building this website and adding features, using a server-side framework like Node.js is a good idea. As it stands right now, we have no way of collecting responses from our site's contact page. Using Node.js on the backend would allow us to collect responses and even add features like online ordering. Node.js would allow us to communicate with the restaurant owner.

Part 2: Host the Website on GitHub Pages

What you need:

- The website we created in Part 1
- A GitHub account

What to do:

1. In a Web browser, go to GitHub
   (`https://github.com/`).

2. If you have a GitHub account already, sign into your
   account. If not, create a new account.

3. When you are logged in, create a new repository.

   a. On the left sidebar of the homepage, click the
      `New` button.

   b. Name your repository "MikesCafe". Make sure
      that the repository is `public` and add a `README`
      as well. You can add a description if you'd like.

   c. Click `Create Repository`.

4. Add the website files to the repository.

   a. On the main page of your repository, click on
      the dropdown button that says `Add file`. (This
      should be next to a green button that says
      `Code`.)

   b. From the opened dropdown menu, click
      `Upload Files`.

   c. On the upload page, use the interface to either
      drag or choose files to upload. You should
      upload all 4 website files (`index.html`,
      `menu.html`, `contact.html`, and `styles.css`).

   d. After uploading all files, it's time to commit the
      changes.

      i. Feel free to change the commit message
         or description if you'd like, but this is not
         necessary.

       ii. Make sure `Commit directly to the main branch` is checked.

      iii. Click the `Commit changes` button.

   e. Go back to the main page of the repository and double check that all four files have successfully been added to the repository.

5. On the main page of your repository, click on the `Settings` tab and use the sidebar to find the `Pages` section.

6. Under `Source`, enable Pages for the code in your repository.

   a. In the first dropdown, replace `None` with `main`.

   b. Make sure the second dropdown says `/(root)`.

   c. Click `Save`.

7. It might take GitHub a minute or two to publish your pages.

8. Visit `https://<username>.github.io/MikesCafe/`.

9. You should be able to access your hosted website!

What Did You Do, and How Did You Do It?

GitHub Pages allows users to quickly create websites without the hassle of registering a domain name and setting up a web server. Thanks to this, we published our new website in a matter of minutes. Now, we have everything we need to generate a QR Code for our digital menu.

Why Do We Need to Host?

We began with the web site on our local machine and copied it to a host provided by GitHub. As we will see in Part 3, in order to generate a code for our website, the QR code generator needs a valid URL. Since we need our website to be accessible by a lot of devices (and devices on different networks), it makes the most sense to host our website on a server on the internet. Fortunately, GitHub Pages makes this easy.

Even when disregarding the QR code and just thinking about the website, it makes sense for us to host the website on an internet connected server. This way, it is accessible from any device with Internet access. Our website will allow potential customers to check out our restaurant and hopefully visit.

I've Never Used GitHub. What Is It?

GitHub is an online platform that lets users store, track, and share code. When users want to store code on GitHub, they do so using repositories. GitHub's version control process uses Git, a very popular source control management tool. Git allows developers to track changes to a codebase and make changes without breaking other parts of the software. Git was created by Linus Torvalds in 2005.

Git and GitHub are crucial software development tools. They make version control and collaboration easy. Without Git and GitHub, a project codebase can easily become disorganized, difficult to modify, and flat-out broken.

Linus Torvalds and Open Source

Linus Torvalds is a Finnish-American software engineer, and he is an important figure in the software development community. In addition to creating Git, he also created and developed a portion of the Linux kernel. In 1991, Torvalds released the first version of the Linux kernel. In contrast to Windows and MacOS, Linux is an *open source* operating system. Everything about the software is documented publicly. This means that the OS can be used, modified, and distributed without regulation.

Open source software is an extremely important aspect of computing. From operating systems and desktop software to Web servers and networks, open source software is ubiquitous and powerful. Some other examples of open source software include Mozilla Firefox, GIMP, Apache Server, the Large Language Model named LLaMA – Large Language Model Meta AI.

GitHub Pages

GitHub Pages allows users to easily publish and host files from a repository on GitHub's servers. These pages can tell readers more about the developer, the project in the repository, or any other information.

GitHub Pages only allows the hosting of static content, which usually comes in the form of HTML and CSS or Markdown files. Users can either build these pages from scratch or use a pre-made theme.

For the average user, GitHub Pages can be a great substitute for a website domain purchased through services like GoDaddy or Namecheap. In our example, this allows our digital menu to be up and running in a matter of minutes.

Part 3: Generate the QR Code

What you need:

- The URL of the website hosted on GitHub

What to do:

1. In a Web browser, go to the QR Code Generator at `https://qr-code-generator.com`. If you have a different tool that you prefer, feel free to use that instead. See Figure 8.3.

2. In the main QR Code Generator interface, click on the `URL` button. It should be the first option.

3. In the main text box below, enter the URL of the `Menu` page of your website. It should be similar to

    `https://<username>.github.io/MikesCafe/menu.html`

4. After a few seconds, the QR code should be auto-generated. From there, the code's frame, shape, color, and logo can be customized.

5. Download the QR code as JPG. There is also an option to download as SVG; feel free to do this if it suits your needs better.

Figure 8.3 QR Code Generator (https://qr-code-generator.com)

What Did You Do, and How Did You Do It?

After following the Part 3 tutorial, the reader should have a working QR code that will produce the URL of our restaurant menu.

How Do QR Codes Work?

The first QR codes were created by DENSO WAVE INCORPORATED, a Japanese manufacturing company, in 1994 [1]. QR codes were created as a more versatile alternative to traditional barcodes. Barcodes were invented by Norman Joseph Woodland and Bernard Silver in 1951, and they became the standard for identifying commercial items.

QR codes are similar to barcodes, in that they use patterns to store information. The contained information gets visually coded as a series of black-and-white chunks. For that reason, each code will look different, depending on its contents. However, QR codes are different from barcodes because they can store two dimensions of information, instead of just one. And, QR codes are scanned faster than bar codes.

Figure 8.4 Comparison of QR codes and barcodes

This is what gives QR codes their square shape. Rather than a single line of coded information, a QR code contains several rows and columns of data. In addition to the chunks of white and black, QR codes also contain boxes in three of the four corners. This helps the QR code scanner identify the correct position and orientation of the QR code.

Norman Joseph Woodland

Norman Joseph Woodland is the co-inventor of the barcode. He was born in Atlantic City, New Jersey, in 1921. During World War II, Woodland served as a technical assistant on the Manhattan Project. After the war, Woodland attended Drexel University, where he studied Mechanical Engineering.

Along with colleague Bernard Silver, Norman Joseph Woodland developed the barcode in 1951. He and Silver invented the barcode as a way of systematically capturing information about commercial goods. The pattern of the barcode is based on Morse code, where the sequence of thin and thick bars represents a series of characters.

In the early 1970s, Woodland helped to develop the Universal Product Code (UPC) barcode system. Today, the UPC system is a widely used system for tracking commercial goods. GS1, a non-profit organization that maintains barcode standards, estimates that over 100 million products use UPC barcodes, and at least 5 billion barcodes are scanned each day.

Static and Dynamic QR Codes

The QR Code Generator tools provide ways to generate QR codes for a variety of data types.

There are two different types of QR codes: static and dynamic codes. Static codes cannot be changed, and they hold static information like URLs, text, and images. On the other hand, dynamic codes cannot be changed either, but always contain a URL that causes an automatic redirect to another URL. This allows us to change what the QR code eventually refers to. For example, suppose we are using a QR code that encodes URL 1 and URL 1 automatically redirects the user to URL 2. When the user scans the code, they only see URL 2. If we decide at a later date that we want the dynamic QR code to send the user to URL 3, we simply change the redirection on the web. The code itself does not change but, from the user's perspective, it did change. These codes are typically used for social media, tracking scans, coupons, and other business-related information.

Alternatives to QR Codes

When considering the wide range of Identification Technologies and identification-based tools, QR codes are only a small part of a larger ecosystem. Depending on the circumstances and the context of use, there are many different tools that can be used. Common alternatives to QR codes are Near-Field Communication (NFC) tags, Bluetooth™ Low Energy (BLE) beacons, and other Radio Frequency Identification (RFID) tags.

Using NFC, RFID, and BLE would require a different set of steps, and the process would differ slightly, but the general idea is the same. For example, NFC depends on the close proximity of a device (like a smartphone) to an NFC tag. Instead of scanning a code, NFC tags can communicate with a device when the device is within 4cm of the tag. Like a QR code, a notification or message would popup on the device's screen when the device has picked up on the NFC signal. BLE beacons function a similar way: the device would pick up the signal from the beacon, and it could then receive the information coming from the beacon.

Part 4: Scan and Use the QR Code

What you need:

- The QR code generated in Part 3
- A smartphone
- A QR code scanner (you likely have one)

What to do:

1. Prepare the QR code to be scanned. This could be in any format: printed on paper and placed on a restaurant's window, displayed on a screen, etc.

2. Open the QR code scanner app on your smartphone.

   a. Most smartphones have a QR code scanner built-in to their camera apps.

   b. If your smartphone does not have a built-in QR code scanner, check your phone's app store for a third-party scanner.

Figure 8.5: Scanning the QR Code using the iPhone camera app

3. Scan the QR code using the QR code scanner.

4. After scanning, your app should present a popup or message that displays the URL of your website's menu. Before navigating to it, always make sure that the address is correct.

5. Navigate to the Menu page on your smartphone. You've successfully used a QR code to view your digital menu!

Figure 8.6: Popup message after successfully scanning QR code with an iPhone

What Did You Do, and How Did You Do It?

The Smartphone as a Gateway to a Proxy Web Service

When a smartphone is used to scan a QR code, the smartphone takes on the role of a gateway device. What does this mean? By itself, the QR code has no way to communicate with other devices or access the Internet. For the process to work, it relies on a device to interact with it. That device, the gateway, will use its own Internet access to complete the transaction. After a smartphone scans the QR code, it then uses the Internet to send packets to the given URL or resource. The QR code provides identifying information, but it relies on the smartphone for internet access.

The web site that is visited is sometimes called a proxy web service. It provides a web presence for the item identified in the QR code.

Using NFC or Beacons

In the case of our restaurant menu, we could easily substitute a QR code for NFC tags or BLE beacons. The setup and usage process would differ slightly, but the overall concept would remain the same.

If we were deploying our QR code menus in an actual restaurant, it would make sense to put a sticker or poster of the QR code at each table. We could also put a single QR code near the door of the restaurant. When customers enter and sit at a table, they can easily scan the code and start looking at the menu.

Using NFC tags or beacons would be the same, just with different technology. Instead of a QR code at each table, there could be an NFC tag with a sign that says "Put your phone here to view the menu". Alternately, there could be a BLE beacon that would advertise the URL of the digital menu, and users can communicate with the beacon using their phones via Bluetooth. Again, the phone would act as a gateway to a proxy web service on the internet.

When deciding which type of Identification Technology to use, the most important thing to consider is the situation and context of use. Each type has its benefits and limitations. For example, NFC tags require close proximity in order to work. In situations where this is not possible, a QR code or beacon may be a better option.

Check Your Understanding

1. What does "QR" stand for, and what is the purpose of QR codes?

2. When a smartphone scans a QR code and then visits a web site, the smartphone is acting as a "gateway" device. Explain what this means.

3. When a smartphone receives a signal from a BLE beacon and then visits a web site, the smartphone is acting as a "gateway" device. Explain what this means.

4. When writing HTML code, why is it important to use semantic markup? What purpose do `meta` tags serve?

5. What is responsive web design, and why is it important?

6. What are some advantages of storing a project on GitHub?

7. Why does the restaurant website need to be hosted on GitHub, rather than on your local machine, for the QR code to work?

8. In addition to URLs, what are some other data types that QR codes can be used to contain? (Hint: check the online generation tool.)

9. What are the similarities and differences between QR codes, NFC tags, and beacons?

Make More / Explore Further

1. Modify the HTML code in your web pages to slightly change the pages' content. Add an address to the home page, change some menu items, or maybe add another form field to the contact form.

2. Modify the CSS code to change some aspects of the website's design or layout. Some ideas include changing the color scheme, importing a different Google Font from `https://fonts.google.com/`, or making a multi-column layout for the menu.

3. Use the QR code generation tool to change the look of your QR code. Depending on the tool used, you may be able to add a frame, change the color and/or shape of the code, or add a logo. For even more customization, consider using an image editor like Photoshop.

4. Use the QR code generation tool to generate a new QR code for a different aspect of the website or digital experience. This new QR code could link to another page of the site, or it could link to an email, image, or social media account.

5. Aside from a restaurant menu, what are some other examples of situations where QR codes can be used?

6. What are some situations in which NFC tags or beacons might be better than QR codes?

7. Our contacts page allows the user to enter text. Currently, that text does not go anywhere. Rather than deploying our restaurant application on GitHib, move it to Node.js and have Node.js send an email to the restaurant owner.

8. Consider the problem of taking roll in a large classroom. We want to give Alice credit for her attendance and penalize Bob if he misses class. It takes too much time

to call each student's name and wait for a response. We want to meet the following requirements:

    a.   If Alice attends class she is noted as such.

    b.   If Bob does not attend class he is marked as absent.

    c.   The instructor is able to see each student's name and photograph on a display.

    d.   As students arrive in class, a seating chart is dynamically generated showing each student's location in the room. Thus, the instructor may easily look at a student and the seating chart and call on him or her by name.

    e.   The instructor is not involved with the mechanics of building the roster. That is, there is no need for the instructor to "call roll".

Design a system using QR-codes and a backend system that meets these requirements. You may assume that the instructor, prior to the class meeting, has an online list of names and photographs of registered students.

9. Ask ChatGPT what the use of QR codes is in IoT.

Summing Up

Using QR codes or NFC tags or beacons as identification technologies, allow us to establish an online presence for every day, non-connected objects. Some example use cases are movie posters, items at the grocery store, or a restaurant menu. In this chapter, we illustrated this concept by creating a website for a restaurant, generating a QR code, and using that QR code to access an online menu.

There are many scenarios where using identification technologies may be a good idea. In this chapter, we saw how QR codes may be cost effective (replacing the need for paper menus), simple to deploy, and utilized to improve sanitation

In general, they can help users easily access more information about an object, place, or event.

With each passing day, these technologies are becoming more popular. And interacting with these devices is easier than ever; most smartphones today have built-in QR, BLE, and NFC functionality.

Looking Ahead

In the next chapter, we will be expanding on our discussion of Bluetooth™ Low Energy (BLE). Our discussion will be in the context of a telemedicine application. Just like QR codes and NFC tags, BLE signals are commonly used for identification. As we will see, they can also be used to transfer data from sensors.

References

1. SproutQR. "Who Invented the QR Code? QR Code History & Creator."
    Accessed July, 2023. https://www.sproutqr.com/blog/qr-code-history.

Chapter Appendix

```
<!DOCTYPE html>
<html lang="en-US">
    <head>
        <title>Mike's Cafe - Home</title>
        <!-- Meta tags tell give important information about our
webpage -->
        <!-- The viewport meta tag is needed for responsive layouts -
->
        <meta charset="utf-8"/>
        <meta name="description" content="The menu for Mike's Cafe"
/>
        <meta name="viewport" content="width=device-width, initial-
scale=1">
        <!-- Including CSS rules from styles.css in our page -->
        <link rel="stylesheet" type="text/css" href="styles.css"/>
    </head>
    <body>
        <!-- Throughout the body, we are using semantic HTML tags to
            give better insight into the content on the page. This
            is thought to be better than simply using <div>
everywhere -->
        <header>
            <h1>Mike's <br/> Cafe + Restaurant</h1>
            <!-- Below is the main navigation menu. Since only the
menu
                page is built, the others have placeholder links -->
            <nav>
                <a class="button" href="index.html">Home</a>
                <a class="button" href="menu.html">Menu</a>
                <a class="button" href="contact.html">Contact</a>
            </nav>
        </header>
        <main>
            <!-- Different parts of the content are contained in
<section>
                tags to make each part smaller and more manageable --
>
            <section>
                <h2>Welcome to Mike's!</h2>
                <p>Mike's is a cafe and restaurant with a
comfortable, laidback atmosphere.
                    When you're at Mike's, you can have a quick
coffee, eat a sandwich, or just sit and do work.
                    We hope you'll stop by!</p>
```

```
                <p>Please navigate to the menu to see the food and
drinks that we offer. </p>
            </section>
            <section>
                <h3>Our Weekly Hours</h3>
                <ul>
                    <li>Monday: 9am-8pm</li>
                    <li>Tuesday: 9am-8pm</li>
                    <li>Wednesday: 9am-8pm</li>
                    <li>Thursday: 9am-8pm</li>
                    <li>Friday: 9am-10pm</li>
                    <li>Saturday/Sunday: 10am-10pm</li>
                </ul>
            </section>
            <section>
                <h3>Customer Reviews</h3>
                <ul>
                    <li><q>I really enjoy coming to Mike's when
trying to finish schoolwork. It's relaxed and not too loud.</q>-
Jimmy S.</li>
                    <li><q>The food at Mike's is so, so good! Please
try the breakfast sandwich!</q> - Sarah T.</li>
                    <li><q>Sometimes, there's a live band playing on
the weekends, and I really like that.</q> - Kieran W.</li>
                </ul>
            </section>
        </main>
        <footer>
            <!-- &copy; is used to generate the copyright symbol on
the page -->
            <p>&copy; 2021 Mike's Cafe.</p>
        </footer>
    </body>
</html>
```

```
<!DOCTYPE html>
<html lang="en-US">
    <head>
        <title>Mike's Cafe - Menu</title>
        <!-- Meta tags tell give important information about our
webpage -->
        <!-- The viewport meta tag is needed for responsive layouts -
->
        <meta charset="utf-8"/>
        <meta name="description" content="The menu for Mike's Cafe"
/>
        <meta name="viewport" content="width=device-width, initial-
scale=1">
        <!-- Including CSS rules from styles.css in our page -->
        <link rel="stylesheet" type="text/css" href="styles.css"/>
    </head>
    <body>
        <!-- Throughout the body, we are using semantic HTML tags to
            give better insight into the content on the page. This
```

```
                    is thought to be better than simply using <div>
everywhere -->
        <header>
            <h1>Mike's <br/> Cafe + Restaurant</h1>
            <!-- Below is the main navigation menu. Since only the
home and menu
                pages are built, the others have placeholder links --
>
            <nav>
                <a class="button" href="index.html">Home</a>
                <a class="button" href="menu.html">Menu</a>
                <a class="button" href="contact.html">Contact</a>
            </nav>
        </header>
        <main>
            <!-- Different parts of the menu are contained in
<section>
                tags to make each part smaller and more manageable --
>
            <section id="intro">
                <h2>Our Menu</h2>
                <p>In addition to the atmosphere at Mike's, we take
pride in the food that we offer.
                    All food is prepared fresh by our chef, and
everything is customizable to your liking.
                    We hope you'll grab a bite to eat while you're
here!
                </p>
            </section>
            <section id="specials">
                <h3>Daily Soup Menu</h3>
                <ul>
                    <li>Monday: Vegetable Soup</li>
                    <li>Tuesday: Beef and Barley</li>
                    <li>Wednesday: Potato Soup</li>
                    <li>Thursday: Broccoli Cheddar</li>
                    <li>Friday: Chicken Tortilla</li>
                    <li>Saturday/Sunday: Chicken Noodle</li>
                </ul>
            </section>
            <section id="appetizers">
                <h3>Appetizers and Sides</h3>
                <!-- By using the class "item" on this div, we can
use CSS to
                    style it. Check the CSS for .item to see the
rules we've applied -->
                <div class="item">
                    <h4>Daily Soup</h4>
                    <p>$3.00 | A bowl of our fresh-made soup. Check
the soup menu for today's option.</p>
                </div>
                <div class="item">
                    <h4>Chef Salad</h4>
                    <p>$4.00 | Romaine lettuce, cherry tomatoes, red
onions, green bell peppers, chickpeas, olives, and banana peppers.
Served with ranch or Italian dressing.</p>
```

```
            </div>
            <div class="item">
                <h4>French Fries</h4>
                <p>$3.50 | Fresh-cut French fries, baked to
crispy perfection. Served with ketchup, hot sauce, or mayonnaise.</p>
            </div>
        </section>
        <section id="sandwiches">
            <h3>Sandwiches</h3>
            <div class="item">
                <h4>Breakfast Sandwich</h4>
                <p>$4.25 | Egg, ham, and cheese, inside a toasted
English muffin. A classic favorite.</p>
            </div>
            <div class="item">
                <h4>Bacon, Lettuce, and Tomato (BLT)</h4>
                <p>$4.00 | Crispy bacon, lettuce, tomato, and
mayonnaise, inside two pieces of fresh-baked bread.
                    (Add egg for an additional cost.)
                </p>
            </div>
            <div class="item">
                <h4>Grilled Cheese</h4>
                <p>$4.50 | A classic three-cheese grilled cheese,
served with a side of your choice.</p>
            </div>
        </section>
        <section id="drinks">
            <h3>Drinks</h3>
            <div class="item">
                <h4>Coffee (Hot/Iced)</h4>
                <p>$1.50 | Both regular coffee and espresso
drinks available. Ask about our lattes and macchiatos!</p>
            </div>
            <div class="item">
                <h4>Tea (Hot/Iced)</h4>
                <p>$1.50 | Black, green, and earl gray teas
available. Mix-ins include milk, sugar, honey, and lemon.</p>
            </div>
            <div class="item">
                <h4>Lemonade</h4>
                <p>$2.50 | Our refreshing in-house lemonade, made
with real, organic lemons.</p>
            </div>
            <div class="item">
                <h4>Soda</h4>
                <p>$3.00 | We offer a variety of Coca-Cola
products, including Coca-Cola, Fanta, Sprite, and more.</p>
            </div>
        </section>
    </main>
    <footer>
        <!-- &copy; is used to generate the copyright symbol on
the page -->
        <p>&copy; 2021 Mike's Cafe.</p>
    </footer>
```

```
        </body>
</html>
```

```
<!DOCTYPE html>
<html lang="en-US">
    <head>
        <title>Mike's Cafe - Contact</title>
        <!-- Meta tags tell give important information about our
webpage -->
        <!-- The viewport meta tag is needed for responsive layouts -
->
        <meta charset="utf-8"/>
        <meta name="description" content="The menu for Mike's Cafe"
/>
        <meta name="viewport" content="width=device-width, initial-
scale=1">
        <!-- Including CSS rules from styles.css in our page -->
        <link rel="stylesheet" type="text/css" href="styles.css"/>
    </head>
    <body>
        <!-- Throughout the body, we are using semantic HTML tags to
            give better insight into the content on the page. This
            is thought to be better than simply using <div>
everywhere -->
        <header>
            <h1>Mike's <br/> Cafe + Restaurant</h1>
            <!-- Below is the main navigation menu. Since only the
menu
                page is built, the others have placeholder links -->
            <nav>
                <a class="button" href="index.html">Home</a>
                <a class="button" href="menu.html">Menu</a>
                <a class="button" href="contact.html">Contact</a>
            </nav>
        </header>
        <main>
            <!-- Different parts of the content are contained in
<section>
                tags to make each part smaller and more manageable --
>
            <section>
                <h2>Contact Us</h2>
                <p>Do you have a question that you'd like answered or
a thought you'd like to share?
                    Let us know with the form below. We'll get back
to you as soon as we can.
                </p>
            </section>
            <section>
                <h3>Contact Form</h3>
                <form>
                    <!-- All form fields have labels and all are
required.
```

```
                              This makes it easier to complete the form
correctly -->
                    <label for="name">Name (required)</label><br/>
                    <input id="name" type="text" required/>
                    <br/><br/>
                    <label for="email">Email Address
(required)</label><br/>
                    <input id="email" type="email" required/>
                    <br/><br/>
                    <label for="type">Message Type
(required)</label><br/>
                    <select id="type" required>
                        <option value="feedback">Feedback</option>
                        <option value="question">Question</option>
                        <option value="other">Other</option>
                    </select>
                    <br/><br/>
                    <label for="msg">Your Message
(required)</label><br/>
                    <textarea id="msg" rows="10" required></textarea>
                    <br/><br/>
                    <input id="submit" class="button" type="submit"/>
                </form>
            </section>
        </main>
        <footer>
            <!-- &copy; is used to generate the copyright symbol on
the page -->
            <p>&copy; 2021 Mike's Cafe.</p>
        </footer>
    </body>
</html>
```

```
/* Style rules for index and menu pages */

/* Importing Google Font 'Josefin Sans' for headers and other
important text */
@import
url('https://fonts.googleapis.com/css2?family=Josefin+Sans:wght@400;7
00&display=swap');

/* General */

* {
    font-family: Arial, Helvetica, sans-serif;
}

.button {
    padding: 10px;
    color: white;
    font-weight: bold;
    text-decoration: none;
    background-color: rgb(138, 109, 90);
    border-radius: 10px;
```

```
        opacity: 0.9;
}

.button:hover {
        background-color: rgb(146, 115, 94);
}

h1, h2, h3, h4, h5, h6, label, .button {
        font-family: 'Josefin Sans', sans-serif;
}

/* Header */

header {
        text-align: center;
        margin: -22px -2% 0;
        padding-bottom: 30px;
        padding-top: 20px;
        border-bottom: 5px solid rgb(138, 109, 90);
        background-color: rgb(206, 162, 133);
        font-family: 'Josefin Sans';
}

/* Main content */

.item {
        border: 1px solid lightgray;
        padding: 0 10px;
        margin: 0px 0;
}

.item h4 {
        margin: 15px 0 5px;
}

.item p {
        margin: 0 0 15px;
}

li {
        padding: 2px;
}

main {
        display: block;
        width: 80%;
        margin: 30px auto;
}

section {
        display: block;
        margin: 30px 0;
}

ul {
        margin-left: -20px;
```

```
}

/* Footer */

footer {
    border-top: 1px solid lightgray;
    padding: 0 2%;
}

/* Form elements */

/* Apply to all input elements that don't have an ID of 'submit' */
input:not(#submit), select, textarea {
    display: inline-block;
    padding: 5px;
    border: 1px solid lightgray;
    border-radius: 5px;
    width: 33%;
}

#submit {
    border: 0;
    padding: 10px;
    font-size: 1.1em;
    cursor: pointer;
}

/* Responsive styles */

/* Apply the following rules on devices with screen widths of 600px
or less */
@media screen and (max-width: 600px) {
    input:not(#submit), select, textarea {
        width: 90%;
    }

    main {
        width: 90%; /* Make main container wider on the screen */
    }
}
```

CHAPTER 9

Constrained Networking

This chapter covers
TeleMedicine
Bluetooth™ Low Energy
IoT Architecture

Healthcare at a distance

Telemedicine During Covid-19

With telemedicine, people can attend health checkups remotely and save on transportation costs. The elderly or people with mild illnesses can meet a doctor without being exposed to others. Patients sick with a virus may meet with their doctor without leaving isolation. Doctor's offices may be temporarily closed and patient care can continue.

There has been an increase in the use of telemedicine since the Covid-19 pandemic.

Even before the Covid-19 pandemic, Doctors Without Borders made important use of telemedicine to help those in need [1]. The right knowledge in the right hands can save a life!

In this chapter, we study how a vital sign such as a person's body temperature can be communicated to a medical doctor using Bluetooth® Low Energy and the World Wide Web.

Bluetooth® Low Energy (BLE) provides short range wireless communication or a Wireless Personal Area Network (WPAN). In this chapter, you will learn how data can be moved from a WPAN to the Web.

"Whenever the art of Medicine is loved, there is also a love of humanity."

Hippocrates

In Part 1, you will deploy firmware to your microcontroller that will communicate with your phone using Bluetooth® Low Energy (BLE). Part 1 is about testing the set up and learning about the binary encodings used for temperature data. In Part 2, you will use the same firmware and BLE to communicate with Node-RED®. In addition, Node-RED® will be programmed to convert the binary codes to English text. In Part 3, you will connect Node-RED®, acting as gateway, to MQTT on the internet. MQTT will communicate with a browser. In Part 4, you will add a temperature sensor to your Photon 2.

Part 1: Testing that your BLE firmware works with an Android or iOS phone.

What you need:

- An Android or Apple phone
- A Particle Photon 2
- An Apple or Windows machine connected to the World Wide Web.
- The free LightBlue® BLE application for your Apple or Android phone

What to do:

1. Copy the firmware named `BLE-Health-Temperature` to the Particle IDE and flash it to your Photon 2. The code may be found at this URL and is also in the chapter appendix.

   https://github.com/sn-code-inside/guide-to-iot/blob/main/Ch09_code/ble-health-temperature.ino

2. The firmware will cause your Photon 2 to advertise itself to its surroundings. When a central device, such as a smart phone, connects to the Photon 2, the firmware publishes random temperature values to the central device. In Part 4, we will configure a thermometer and publish actual temperature values.

   You need to install appropriate software on your phone so that it behaves as a BLE central device. The software that you need to install on your phone is called LightBlue®.

3. Test your Photon 2's BLE signals by installing the LightBlue® application on your phone. The URL for LightBlue® is here:

   `https://punchthrough.com/LightBlue/`

   a. LightBlue® will cause your phone to behave as a BLE central device and will scan for peripheral device advertisements. Your Photon 2 is behaving as a peripheral and is advertising its existence. Your goal is to connect your phone to the Photon 2. After you connect, your phone (running LightBlue®) becomes a client of the Photon 2.

   b. Note that finding the Photon 2 may require a bit of browsing and experimenting with LightBlue®. There are likely to be several BLE sources in your surroundings. The dBm value (decibels relative to one milliwatt) is used to define the strength of the BLE signal. Anything greater than -75 dBm is considered to be a reliable signal. The closer that you get to 0 (from the negative side of 0) , the more reliable the signal.
   c. On LightBlue®'s PunchThrough application, you can use signal strength to help locate which signal is coming from your Photon 2.
   d. Holding my Photon 2 a few inches away from my phone gives me -34 dBm. That is a very strong signal.
   e. The Photon 2, running ble-health-temperature.ino, will also display a WiFi MAC address on the console. This WiFi MAC address is only slightly different from the BLE MAC address and should help you locate which BLE device to connect to.
   f. Within the firmware, there is code that defines the temperature characteristic as a `notify` characteristic. This means that a client does not have to perform explicit read requests. The client (your phone) can sit back and receive the temperature values.

4. Using the LightBlue® application, you will need to use the `subscribe` or `listen` selection to receive these temperature values. This is the publish subscribe pattern that we saw when we studied MQTT in Chapters 6 and 7.

What Did You Do, and How Did You Do It?

The reader should take some time to review the firmware named `BLE-Health-Temperature`.

The temperature measurement data is transmitted to your phone in 6 bytes. Each byte is represented by two hexadecimal digits. Each hexadecimal digit represents exactly four bits of binary data. The user of the LightBlue® application should see a list of values coming from the Photon 2. For example, the following 6 bytes represent one temperature report from the Photon 2.

```
04  E1  0E  00  FE  06
:
:
```

What do these numbers mean?

The meanings of these values are defined by the BLE Special Interest Group (SIG). Descriptions of how these values are to be interpreted is available to anyone with an interest. In other words, the health thermometer service is an open standard.

Let's take a look at each byte.

By referring to the documentation openly published by the Bluetooth® SIG, we learn that the leftmost byte (0x04) is a flags value. This means that each bit acts as a flag – specifying whether some property is on or off. Each bit in this flags value is defined by the SIG. By consulting the documentation, we learn that the rightmost bit (bit 0) is 0 for temperatures measured in Celsius and 1 for temperatures measured in Fahrenheit. The hexadecimal value of 0x04 is 0000 0100 in binary. The rightmost bit (bit 0) is 0. So, this report is in Celsius.

There is more information in the hexadecimal value 0x04. Bit 2 in this value is 1. This tells the receiver that the message being sent includes a temperature value in the next four bytes.

In summary, 0x04 tells the receiver that the following 4 bytes encode a temperature value measured in Cesius.

The right most byte (0x06) is also an encoded value. The hexadecimal value of 0x06 tells the receiver that the temperature was taken with a thermometer placed in the mouth. If, instead, the temperature was taken from the armpit then this value would have been 0x01. These encodings are part of the health thermometer service definition provided by the Bluetooth® SIG.

But what about the four bytes in the middle? In this example we have 0xE1 0x0E 0x00, and 0xFE. How do these bytes represent a temperature recording?

The first three bytes of these four represent a number. The last byte of these four (0xFE) represents an exponent. Let's look at the first three bytes (0xE1 0x0E 0x00).

Here we note that the BLE standard specifies that these numbers are being sent in little-endian notation. That means that the byte that arrives first will represent the least significant byte. So, the first thing we will do to interpret the meaning of bytes (0xE1 0x0E 0x00) is to reverse their order. Why? Because, we as humans, are used to reading numbers from left to right and the most significant digits are always placed on the left.

OK, now we need to interpret the bytes 0x00 0x0E 0xE1 or (in binary) 0000 0000 0000 1110 1110 0001. This base 2 value gives 3809 in base 10. That is a very high temperature! But we are not done. We need to take into account the exponent.

How do we handle the exponent? The exponent is written in a standard representation called two's complement notation. To interpret the number 0xFE, we first look at its leftmost bit in binary. 0xFE in base 16 is equal to 1111 1110 in binary. The leftmost bit is a 1. So, according to two's complement notation, we know the number is negative. To find its value, we follow a two step process. First, we flip the bits, giving 0000 0001. Second, we add 1 to the result. In binary, we perform the addition:

```
    0000  0001

    +         1
```

```
---------

0000 0010
```

That is equal to 2 in base 10. Thus, the exponent is -2.

Finally, we can compute value $3809 \times 10^{-2} = 38.09$.

So, it turns out that "04 E1 0E 00 FE 06" means that the temperature was taken in the mouth and was 38.09 degrees Celsius.

To a medical doctor, that might mean that the patient has a fever or perhaps even an infection. But we do not want to display 04 E1 0E 00 FE 06 to a medical doctor. We will see how we can format the data differently in the next section. For now, since we are not developing a smartphone application, we will leave the data as it is: 04 E1 0E 00 FE 06.

Part 2: Using Node-RED® ™ to receive BLE signals from your microcontroller

Our goal is to establish a connection between Node-RED® and the Photon 2 using BLE. In addition, we want to convert the messages encoded in binary to a message encoded in English text.

What you need:

- Node-RED® running on your computer
- A Particle Photon 2 running the same firmware from Part 1.
- An Apple or Windows machine connected to the World Wide Web.

What to do:

1. Install two BLE Nodes in Node-RED® with the following shell commands.

On a MAC:
```
cd ~/.Node-RED
npm install Node-RED-contrib-generic-ble
```

On Windows:
   Change to where your Node-RED® is installed and run:
```
npm install Node-RED-contrib-generic-ble
```

2. Test if the two nodes were properly installed by running Node-RED® from a shell:

```
Node-RED
```

3. With a browser, visit Node-RED® at this URL:

```
http://127.0.0.1:1880/
```

4. Within Node-RED®, expand the `Network` icon on the left and verify the presence of two BLE nodes: `Generic BLE In` and `Generic BLE out`.

5. Using the + sign, create a new flow entitled `BLE-To-Node-RED`.

6. Add an `Inject node` to the palette.

7. In the `Inject node`, set the message payload type to JSON and set the message payload text to the JSON message `{"notify": true, "period": 0 }`. This message will tell the `Generic BLE In` node to listen for notify messages coming from the BLE connection. Name this node `Start the BLE Node Listening`. See Figure 9.1.

Figure 9.1 Configure a Node-RED® node to inject JSON

8. Drag the `Generic BLE In` node onto the palette. Create a wire from the `Inject` node in step 6 to the new `Generic BLE In` node.

9. On your computer, make sure that Bluetooth® is turned on.

10. Run the BLE firmware on the Photon 2. This is named `BLE-Health-Temperature` from Part 1.

11. Double click the `Generic BLE In` node and select the two check boxes: `Stringify in payload` and `Emit notify events`. Leave the node name empty.

12. Double click the `Generic BLE In` node and select the pencil symbol to edit the properties. Select the `BLE Scanning` check box and select `Apply`. This will cause your computer to scan for BLE signals. There may be several devices broadcasting their existence. You will need to select a BLE signal (choosing one nearby) and then clicking the `Apply` button. Continue this until you find the one with a GATT characteristic of `Temperature Measurement`.

13. Once you see `Temperature Measurement`, select the `Update` button and then the `Done` button.

14. Drag a debug node onto the palette and connect it to the output of the `Generic BLE In` node. In this way, the data that is received over BLE will appear in the debug pane on the right. The debug node will display the `msg.payload` property.

15. Deploy the flow. The `Generic BLE In` node will be marked `missing`. To start listening for notifications, click on the far left side of the `Inject node` icon. With the Photon 2 running, you should see the publications (notifications) from the Photon 2 in the debug window. See Figure 9.2

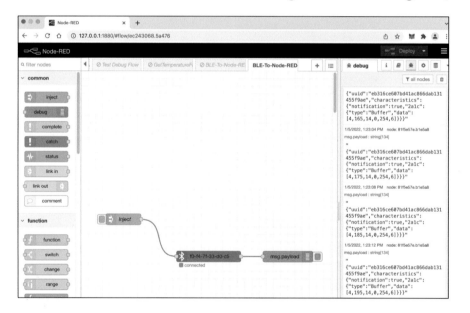

Figure 9.2 Viewing BLE data in Node-RED®

16. Add a new `Inject node` and set the `msg.topic` to `connect`. Name the node `Connect to Photon 2`. It is important that the `msg.payload` and `msg.topic` types be set as string. You should see `Message.payload = a/z` and `msg.topic = a/z`. See Figure 9.3.

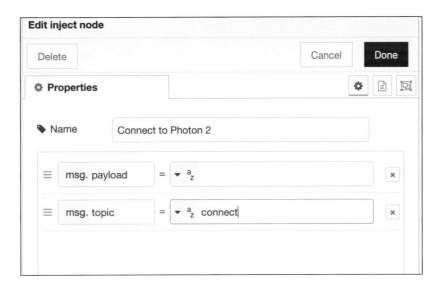

Figure 9.3 Creating an inject node with a connect string

17. Add a new `Inject node` and set the `msg.topic` to the value `disconnect` – with no quotes. Name the node `Disconnect from Photon 2`. Again, it is important that the `msg.payload` type and `msg.topic` type be set be set as string. You should see `Message.payload = a/z` and `Message.topic = a/z`.

18. See Figure 9.4 and wire the two new `Inject nodes` to the input of the `Generic BLE In` node. The `BLE In` node should now have three inject nodes wired to it. Deploy the flow and experiment. Start and stop the BLE connection using these new nodes. After the connection is started, inject a listening request from the middle inject node. Watch the output from the debug node.

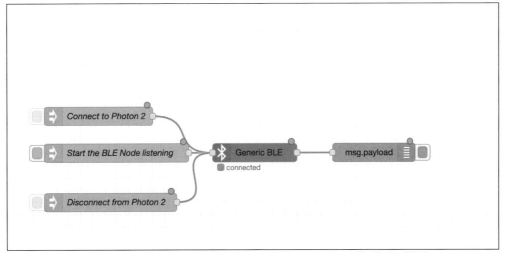

Figure 9.4 BLE- connecting, listening, and disconnecting with Node-RED®

19. Your Node-RED® palette should now be showing the messages arriving from the Photon 2. See Figure 9.5.

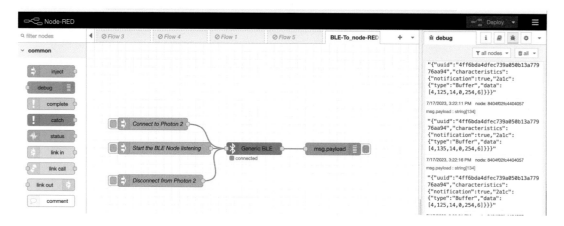

Figure 9.5 Messages displayed after arriving over BLE

20. Drag a new function node onto the Node-RED® palette and place it between the `Generic BLE In` node and the `Debug node`.

21. Copy and paste the code found at this URL into your function node. Name this function node `FromBinaryToText`. This code is also found in the chapter appendix.

    https://github.com/sn-code-inside/guide-to-iot/blob/main/Ch09_code/FromBinaryToText.js

22. Your output should now appear as Figure 9.6

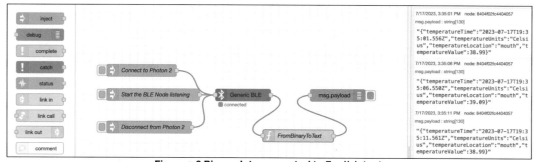

Figure 9.6 Binary data converted to English text

What Did You Do, and How Did You Do It?

The reader should take some time and read over the comments and the code in the file named `FromBinaryToText.js`. The following discussion assumes that you have done so.

The Node-RED® flow that we built in Part 2 does two things. First, it interacts with a BLE peripheral device (your Photon 2) and then it transforms the binary payload to text.

Bluetooth® Low Energy (BLE) and Open Systems

BLE is an open wireless network technology that uses very little power and communicates over a fairly short distance (typically less than 100 meters).

At a high level, here is how it works. Peripheral devices periodically broadcast radio signals to any listener that might be nearby. This is called *advertising*. Another device (called a central device in BLE) may decide to *scan* for these signals. These advertising signals include information on the services the device has on offer. The central device may then decide to *connect* to the peripheral. The messages being transmitted during these interactions (advertising, scanning, and connecting) are all carefully defined by the Bluetooth® SIG.

Once a connection is established, that is, once the peripheral and the central have exchanged the appropriate messages, the peripheral stops advertising and acts as a server to its new client. The central device may then request and receive data values from the peripheral. In BLE, these data values are called *characteristics*.

In the example in Part 2, the characteristic that we are interested in is the temperature characteristic. This data value (a block of binary data) includes information on the units used (Celsius or Fahrenheit) as well as the location on the human body where the temperature was taken and, of course, the temperature itself.

Each characteristic in the Bluetooth® SIG specification has an associated unique name (an integer chosen by the SIG). In the example in Part 2, the characteristic was named `2a1c`. This name was used in the Node-RED® function that converted the data from binary to text. In BLE, characteristics are associated with a higher level concept called a *service*. A service may provide several related characteristics. And services are associated with a still higher level concept called a BLE *profile*. A profile may provide several related services.

The important thing to note here is that the services and characteristics have assigned numbers (names) that allow for unambiguous communication. When you ask for `2a1c` from a standard BLE device, you are asking for the temperature characteristic. Research this. Visit this web site and open the document named Assigned Numbers Document. Search for `2a1c` and you will see that this is the Temperature Measurement characteristic.

```
https://www.bluetooth.com/specifications/assigned-numbers/
```

Search the same document for `1809` and you will find the Health Thermometer service. This is the service that contains the Temperature Measurement characteristic.

Note that the Temperature Measurement characteristic is being unambiguously defined. By browsing this web site, you can clearly see what it means to be an "open" system. Every detail about the characteristics and services and profiles is defined and is available for inspection by anyone. While this exemplifies an "open" system, the reader should note that many modern IoT systems are not "open".

Have you ever attended a sporting event and became hungry for popcorn? You may have decided to listen for popcorn advertisements. And, sure enough, a person walks by yelling "POPCORN, GET YOUR FRESH POPCORN HERE!". You signal to the popcorn vendor that you want to engage in a transaction. At that point, money is exchanged for a warm box of popcorn. This is an example of wireless service discovery – very much like BLE. It is also an "open" system. Everyone knows how to play.

Constrained Devices

Suppose we were to build a device that a user could wear to monitor his or her blood pressure. This might be useful in a telemedicine application. We might want to collect the data and use it in a report to a medical doctor.

The device will likely be battery powered (we don't want the person to have to walk around with an attached wire) and we would prefer not to have to change or charge the batteries every day. Thus, we have a significant constraint on how much power we can consume.

Such a constraint will dictate what features are and are not provided by the device.

We may not be able to provide data storage on the device and may need to transfer the data to a more capable device. So, we need a network.

The device has no wires (it's a wearable device) and so our networking needs to be wireless.

We would likely turn to a technology like BLE for a solution. It provides a low energy network but can only communicate over short distances. We can't use BLE to make an HTTP request to an arbitrary host on the internet. That would require a lot of bits being transmitted over a long distance and that requires a lot of energy.

Our low energy constraint will mean that we prefer short binary messages – each encoding the information that we want to transmit.

But, for our device to get its data over to the web, we need a gateway device that converts these binary (short) messages to textual (verbose) messages. The gateway device is less constrained than the wearable device. It has access to the internet and may have a more abundant source of storage and power. A phone or a computer will do just fine.

In Part 2, we are using Node-RED®, running on a gateway device (our computer), to collect data from a constrained device (our Photon 2). We used a function to convert the binary data 04   E1   0E   00   FE   06 into a readable text message. See the JSON string on the right in Figure 9.6.

Now it is time to transfer this textual message to the internet. Node-RED® is perfectly capable to carry out this mission. It knows how to talk to an MQTT broker and MQTT may be just what the doctor ordered – no pun intended. After all, we may have many patients and many health care professionals. See Chapters 6 and 7 to understand why MQTT is appropriate.

Part 3: Using Node-RED®, publish the BLE messages to MQTT and provide a browser that subscribes.

Our goal is to publish the formatted messages to an MQTT broker and have a browser subscribe to these measurements.

What you need:

- Node-RED® running on your computer
- A Particle Photon 2 running the same firmware from Part 1.
- An Apple or Windows machine connected to the World Wide Web.
- The Node-RED® flow established in Part 2.
- An MQTT broker (mosquitto) running locally.

What to do:

1. We will use mosquito as our MQTT broker. Prior to running mosquito, change mosquitto's configuration file. We are not using password protection in this example.

   a. On a Mac, depending on the setup, the configuration file may be found at:

      ```
      /usr/local/etc/mosquitto/mosquitto.conf
      ```

   b. Also on a Mac, the configuration may be found at:

      ```
      /opt/homebrew/etc/mosquitto/mosquitto.conf
      ```

   c. On a Windows machine, the configuration file is typically found at:

      ```
      C:\Program Files\mosquitto\mosquitto.conf
      ```

   d. At the very bottom of the `mosquitto.conf configuration file`, add the following five lines:

      ```
      listener 1883
      protocol mqtt
      listener 9002
      protocol websockets
      allow_anonymous true
      ```

2. In a command shell, start mosquitto (picking up the new configuration file) with the following command. See Figure 9.7.

mosquitto -c /opt/homebrew/etc/mosquitto/mosquitto.conf -v

```
$ mosquitto -c /opt/homebrew/etc/mosquitto/mosquitto.conf -v
1638666336: mosquitto version 2.0.14 starting
    1638666336: Config loaded from
    /usr/local/etc/mosquitto/mosquitto.conf.
    1638666336: Opening ipv6 listen socket on port 1883.
    1638666336: Opening ipv4 listen socket on port 1883.
    1638666336: Opening websockets listen socket on port 9002.
    1638666336: mosquitto version 2.0.14 running
```

Figure 9.7 Running Mosquitto from the command line

3. Run Node-RED® and begin with the flow we created in Part 2.

```
Node-RED
```

4. Add an "MQTT OUT" node to the Node-RED® palette. Configure the new node to publish to the topic `patient/temperatureReport`. The quality of service (QoS) is 0 and Mosquitto's port is 1883 running on localhost. The name of this Node is `To MQTT`. Hint: You may need to use the pencil icon to change to localhost.

5. Connect the output of the node named `FromBinaryToText` to the input side of the node named `ToMQTT` and perform a `Deploy` operation. See Figure 9.8.

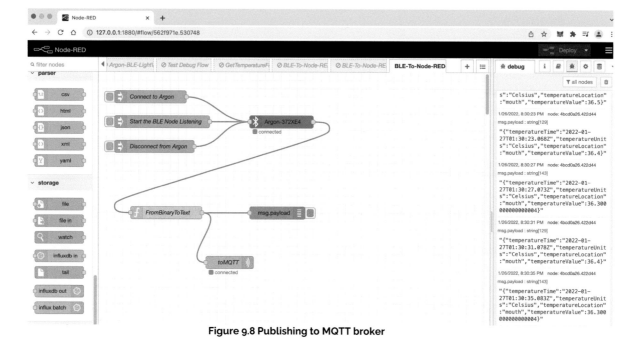

Figure 9.8 Publishing to MQTT broker

6. To test if everything is working properly, subscribe to MQTT messages from the command line. See Figure 9.9.

```
mosquitto_sub -t localhost -t patient/temperatureReport
{"temperatureTime":"2023-07-
17T20:03:21.847Z","temperatureUnits":"Celsius","temperatureLocation":
"mouth","temperatureValue":36.9}
{"temperatureTime":"2023-07-
17T20:03:26.843Z","temperatureUnits":"Celsius","temperatureLocation":
"mouth","temperatureValue":36.800000000000004}
```

Figure 9.9 Subscribing from the command line

7. As we did in Chapter 6, create a web application using Node.js.

    a. Create an empty directory named Chapter9_Part3.

        ```
        mkdir Chapter9_Part3
        ```

    b. Use cd to change into the directory
        `Chapter9_Part3`.

        ```
        cd Chapter9_Part3
        ```

    c. Create a file named `index.js` and save the content found at this URL.
        The code may also be found in the chapter appendix.

        https://github.com/sn-code-inside/guide-to-
        iot/blob/main/Ch09_code/Chapter9_Part3/index.js

    d. Within the directory, `Chapter9_Part3`, create a sub directory named
        public.

        ```
        mkdir public
        ```

    e. Use `cd` to change into the `public` directory.

        ```
        cd public
        ```

    f. Save the file at this URL in the `public` directory with the name
        `index.html`. The code may also be found in the chapter appendix.

        https://github.com/sn-code-inside/guide-to-
        iot/blob/main/Ch09_code/Chapter9_Part3/public/index.html

    g. Use cd to change into `Chap9_Part3` (the parent of `public`).

        ```
        cd ..
        ```

    h. Within the `Chap_Part3` directory, run the following two commands:

        ```
        npm init     # Note: choose the defaults
        npm install express
        ```

    i.   And, to start our web server serving a web page, run the following command:

```
node index.js
```

    j.   Visit the web page at `http://localhost:3000/index.html`.

5. After a few seconds, your browser should begin displaying a Google Chart Gauge with temperature data as reported by the microcontroller. See Figure 9.10.

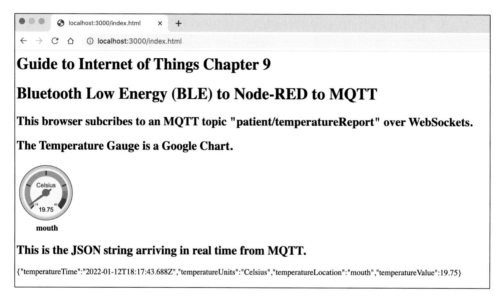

Figure 9.10 Showing room temperature in a Google Chart

What Did You Do, and How Did You Do It?

By working through the steps in this chapter, the reader has gained hands on experience with the three architectural parts of modern IoT systems. Here we will describe these three architectural parts. But let's first review what is meant by "architecture" and then consider how the concept applies to a wide variety of IoT systems.

Architecture

What is "Computer Architecture" ? Here is one popular way computer architecture is defined:

 "Computer architecture, like other architectures, is the art of determining the needs of a user of a structure and then designing to meet those needs as effectively as possible within economic and technological constraints." [2]

According to this definition, architecture is concerned with user needs, technological constraints , and economic constraints. Let's examine how these ideas apply to the example in this chapter.

With respect to user needs, our telemedicine application requires that patients and doctors communicate vital signs over a long distance. They will need information technology to do this. Since the patients may not be physically well and are unlikely to be IT specialists, the system itself should be easy to set up and use. Ease of use is also important from the doctor's perspective. Graphical displays, for example, are often more informative than text. From both the patient and the doctor perspectives, the technology should only enhance and not get in the way of the patient doctor relationship. We cannot stress this enough. In this scenario, the technology has to be dead simple to use. The system should be so simple that the technology disappears into the background.

Let's consider technological constraints. As we have seen, on the patient side of this communication, we may need battery power and wireless connectivity for devices that are unobtrusive and perhaps even wearable. Fortunately, requirements for low power wireless connectivity are satisfied by devices that support standards such as Bluetooth® (developed by the Bluetooth® SIG) or Zigbee ® (developed by the Connectivity Standards Alliance). But these requirements also imply the need for a less constrained device – acting as a gateway between the constrained network and the internet. This gateway requirement is satisfied by a smart phone or computer - able to communicate over the internet. The gateway can use the TCP/IP protocol stack to talk to the internet and the BLE protocol stack to talk to local, wireless, and battery powered devices.

The definition also mentions economic constraints. If the internet is available, it is able to carry signals over a long distance and at a minimal cost. Doctors need to be fitted with smart phones or computers connected to the internet – typically using WiFi, ethernet, or cellular networks. The patients will need to be able to afford the cost of the devices running on the constrained network (Bluetooth®, Zigbee®, etc.) as well as the cost of a gateway device (smart phone or computer) that is able to interact with devices on the constrained network as well as the internet. So, the patient will also typically need access to a WiFi, ethernet, or cellular network.

Finally, there are usability, technological, and economical concerns associated with the applications that are used by the doctors and the patients. Both types of users will be running applications (recall the end-to-end principle from Chapter 8) and these applications will often need to be inexpensive at scale, reliable, fault tolerant, secure, and private.

The definition of "architecture" seems to be useful – providing an overall description of the systems we are building.

If we abstract away from any particular use case, and focus on technology rather than economics or user needs, we find that many IoT systems are architected around three important layers: the *transducer* layer, the *gateway* layer and the *agent* layer.

Transducer Layer

A transducer is a device that converts energy from one form to another. It is in this layer that we find sensors and actuators. There is a wide variety of transducers and many are still being developed. In Part 4 of this chapter, the transducer that we use converts heat energy into a digital signal.

Many IoT systems (smart city, smart agriculture, smart factory, smart home, smart medicine) employ a transducer layer in their architectures. This is where the rubber meets the road and where our devices interact with the environment.

Gateway Layer

A gateway is a device that is able to communicate with more than one network protocol. It is in the gateway layer where a device communicates with a constrained network as well as the internet.

For example, a gateway device may communicate with local devices using short binary messages over BLE. And, at the same time, it may communicate with remote machines - using more verbose messages over TCP/IP. These messages may be carried over cellular, Wi-Fi, or ethernet networks.

A gateway may also add value in other ways. For example, before sending data packets to the internet, a gateway may add relevant information to the data values arriving from sensors. The information added may consist of timestamps or identifiers or topics for publish and subscribe scenarios. The gateway may be leveraged to add application level signatures or encryption.

Many IoT systems will use a tool like Node-RED® in the gateway layer. It is able to communicate with the sensors and actuators over BLE. It is able to add information to the raw data it receives from nearby devices. It is able to format messages and transmit them to receiving applications on the internet. And, it is able to receive instructions from the internet and transform them into an appropriate form for local receivers.

Agent Layer

The agent layer includes the IoT applications that are run on capable machines on the internet. It is in this layer where we find applications such as MQTT brokers, databases, data analytics and data visualization tools. Programs in this layer may make decisions (with or without human involvement) and these decisions may, in turn, result in messages being sent to gateways. The gateways may then interact with sensors or actuators and have a direct impact on our environment.

It is through this agent layer that we, as humans, normally interact with the IoT (perhaps via standard web protocols).

In this chapter, we used MQTT and a web application in the agent layer. End users were able to subscribe to temperature values and view them on the web in Google Charts.

Part 4: Add a real thermometer to your temperature reporting system.

Finally, we will complete our system by adding a temperature sensor. We can leverage the hardware setup from Chapter 5 to collect temperature data from a temperature sensor. We will communicate the temperature data over BLE to our gateway and view the real time results using Google charts on the web. So, all of our work from Part 3 will be reused here.

What you need:

- Particle Photon 2 and breadboard
- SHT30-D temperature sensor
- Work from Part 2 and Part 3

What to do:

1. Connect your SHT30 to the Photon 2 as we did in Chapter 5. See Figure 9.11.

2. Using the Particle Web IDE, flash the code found at this URL to your Particle Photon 2. This code is also available in the chapter appendix.

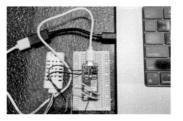

Figure 9.11: The SHT30 connected to the Photon 2

https://github.com/sn-code-inside/guide-
to-
iot/blob/main/Ch09_code/sht30_to_ble.ino

3. Note that this firmware communicates
    with two constrained networks. It
    communicates with the temperature
    sensor as well as our computer over
    BLE.

What Did You Do, and How Did You Do It?

In this Part, we added an actual transducer to our application. Using the same hardware configuration as the one that we built in Chapter 5, we were able to visualize real temperature data in a Google Chart.

Check Your Understanding

1. How does advertising provide for discovery?

2. Describe how BLE `notify` is similar to the publish subscribe pattern.

3. Describe how BLE `notify` differs from the way MQTT works.

4. Describe how a BLE service differs from a BLE characteristic.

5. Describe what a BLE service has in common with a BLE characteristic.

6. Suppose a phone, acting as a central node, connects to a BLE device, acting as a peripheral. Which of these devices now acts like a server? Which of these devices now acts like a client?

Make More / Explore Further

1. Do some research on BLE. How does a BLE profile differ from a BLE service.

2. Do some research on BLE. How does a BLE profile differ from a BLE characteristic.

3. Is a BLE connection between a central device and a peripheral device automatic or must the connection be initiated by the central device?

4. Describe how a hospital might use BLE in a wayfinding application?

5. Our application is missing a patient identifier – this would be important in a real situation where there may be many patients and many health care providers

interested in a particular patient's vital signs. Add a patient identifier at the gateway layer. Make sure that it makes its way through the broker and onto the browser.

6. See question 5 and explain why it makes good sense to add the patient identifier at the gateway layer and not in the transducer layer?

7. Currently, our Google Chart Gauge is hard coded to handle only Celsius temperatures. Make the necessary modifications to index.html so that either Celsius or Fahrenheit temperatures may arrive from the broker.

8. Require that Node-RED® provide a user name and password to the broker. Require that the subscribing browser also provides a user name and password. (See Chapter 7 Part 3 for help.)

9. Add logic to Node-RED® so that the temperature sensor data is only published to mosquito if the temperature reaches a threshold.

10.   Explore some major IoT platforms (Google Cloud IoT, AWS IOT, Azure IoT) and analyze each one in terms of the architectural components presented in this chapter, i.e., transducer layer, gateway layer, and agent layer. The names used in these systems may differ slightly from those used here. But the careful reader will see these same ideas used time and time again across the IoT landscape.

11. Use a Large Language Model, such as ChatGPT, to compare and contrast Google Cloud IoT, AWS IOT, and Azure IoT.

Summing Up

This is a central chapter in this book. For the first time, the reader is taken through a complete example that illustrates the three important architectural layers of modern IoT systems: the transducer layer, the gateway layer, and the agent layer.

A temperature sensor and microcontroller was used in the transducer layer – communicating over Bluetooth® Low Energy to a computer running Node-RED®. Node-RED®, running as a gateway, transformed incoming messages and communicated with an MQTT broker running in the agent layer. A web visualization, provide by Google Charts and Node.js, also ran in the agent layer.

This chapter's overall theme was telemedicine. The Covid-19 pandemic has spawned an increase in the use of this important application of IoT.

Looking Ahead

In this chapter, we saw how we can display data on the Web using a Google Chart. But there was no attempt to store the data to a database.

In the next chapter, we explore another important application in the agent layer. The reader will get hands on experience using an exceptionally popular database - SQLite.

References

1. Doctors Without Borders. "Telemedicine on the Front Lines." Last modified May 31, 2017. Accessed July 17, 2023. https://www.doctorswithoutborders.org/latest/telemedicine-front-lines
2. Buchholz, Werner. *Planning a Computer System*. New York: McGraw-Hill, 1962, p.5.

Chapter Appendix

```
// BLE-Health-Temperature

// Guide to Internet of Things Chapter 9 Constrained Networking
// This firmware was adapted from the BLE tutorial
// found here: https://docs.particle.io/tutorials/device-
os/bluetooth-le/

// The BLE class documentation is here:
// https://docs.particle.io/cards/firmware/bluetooth-le-ble/ble-
class/

// There is a license here:
// https://github.com/particle-iot/docs/blob/master/LICENSE.txt

boolean DEBUG = true;

// After a connection is established, publish the encoded temperature
every 5 seconds.
unsigned long  interval = 5000;

// Track milliseconds since last update.
unsigned long lastUpdate = 0;

// In C++, the function declaration (prototype) must be seen before a
call.
float getTempC();

// We need to encode a float temperature with a standard encoding.
uint32_t encoding_from_float_using_ieee11073(float temperature);

// The "Health Thermometer" GATT service is 0x1809.
// See https://www.bluetooth.com/specifications/assigned-numbers/
// and look in the document 16-bit-UUIDs.

// Create a UUID object for the service.
BleUuid
healthThermometerService(BLE_SIG_UUID_HEALTH_THERMONETER_SVC);

// The Temperature Measurement GATT chacteristic is 0x2A1C.
// See https://www.bluetooth.com/specifications/assigned-numbers/
// and look in the document 16-bit-UUIDs.
```

```
// Create a BLE Characteristic object with a name and a reference to
its service.
// By 'notify' we specify this as a value that may be subscribed to.
The user can sit
// back and receive these values.
// The value 0x2A1C will be available to the central device.

BleCharacteristic temperatureMeasurementCharacteristic("temp",
BleCharacteristicProperty::NOTIFY, BleUuid(0x2A1C),
healthThermometerService);

// We don't actually have a thermometer here, we just randomly adjust
this value.
float lastValue = 37.0; // 98.6 deg F;

// A byte array to hold 6 bytes for the WiFi mac address.
byte mac[6];

void setup() {

    // If we want to print to the serial port we call 'begin' with a
baud rate.
    Serial.begin(9600);

    // Turn the BLE radio on.
    BLE.on();

    // We want to publish this value.
    BLE.addCharacteristic(temperatureMeasurementCharacteristic);

    // We want to advertise this service.
    BleAdvertisingData advData;
    advData.appendServiceUUID(healthThermometerService);

    // Continuously advertise when not connected to a central
device.
    BLE.advertise(&advData);

    // The mac address of the WiFi interface will be close to the
    // mac address of the BLE interface. We can use the mac
address
    // of the WiFi interface to help locate the BLE mac address.

    WiFi.macAddress(mac);
}

void loop() {


    // Only on occasion, let the if be true.
    if (millis() - lastUpdate >= interval) {
            lastUpdate = millis();


            // If a central has connected to this device then send an
array of 6 bytes.
```

```
            if (BLE.connected()) {

                // Prepare room for standard response data.
                // The Temperature Measurement characteristic data
formatis defined in detail in this XML document.
                // The BLE standard defines the encoding of the 6
bytes

                uint8_t buf[6];

                // First byte is flags. We're using Celsius
units (bit 0 == 0), no timestamp (bit 1 == 0), with temperature type
(bit 2 == 1), so the flags are 0x04.
                // Remaining flags (3,4,5,6,7) are for future
use.
                buf[0] = 0x04;

                // Last byte describes where in the body the
temperature was taken.
                // For example, 1 == armpit, 4 == finger, and 6 ==
mouth.

                buf[5] = 6; // Mouth

                // We have 4 bytes to encode the actual
temperature.
                // buf[1],buf[2],buf[3], and buf[4]
                // This is a 32 bit encoding.

                // Get the temperature and encode in 32 bits.
                // ieee 11073 defines how to do this encoding
                uint32_t value =
encoding_from_float_using_ieee11073(getTempC());
                // copy 4 bytes into buf[1], buf[2], buf[3], and
buf[4]
                memcpy(&buf[1], &value, 4);
                // Include this data in the characteristic.
                temperatureMeasurementCharacteristic.setValue(buf,
sizeof(buf));
            }
        else {
            // If no central has tried to connect, display a MAC
address that is close to the BLE interface.
            // This may be helpful for a user trying to connect.
            if(DEBUG) {
                Serial.println("Not connected to BLE");
                Serial.printlnf("Scan for a mac address that is
close to this WiFi mac: %02x:%02x:%02x:%02x:%02x:%02x", mac[0],
mac[1], mac[2], mac[3], mac[4], mac[5]);
            }
        }


    }
}

float getTempC() {
```

```
    // This function returns a random temperature.
    // Half the time, increase the value by 0.1.
    if (rand() > (RAND_MAX / 2)) {
        lastValue += 0.1;
    }
    else {
    // Half the time, decrease the value by 0.1.
        lastValue -= 0.1;
    }

  if(DEBUG) Serial.println(lastValue);

    return lastValue;
}

uint32_t encoding_from_float_using_ieee11073(float temperature) {

    // The standard way to represent a float as an integer
    // is described by ISO/IEEE 11073 Personal Health Data Standards.
    // Precondition: health temperature > 0.
     // Postcondition: Returns 32 bits of encoded data.
    // We will multiply the temperature by 100 and so we need to
store an exponent of -2 in the encoding.
    // The receiver will then know to divide the temperature by 100.
    // Let's step through how to represent -2 in 8 bits.
    // First, represent it as positive.
    uint8_t posInt = 0b00000010;
    // Second, flip the bits using a bitwise not.
    uint8_t flippedBits = ~posInt;
    // Third, add one
     uint8_t exponent = flippedBits + 1;
    // Now, we have represented the -2 as an 8 bit integer in 2's
compliment notation.
       // place the exponent on the left of a 32 bit unsigned integer
        uint32_t result = ((uint32_t)exponent) << 24;
        // multiply the temperature by 100 to shift the decimal point
to the right two places.
        float shiftedTemperature = temperature * 100;
        // truncate the fractional portion and store the result in
mantissa.
        uint32_t mantissa = (uint32_t)(shiftedTemperature);
        // combine the exponent with the mantissa using a bitwise or
        result = result | mantissa;
        if(DEBUG) Serial.printlnf("TEMPERATURE %08X",result);
      return result;
}
```

```
```
// Guide to Internet of Things Chapter 9
// FromBinaryToText

// This is Javascript logic that is placed inside
// a Node-RED function node.

// It takes a message object as input, modifies its
```
```

```
// payload and returns the same message object.

// When working with a Node-RED function node, we need to
// return an object - usually a message object - never
// a number or a string.

// Note: when debugging use node.warn("x == " + x);

// This function converts a binary payload to text.
// We have a msg object as input.
// The incoming msg.payload is a JSON string.
// We want to convert the string in msg.payload
// into a Javascript object.
var msgInObject = JSON.parse(msg.payload);

// We need the data from the array.
// The array is within a JSON string.
// Drill down in the object to the array.
// Note that "2a1c" is a BLE standard number for the
// temperature characteristic. It is a key in the JSON string
// that we interrogate here.
var arrObj = msgInObject["characteristics"]["2a1c"]["data"];

// Create an object to collect the new output.
var msgOutObject = new Object();

// Place the time in the object
msgOutObject.temperatureTime = new Date();

// Let's examine the least significant bit in the first byte.
// We will perform an AND operation with 1.
// If the result is 1 then the temperature is in Fahrenheit.
// If the result is 0 then the temperature is in Celsius.
if ((arrObj[0] & 1) === 1) {
    msgOutObject.temperatureUnits = 'Fahrenheit';
}
else {
    msgOutObject.temperatureUnits = 'Celsius';
}
// Consult the BLE documentation for exact encodings
// for each body location. There are several not covered here.
// Here, we test only for mouth or finger.
if (arrObj[5] === 6) {
    msgOutObject.temperatureLocation = 'mouth';
}
else if (arrObj[5] === 4) {
    msgOutObject.temperatureLocation = 'finger';
}

// Create a number from bytes[1], [2], and [3].
// arrObj[3] is most significant and arrObj[1] is least significant.
var numericValue = arrObj[1];   // 1's place
numericValue = arrObj[2] * 256 + numericValue;
numericValue = arrObj[3] * 256 * 256 + numericValue;

// The encoding includes an exponent.
```

```
// The exponent is in 2's complement notation.
// If the leftmost bit is 1, the number is negative.
// If the number is negative, we flip the bits and add 1.
var exponent = 0;

// Find the value of the exponent in byte [4].
// Is the leftmost bit on ?
if((arrObj[4] & 0x80) !== 0) {
    // the number is negative. Flip the bits with XOR 1.
    exponent = arrObj[4] ^ 0xFF;
    // add 1
    exponent = exponent + 1;
    // make it negative
    exponent = (exponent * (-1));

}
// raise the numericValue to the exponent

msgOutObject.temperatureValue = numericValue *
Math.pow(10.0,exponent);

// Change the message payload to include a new JSON string.
// We do this by calling stringify on the output object.
msg.payload = JSON.stringify(msgOutObject);


return msg;
```

```
// Guide to Internet of Things
// Chapter 9 Node.js server code

// This file is named index.js.
// This code is used to serve up the single file in the public directory.
// The file being served is named index.html.

// A directory named "public" is available in the current directory.
// The public directory holds index.html containing HTML and Javascript.
// A browser will visit with http://localhost:3000/index.html.
// The file index.html will be fetched by HTTP and loaded into the browser.
// The browser is able to render the HTML and execute the Javascript.

const express = require('express')
const port = 3000
app = express();
// allow access to the files in public
app.use(express.static('public'));

app.listen(port, () => {
  console.log(`Patient temperature data available at
http://localhost:${port}/index.html`)
})
```

```
<!--
   Guide to Internet of Things
```

```
   Chapter 9 index.html

   This web application will cause the browser to connect to a
   running instance of an MQTT broker and subscribe to messages
   published to the patient/temperatureReport topic.

   The broker was started with:
   mosquitto -c /usr/local/etc/mosquitto/mosquitto.conf -v

   A Google Chart gauge is used to display the temperatures.
-->

<html>
  <head>

    <!-- Using a simple inline css style -->
    <style type="text/css">
        <!--
          .tab { margin-left: 40px; }
        -->
    </style>

    <!-- Get Google charts -->
    <script type="text/javascript"
src="https://www.gstatic.com/charts/loader.js"></script>
    <!-- Get the MQTT library -->
    <script src="https://cdnjs.cloudflare.com/ajax/libs/paho-
mqtt/1.0.1/mqttws31.js" type="text/javascript"></script>

    <!-- Load the gauge -->
    <script type="text/javascript">
        google.charts.load('current', {'packages':['gauge']});
        google.charts.setOnLoadCallback(drawGauge);

        var data = null;
        var chart = null;
        var options = null;

        <!-- Setup the parameters for the gauge and call changeGauge. -->
        function drawGauge() {

          data = google.visualization.arrayToDataTable([
            ['Label', 'Value'],
            ['Celsius', 0]
          ]);

          options = {
            width: 400, height: 120,
            yellowFrom:19.0, yellowTo:36.0,
            greenFrom:36.0, greenTo:37.8,
            redFrom: 37.8, redTo: 40.0,
            minorTicks: 0.1, min:19.0,max:40.0
          };

          chart = new
google.visualization.Gauge(document.getElementById('chart_div'));
          // The initial gauge value is 34.0 degrees Celsius.
          changeGauge(34.0);
        }
        <!-- Update the gauge -->
        function changeGauge(tempValue) {
          data.setValue(0, 1, tempValue);
```

```
            chart.draw(data, options);
        };
    </script>

    <!-- MQTT connection logic -->
    <script>
        // Create a client instance
        client = new Paho.MQTT.Client('localhost', Number(9002),
'doctorID'+Math.floor(Math.random() * 100));

        // set callback handlers
        client.onConnectionLost = onConnectionLost;
        client.onMessageArrived = onMessageArrived;

        // connect the client
        client.connect({onSuccess:onConnect});

        // called when the client connects
        function onConnect() {
            // after connetion, subscribe to the topic
            client.subscribe("patient/temperatureReport");

        }

        // called when the client loses its connection
        function onConnectionLost(responseObject) {
            alert('onConnectionLost error' + responseObject);
            if (responseObject.errorCode !== 0) {

console.log("onConnectionLost:"+responseObject.errorMessage);
            }
        }

        // This function is called when a message arrives from MQTT.
        function onMessageArrived(message) {
            // Place the contents in the document.
            var payloadObj = JSON.parse(message.payloadString);
            document.getElementById("json_arrival").innerHTML
=message.payloadString;
            document.getElementById("body_location").innerHTML
=payloadObj.temperatureLocation;
            // Update the gauge with this new data.
            changeGauge(parseFloat(payloadObj.temperatureValue));
        }
    </script>
    <!-- HTML document -->
    <body>
    <h1>Guide to Internet of Things Chapter 9 </h1>
    <h1>Bluetooth Low Energy (BLE) to Node-RED to MQTT</h1>
    <h2>This browser subcribes to an MQTT topic "patient/temperatureReport"
over WebSockets.</h2>
    <h2>The Temperature Gauge is a Google Chart.</h2>
    <div id="chart_div" style="width: 400px; height: 120px;"></div>
    <b><div class="tab" id="body_location"></div></b>
    <h2>This is the JSON string arriving in real time from MQTT.</h2>
    <p id="json_arrival"></p>
    </body>
</html>
```

```
// Guide to Internet of Things
// Chapter 9
// This code combines SHT30 temperature sensing with BLE wireless
communication.

// sht30-to-ble.ino monitors temperature data from a SHT30-D temperature
sensor.
// It then sends this over wireless BLE.
// Be sure to include the adafruit-sht31 library in this project.
// Include the header file for this library.

#include <adafruit-sht31.h>

// Set debug to true for particle serial monitor
bool DEBUG = TRUE;

// Get access to an Adafruit_SHT31 object.
Adafruit_SHT31 sht31 = Adafruit_SHT31();

// Prototypes for functions
// Send to temperature to a BLE central device
void sendToBLE(float celsius);
// Get the temperature from a SHT30 sensor.
float getTempFromSHT30();

// We need to encode a float temperature with a standard encoding for BLE
transmission.
uint32_t encoding_from_float_using_ieee11073(float temperature);


// The "Health Thermometer" GATT service is 0x1809.
// See https://www.bluetooth.com/specifications/assigned-numbers/
// and look in the document 16-bit-UUIDs.

// Create a UUID object for the service.
BleUuid healthThermometerService(BLE_SIG_UUID_HEALTH_THERMONETER_SVC);

// The Temperature Measurement GATT chacteristic is 0x2A1C.
// See https://www.bluetooth.com/specifications/assigned-numbers/
// and look in the document 16-bit-UUIDs.

// Create a BLE Characteristic object with a name and a reference to its
service.
// By 'notify' we specify this as a value that may be subscribed to. The
user can sit
// back and receive these values.
// The value 0x2A1C will be available to the central device.

BleCharacteristic temperatureMeasurementCharacteristic("temp",
BleCharacteristicProperty::NOTIFY, BleUuid(0x2A1C),
healthThermometerService);

// A byte array to hold 6 bytes for the WiFi mac address.
byte mac[6];

// used to avoid use of the delay()
```

```
unsigned long loop_timer = 0;

void setup() {
  // The variable connected will be true or false depending on the
connection to SHT31-D.
  bool connected;
  // We may use the USB connection as well.
  Serial.begin();

  // Establish a connection to temperature sensor.
  // The SHT30-D's address is 0x44. Other I2C sensors will
  // have other addresses. These addreeses are specified in the datasheet
  // for the device.
  connected = sht31.begin(0x44);
  // Inform the user if the connection was established.
  if (connected) {
    Serial.println("Connected to SHT31");
  }
  else {
    Serial.println("Error: Not connected to SHT31");
  }

 // Turn the BLE radio on.
 BLE.on();

  // We want to publish this value.
  BLE.addCharacteristic(temperatureMeasurementCharacteristic);

  // We want to advertise this service.
  BleAdvertisingData advData;
  advData.appendServiceUUID(healthThermometerService);

  // Continuously advertise when not connected to a central device.
  BLE.advertise(&advData);


  // The mac address of the WiFi interface will be close to the
  // mac address of the BLE interface. We can use the mac address
  // of the WiFi interface to help locate the BLE mac address.

  WiFi.macAddress(mac);
  // initialize timer
  loop_timer = millis();
} // end of setup

void loop(void) {

  float celsius;

  if(millis() - loop_timer >= 5000UL) {
      loop_timer = millis();
      // Get temp from sensor
      celsius = (float) getTempFromSHT30();
      // and send over BLE to a central device
      sendToBLE(celsius);
  }
}

float getTempFromSHT30() {
  // The device reports temperatures in celsius.
  float celsius = sht31.readTemperature();
  if(DEBUG) Serial.println(celsius);
```

```
    return celsius;
}

void sendToBLE(float celsius) {

    // If a central has connected to this device then send an array of 6
bytes.
    if (BLE.connected()) {

                    // Prepare room for standard response data.
                    // The Temperature Measurement characteristic data
formatis defined in detail in the SIG.
                    // The BLE standard defines the encoding of the 6
bytes

                    uint8_t buf[6];

                    // First byte is flags. We're using Celsius units
(bit 0 == 0), no timestamp (bit 1 == 0), with temperature type (bit 2 == 1),
so the flags are 0x04.
                    // Remaining flags (3,4,5,6,7) are for future
use.
                    buf[0] = 0x04;

            // Last byte describes where in the body the temperature was
taken.
            // For example, 1 == armpit, 4 == finger, and 6 == mouth.

                    buf[5] = 6; // Mouth

                    // We have 4 bytes to encode the actual
temperature.
                    // buf[1],buf[2],buf[3], and buf[4]
                    // This is a 32 bit encoding.

                    // Get the temperature and encode in 32 bits.
                    // ieee 11073 defines how to do this encoding
                    uint32_t value =
encoding_from_float_using_ieee11073(celsius);
                    // copy 4 bytes into buf[1], buf[2], buf[3], and
buf[4]
                    memcpy(&buf[1], &value, 4);
            // Include this data in the characteristic. That will cause
transmission over BLE.
            temperatureMeasurementCharacteristic.setValue(buf,
sizeof(buf));
            }
          else {
                // If no central has tried to connect, display a MAC
address that is close to the BLE interface.
                // This may be helpful for a user trying to connect.
                if(DEBUG) {
                    Serial.println("Not connected to BLE");
                    Serial.printlnf("Scan for a mac address that is close
to this WiFi mac: %02x:%02x:%02x:%02x:%02x:%02x", mac[0], mac[1], mac[2],
mac[3], mac[4], mac[5]);
                    }
                }

}
uint32_t encoding_from_float_using_ieee11073(float temperature) {
```

```
    // The standard way to represent a float as an integer
    // is described by ISO/IEEE 11073 Personal Health Data Standards.
    // Precondition: health temperature > 0.
     // Postcondition: Returns 32 bits of encoded data.
    // We will multiply the temperature by 100 and so we need to store an
exponent of -2 in the encoding.
    // The receiver will then know to divide the temperature by 100.
    // Let's step through how to represent -2 in 8 bits.
    // First, represent it as positive.
    uint8_t posInt = 0b00000010;
    // Second, flip the bits using a bitwise not.
    uint8_t flippedBits = ~posInt;
    // Third, add one
     uint8_t exponent = flippedBits + 1;
    // Now, we have represented the -2 as an 8 bit integer in 2's compliment
notation.
        // place the exponent on the left of a 32 bit unsigned integer
        uint32_t result = ((uint32_t)exponent) << 24;
        // multiply the temperature by 100 to shift the decimal point to
the right two places.
        float shiftedTemperature = temperature * 100;
        // truncate the fractional portion and store the result in
mantissa.
        uint32_t mantissa = (uint32_t)(shiftedTemperature);
        // combine the exponent with the mantissa using a bitwise or
        result = result | mantissa;
        if(DEBUG) Serial.printlnf("TEMPERATURE %08X",result);
    return result;
}
```

CHAPTER 10

Persistence and Visualization

This chapter covers
   Water sensing
   Node-RED Http Nodes
   Node-RED SQLite Node
   Visualization
   CMU's OpenChirp

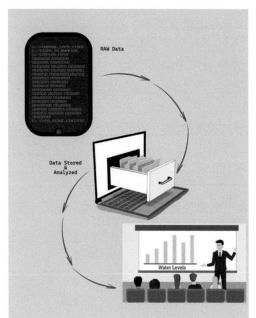

Provide meaning with visualization

"It is a capital mistake to theorize before one has data."

Sherlock Holmes in "A Study of Scarlet" by Arthur Conan Doyle

Climate Change Threatens Water Quality

Due to climate change, scientists expect an increase in the severity of storms. These storms are predicted to have heavier downpours leading to greater storm water runoff – imagine a parking lot overflowing with water. The runoff may contain garbage, pesticides, and bacteria.

Don't get us wrong – we know that we need rain. But we want the rain to be soaked up near where it falls.

Unlike sewage, stormwater does not run into a treatment plant. It is often channeled through stormwater drains, pipes and ditches and then into our streams and waterways. This often results in polluted water and flooding.

Organizations are stepping up to reduce pollution and improve the quality of our water.

Carnegie Mellon University, for example, is collecting rain water from the roofs of buildings to be used for flushing toilets [1]. The University adheres to the U.S. Green Building Council Leadership in Energy and Environmental Design (LEED) building rating system [2].

In this chapter, you will use a simple moisture sensor to detect water levels. The sensor will generate data that will be visualized (using Node-RED) and stored in a database (using SQLite).

Water level detection has a wide variety of use cases. It may be used in a storm water control system that monitors and then reroutes rainwater flows. It is better to route water to a local destination than to leave it to flow and gather dirt and debris and pollute an otherwise clean stream.

Water level detection might also be used in a smart farm sprinkler system. A water level sensor can provide data to a microcontroller which also has remote access to a weather forecasting API. If there is rain in the immediate forecast then there is no need to water the farm – even if the soil is dry. The microcontroller will note the likelihood of rain and leave the sprinkler turned off. If, on the other hand, the soil is dry and no rain is in the local forecast, the microcontroller can direct that a sprinkler be turned on. Scientists at IBM have built such a system and there is an interesting presentation at this link:

```
https://www.youtube.com/watch?v=Rvc1CqNJkOA&list=PLhZR82i0P9NqrksME13f
2t8tDMIhxUtCH
```

Many IoT applications are designed to repeatedly produce data values. These data streams are often described as "time series data".

Time series data consists of measurements that are taken repeatedly and recorded with timestamps over a specific period. These measurements must be monitored, stored, and visualized for analysis. In this chapter, we will treat water level measurements as time series data. The reader should note that this general approach of monitoring, storing, and visualizing data can be applied to a wide range of use cases.

In this chapter, in order to gather and store time series data, we use the very popular SQLite database.

Part 1: Setting up a water sensor and firmware on the Photon 2

What you need:

- A Windows or Apple computer
- A connection to the internet
- A DGZZI Water Level Sensor

What to do:

1. There are three pins on the water level sensor (signal, positive, and negative). Using female pins, connect the negative pin (labelled with a minus sign) to the microcontroller GND. Connect the positive pin (labelled with a plus sign) to the microcontroller 3V3. Connect the signal pin (labelled with an S) to the microcontroller A0. See Figure 10.1.

Figure 10.1 A Photon 2 connected to DGZZI Water Level Sensor

2. Using the Particle Web IDE, flash the firmware named `WaterSensor.ino` to your microcontroller. This firmware is also available at this URL:

    https://github.com/sn-code-inside/guide-to-iot/blob/main/Ch10_code/WaterSensor.ino

```
// Guide to Internet of Things

// Chapter 10

// Part 1 WaterSensor.ino



// WaterSensor firmware

// A0 is connected to the signal pin on the DGZZI Water Level
Sensor

const int waterLevelPin = A0;

// We want a report on the level every 5 seconds

const int NUMSECONDS = 5;

int timeCtr = 0;
```

```
// Use an int to hold the water level

int waterValue = 0;

// Use the command line and the command:

// "particle serial monitor" to view these values.


// Set up serial speed.

void setup() {

    Serial.begin(9600);

}


void loop() {


    //Make a report every 5 seconds

    if (timeCtr <= millis()) {

        // get the value from A0

        waterValue = analogRead(waterLevelPin);

        // display on the command line

        Serial.println(waterValue);

        // update timeCtr to be 5 seconds greater than current
time

        timeCtr = millis() + (NUMSECONDS * 1000);

    }

}
```

3. Note that the output of Part 1 will be visible in your command line shell. You will need to run the command `particle serial monitor`. Experiment with a jar of water. Dip the sensor into the water (not too far) and note the changing values in your command line monitor. See Figure 10.2.

```
particle serial monitor
particle—cli v3.4.0

Opening serial monitor for com port: "/dev/tty.usbmodem101"
Serial monitor opened successfully:
2
0          Sensor not submerged
667
683        Sensor lightly submerged
785
1093       Sensor deeply submerged
1238
632
868
999
125
52
47
```

Figure 10.2 Command line reports of DGZI Water Level Sensor

What Did You Do, and How Did You Do It?

Pure water is not a good conductor of electricity. Water with impurities, however, serves as a fine conductor. As the sensor is submerged deeper into the water, conductivity increases. So, the deeper the sensor is placed into the water the higher the values that are generated on the signal pin. As mentioned, these values are dependent on the amount of impurities in the water and will vary depending on the quality of water.

The firmware that we deployed reads the input from the sensor every five seconds and writes those values to the serial port. These values are visible using the Particle serial monitor in the command line shell.

Virus Detection

Sewage as Gold

According to an article in the New York Times on August 17, 2022, sewage waste is gold. Or, perhaps, it makes more sense to say that the data we collect from sewage water can be very valuable.

Viruses such as Covid-19, Polio, and Monkey Pox may be spreading in a community and still go undetected. This is due to the fact that many people may not yet be showing symptoms or may simply refrain from being tested.

Viruses pass through in our stool and devices have been built to detect and recognize different viruses. From these data, public health officials are able to learn what viruses are in our community and the degree to which the viruses have spread.

See:
https://www.nytimes.com/interactive/2022/08/17/health/wastewater-polio-covid-nyc.html

Part 2: Communicating water level data to Node-RED

So far, we are able to detect the presence of water with a sensor. Our next step is to communicate the data values using a standard web protocol – HTTP.

We will configure Node-RED to behave as an HTTP server and configure our microcontroller to behave as an HTTP client.

What you need:

- A Particle Photon 2
- Node-RED
- Particle IDE

What to do:

1. In the chapter appendix is firmware that you will flash to your microcontroller. This firmware may also be found at this URL:

   https://github.com/sn-code-inside/guide-to-iot/blob/main/Ch10_code/WaterSensorWithHTTP.ino

2. In the Particle Web IDE, include the library named `HTTPClient` into your project holding `WaterSensorWithHTTP.ino`. To do this, click the `Libraries` icon and type `HTTPClient` into the search bar. Select `Include in Project` and then select the project named `WaterSensorWithHTTP.ino`.

3. Before flashing the firmware, modify the `WaterSensorWithHTTP.ino` firmware so that it contains the correct IP address and port. The IP address is the IP address of your computer – not `localhost` and not `127.0.0.1`. The port must be the port that Node-RED listens on (normally 1880). This is visible when you run Node-RED and then visit Node-RED with a browser. It appears after the colon in the URL.

4. Using the Particle Web IDE, compile (and verify) the firmware. Flash `WaterSensorWithHTTP` to your device.

5. Run Node-RED. In Node-RED, drag an `http in` node onto the workspace. Name this node `Listen for HTTP Request`. Configure this node to handle `post` requests to the url `/stormWaterReading`.

6. In Node-RED, drag an `http response` node onto the workspace. Name this node `Generate HTTP Response`. Configure its status code to 200.

7. In Node-RED, drag a `debug` node onto the workspace. Name this node `View Request`.

8. Connect the `Listen for HTTP Request` node to both the `Generate HTTP Response` node and the `View Request` node.

9. Deploy the flow. The microcontroller will begin making HTTP requests to your Node-RED server. See Figure 10.3.

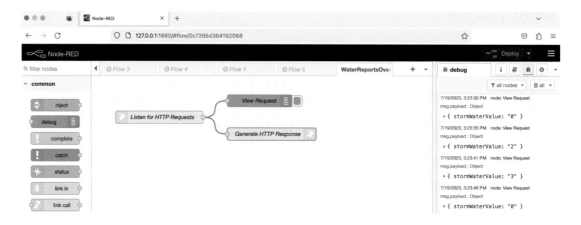

Figure 10.3 Handling microcontroller HTTP requests and responses using Node-RED

What Did You Do, and How Did You Do It?

The microcontroller is able to communicate over a Wi-Fi network. The firmware that we used in Part 2 leverages Wi-Fi to communicate textual messages constructed according to the HTTP standard.

The reader should read the code and comments in the file WaterSensorWithHTTP.ino.

The firmware used an `http_request_t` object to make HTTP requests to the computer running Node-RED. The firmware used the IP address and port of the machine running the Node-RED server. This IP and port were used to locate the machine and the application. The firmware also specified the path to the particular service it was interested in:

```
request.path = "/stormWaterReading";
```

The firmware also created a particular JSON string that was used to hold a single name, value pair:

```
{"stormWaterValue":"188"}
```

The firmware included timing logic so that an HTTP request (along with the JSON string) is transmitted over Wi-Fi every 5 seconds.

We used Node_RED to display the incoming JSON strings and generate an HTTP response to the microcontroller. If you run the `particle serial monitor` command in a command line shell, you should see the response and the response code (200) arriving back to the microcontroller.

In Node-RED, each `http-in node` must be followed by an `http-response node`. The `http-response node` uses the `msg.payload` property of the incoming message for its response. See the Check Your Understanding section below and experiment with changing the `msg.payload`.

Part 3: Writing water level data to a file using Node-RED

So far, we are collecting ephemeral data on our Node-RED server. We say that the data is "ephemeral" because it is short lived and not being saved.

Our next step is to ensure that the data is persisted to a long living data store. These data may then be processed at a later time by a wide variety of applications.

What you need:

- A Particle Photon 2
- Node-RED
- A MAC or Windows computer
- Work from Part 2

What to do:

1. Working from Part 2, after the `Listen for HTTP Request node`, connect a function node named `PrepareForFileWrite` with the following Javascript. This code may also be found at the following URL:

   https://github.com/sn-code-inside/guide-to-iot/blob/main/Ch10_code/PrepareForFileWrite.js

   ```
   // Guide to Internet of Things
   // Chapter 10
   // Part 3 PrepareForFileWrite.js

   // Chapter 10, Part 3
   // for testing, use node.warn(msg.payload);

   // take water value from http message
   var value = msg.payload.stormWaterValue;
   // take the current time
   var time = new Date();
   // create a new message object, including topic
   msg.payload = {topic:'Photon 2 Water Level', payload:value,
   timeStamp:time}
   // forward to the next node
   ```

```
return msg;
```

2. Select `Done` and connect a `write file` node after the `PrepareForFileWrite` function node. Name this node `WriteToFile`.

3. Configure the `WriteToFile` node. The `Filename` field is a complete path. For example, my `Filename` field is `/Users/mm6/mm6/IOTBook/Ch10_code/data/WaterLevelLog` with no quotes. The action is `append to file`. Choose to add a newline to each payload. Use the default encoding. Select `Create directory if it does not exist`.

4. Select `Done` and deploy the new flow. Examine the file named `WaterLevelLog`. It should be populated with a new line of JSON every 5 seconds.

5. An example line looks like the following:

```
{"topic":"Photon 2 Water Level","payload":"2","timeStamp":"2023-
07-19T19:37:00.987Z"}
```

6. See Figure 10.4.

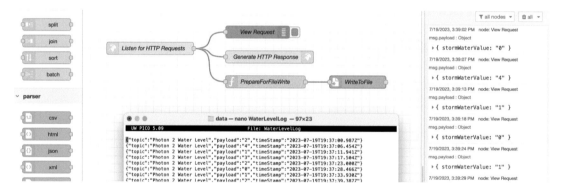

Figure 10.4 Writing water level data to a file using Node-RED

What Did You Do, and How Did You Do It?

In this part, we added a function node to reformat the data arriving from the microcontroller. Initially, the data arrived as a JSON formatted string but only held a single name-value pair describing the water level detected by the sensor. The function node added a timestamp and a topic to each arriving message.

In addition, we added a node to persist the incoming data to a file. Node-RED made this process easy to perform. Behind the scenes, Node-RED made use of the file system offered by the operating system.

What is a file system? One of the most important jobs of a modern operating system, such as Mac OSX, Microsoft Windows, or Linux, is to maintain a file system. A file system is used to give names to directories (also known as `folders`) and various types of files. It is also needed to locate those directories and files on persistent storage – such as a disk.

Figure 10.5 shows a layered architecture and how Node-RED makes use of the file system provided by the operating system.

Node-RED
Filesystem
Physical Files

Figure 10.5 The Layered architecture of Part 3

Node-RED makes requests to the file system for services. These services may be location services or naming services and provide a Node-RED node convenient access to the data on these files.

Node-RED and the file system ensure that if a particular file already exists, data will be appended to the file. If the file or directory does not exist, it is named and created for you.

The file system does a lot of work for us (behind the scenes). It provides an important abstraction layer (we don't need to know how it works, it just does!). This allows the Node-RED application developer to separate concerns. He or she is allowed to focus on the problem at hand – storing water data readings – and to ignore the myriad of details associated with writing bits to disk.

The principle that one should *separate concerns* is a central one in computer science and in system building in general.

Monitoring and Surveillance Capitalism

Can I Be Monitored While I Sleep?

Sure! You may be told by your doctor that you need to use a continuous positive airway pressure (CPAP) machine. This medically important device helps people with sleep apnea breathe more freely while they sleep. Some of these devices are both smart and connected and transfer data over networks to persistent storage. The question is, who has access to these data? It makes good sense that your doctor has access and is therefore better able to monitor your condition. The device manufacturer may also make good use of the usage data to improve the design of future devices and detect failures and the need for repair.

It is far less clear that other players should have access to these data. Medical treatment information is usually considered to be well within a person's sphere of privacy. Should an insurance company, for example, have access to your sleep data? Some devices and systems make this data available to anyone with the appropriate cryptographic key. The data might even have monetary value.

In an attempt to capture, from an economic point of view, what is going on, Shoshana Zuboff, a Harvard Business School professor, coined the term "Surveillance Capitalism" in 2014. For more, see the article in ProPublica entitled "You Snooze. You Lose: Insurers Make The Old Adage Literally True".

https://www.propublica.org/article/you-snooze-you-lose-insurers-make-the-old-adage-literally-true

Part 4: Persisting and Visualizing the data

What you need:

- A Particle Photon 2
- Node-RED
- Running firmware on a Photon 2 from Part 3
- A Node-RED dashboard node - directions follow

What to do:

1. In Node-RED, use the hamburger icon, select manage palette and install the `node-red-dashboard` series of nodes.

2. From the `Dashboard` category on the left, copy a `chart` node onto the workspace. Double-click this node and configure it as follows: Name this chart node `Water Level Chart`. In the `Group` field, enter `Time Series Water Level`. In the `Label` field, enter `Time Series Chart`. In the `Type` field, select `Line Chart`. In the `x-axis` field, choose `last 20 minutes`. In the `X-axis Label` field, choose `HH:MM:ss`. Check the `as UTC` check box. For the `Y-axis`, choose a minimum of 0 and a maximum of 4000. The `Legend` should be set to `Show`. The blank label should read `no data has arrived`. Choose the remaining defaults and select `Done`. See Figure 10.6.

Figure 10.6 Configuring a Node-RED chart node

3. Just below the hamburger icon, on the top right corner, there is a down arrow. Use this to configure the Dashboard. `Choose Dashboard` and then select the `Site` tab and set the `Horizontal 1 x 1` widget size to 80. Also, set the `Vertical 1 x 1` widget sizes to 80. See Figure 10.7.

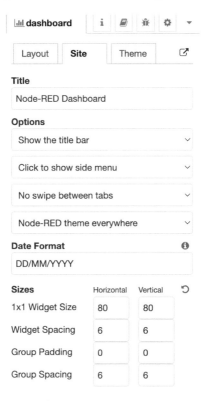

Figure 10.7 Configuring the Dashboard in Node-RED

4. Before the `Water Level Chart` node, add a new function node named
    `Prepare to chart`. This new function node's output will be connected to
    the `Water Level Chart` node's input. Under the `On Message` tab, add the
    following code to the `Prepare to chart` node:

```
msg = msg.payload;

// to clear the chart use msg.payload = []

return msg;
```

5. Connect the output of the node named `PrepareForFileWrite` to the input
    of the node named `Prepare to chart`. See Figure 10.8.

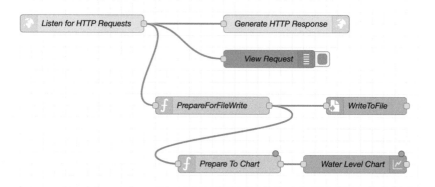

Figure 10.8 Charting the water levels in Node-RED

6. Connect your microcontroller, deploy the flow, and view the resulting chart.
    See Figure 10.9. Note, to view the chart, click the small box with the diagonal
    up arrow on the top right of the dashboard. Experiment by dipping the sensor
    into your coffee or water.

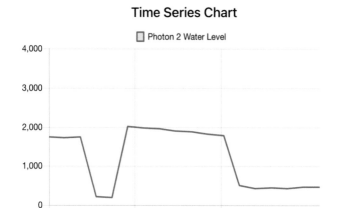

Figure 10.9 Charting the water levels in Node-RED

What Did You Do, and How Did You Do It?

In this part, we were able to visualize our data by including a Node-RED charting tool in our Node-RED flow. We modified our flow so that the writing of a file could take place in parallel with the displaying of a graph of arriving values.

Why is visualization important? By using a graph or an animation, trends may be easier to discern and anomalous events may be easier to detect. In the IoT space, various graphing tools are widely available.

Part 5: Persisting and Querying IoT Data using SQLite

So far, we have written our water data to disk and created a line graph of the water levels. And this, by itself, can be quite useful. Other applications can be written that consume the data file and deliver real value to users. The graphic visualization may be of use to decision makers.

In this Part, we will add a database to the Node-RED flows. We will use the very popular SQLite database.

What you need:

- A Particle Photon 2
- Node-RED
- The flow from Part 4
- Particle IDE
- Widely available SQLite Database - directions follow

What to do:

1. Continuing with the flow from Part 4, click the hamburger icon and select `Manage palette`. Install the node named `node-red-node-sqlite`.

2. We need to add a new flow that will allow us to create a database. Create a second flow on the same workspace. It will begin with an `inject` node named `Click to create database`. Its `message.topic` field will be of type boolean and set to true. In the `inject` node, delete the `msg.payload` field. The `inject` node will be piped to an `sqlite` node named `Create Table`. Drag an `sqlite` node onto the workspace and name it `Create Table`.

3. Edit the `Create Table` node. Use the pencil icon and set the database to a path. For example, my database field is set to `/Users/mm6/mm6/IOTBook/Ch10_code/data/WaterLevelLogDB`, with no quotes. The mode is `Read-Write-Create`. Be sure to include the `Create` selection, that is, do not simply select `Read-Write`. Select the `SQL Query` as `Fixed Statement` and enter the following line of SQL:

```
CREATE TABLE waterValues(myTimeStamp integer not
null,dataRecordJSON TEXT not null);
```

4. The `Create Table` node should only be run once - to create the table. If you run it more than once it will simply produce an error saying that the table already exists. It will do no damage to run it more than once. Deploy the flow and click the far left side of the `Click to Create Database` node. This should create the database file named `WaterLevelLogDB` in the directory that you specified. Use the file system to check that the database file exists (WaterLevelLogDB) and that its size is 0 bytes.

5. So far, we have created a database and after every five seconds, we are writing a record to a file (but not the database). Prior to writing the data to the file, we used a function node named `PrepareForFileWrite`. Now, we will do the same thing for the database.

6. Add a new function node named `PrepareForDatabaseWrite` to the workspace. Pipe the output of the `Listen for HTTP Request` node to the `PrepareForDatabaseWrite` node. This function node, `PrepareForDatabaseWrite`, will contain the following JavaScript. Note that this code may also be found at this URL:

    https://github.com/sn-code-inside/guide-to-iot/blob/main/Ch10_code/PrepareForDatabaseWrite.js

```javascript
// PrepareForDatabaseWrite
// take water value from http message
var value = msg.payload.stormWaterValue;
// Show the value in debug window
// node.warn(value);
// take the current time
var time = Date.now();
// Show the time in debug window
// node.warn(time);

// create a new object to hold a database record
msgRecord = {topic:'Photon 2 Water Level', payload:value,
timeStamp:time}
// make it a JSON string
msgRecordString = JSON.stringify(msgRecord);
// add it to the msg object
// Sqlite wants the data in the params property
msg.params = { $thetime:time, $thevalue:msgRecordString}
return msg;
```

7. Pipe the node named `PrepareForDatabaseWrite` to a new `sqlite` node. Double click the `sqlite` node and name this node `Insert SQLite Record`. Use the pencil icon and set the database to the same path as in step 3. My database field has no quotes and is set to: `/Users/mm6/mm6/IOTBook/Ch10_code/data/WaterLevelLogDB`. The

mode should be set to `read-write-create` and the `SQL Query` is `Prepared Statement`. The prepared SQL statement is:

```
insert into waterValues(myTimeStamp,dataRecordJSON) values
($thetime,$thevalue)
```

8. Deploy the flow. Every five seconds, a new database record should be written. Use the file system to check that the database file exists (WaterLevelLogDB) and that its size is no longer 0 bytes.

9. To query our database, add a new flow to the same workspace. This flow will also begin with an `inject` node. Name the inject node `Click to Query`. Set the `msg.topic` to true and the `msg.params` to an empty JSON object. You can add msg.params with the plus sign near the botom left. See Figure 10.10 and note that the `{}` symbols appear twice. Pipe the output to a new `sqlite` node named `Query all`. It will use the same database path that we used before and will generate a `Prepared Statement` and will be set to `Read-Write-Create`. The SQL prepared statement will be the following:

```
select * from waterValues;
```

Figure 10.10 Configuring the eject node prior to a query node

10. Pipe the output of the `Query all` node to a new debug node named `Display Query Results`.

11. Deploy the entire flow (now with three separate flows). An HTTP request is being made by your microcontroller every 5 seconds. You should be able to view the entire database by clicking the inject node just before the

`Query for all` node. It will show the result as a list of objects that you can expand.

12. See Figure 10.11.

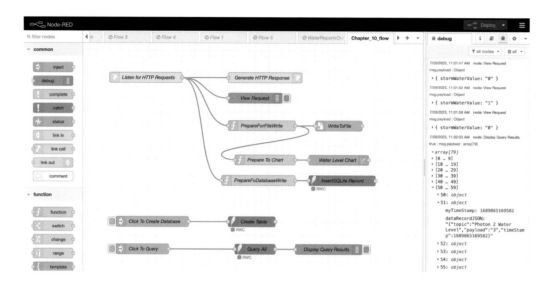

Figure 10.11 Database administration and storing water level records

What Did You Do, and How Did You Do It?

Recall Figure 10.5. In that figure we showed that Node-RED requested services from the file system and the file system was concerned with the low level details associated with the naming and processing of data files.

How can we describe the database layer that was introduced in Part 5? The application developer is using a particular Node-RED node and, behind the scenes, a database is built. The database needs access to files and needs the services provided by the file system. So, we have this particular layering (see Figure 10.12):

Node-RED
SQLite
Filesystem
Physical Files

Figure 10.12 The Layered architecture of Part 4

Since the operating system designers used a layered architecture and separated concerns, it was an easy matter for the SQLite developers to plug right in to Figure 10.5. SQLite offers services to Node-RED and uses the services provided by the file system.

In Part 5, we are using a simple SQLite database. It is very popular and is easy to use. It provides an application programmer with access to database files using the Structured Query Language (SQL). This query language allows the developer to work at a higher level of abstraction. Rather than asking for services from the file system directly, the SQLite layer provides additional support for complex queries.

In this part we used the following SQL statements:

CREATE TABLE	This statement was used to create a table inside of the file named `WaterLevelLogDB`. Note that the database schema is found in the create table command. The schema describes the name of each column and the type of data that it contains.
INSERT INTO	This statement was used to add records to our database. We specified the table name as `waterValues`.
SELECT	This statement was used to perform a query on the existing database. We selected all of the columns from the table named `waterValues`.

With respect to the IoT, rather than using the simple SQLite, more sophisticated and larger scale databases are often used. These time series databases may be specifically tailored to IoT. They are used for anomaly detection (looking for what may be out of the ordinary), prediction (trying to guess what the future data will look like), analytics (the gathering and processing of summary statistics), storage (on disk or in the cloud), and visualization (using graphs or animations). Some of them are optimized to perform very fast queries over timestamped data.

General Data Protection Regulation (GDPR)

European privacy and security law

Since the invention of the World Wide Web, applications have been designed to collect massive amounts of data on their users. This data can be used for good or bad. It may improve user experience or be sold or stolen for nefarious reasons.

The General Data Protection Regulations (GDPR) are European Union laws designed to protect data and user privacy. The Internet of Things will likely increase the need for such laws and regulations. Data will be collected on a wide variety of things, users, and events.

To be compliant with GDPR, systems must be built in such a way as to preserve:

-the right to be forgotten. People must be able to delete data that is associated with them.
-the right to consult. People must have access to the data that is associated with them.
-data portability. People must be able to transfer their data from one organization to another without having to reformat the data associated with them.
-data log access. Access to the data must be monitored, controlled, and recorded.
-anonymization. Techniques must be employed that ensure that personal data is not associated with identifiable individuals.

While this chapter provides instructions on how to persist IoT data, the reader should keep in mind the issues that the GDPR is designed to address. There are plenty of ways that IoT date can be misused.

The main GDPR web site is at this URL: `https://gdpr.eu/`

Carnegie Mellon's OpenChirp [3]

We conclude this chapter with a brief overview of the OpenChirp system built by researchers at Carnegie Mellon University. See Figure 10.13. for a brief description of the architecture. For the full description, be sure to see the OpenChirp paper in the footnote below. If you have worked through this text, much of what we are about to say should make good sense and the architecture should be understandable.

In the OpenChirp architecture, LPWAN nodes are in the transducer layer.
The transducer layer contains sensors and actuators. These particular sensors and actuators use low power – they may be battery powered - but operate over a wide area network. Thus, they are Low Power Wide Area Network devices (LPWAN nodes).

Since these transducers utilize very little power, they may only transmit a small number of bits over a wide area. This is quite appropriate for some applications. In some settings, you may only require that your devices communicate rarely and, when they do decide to communicate, transmit only a small amount of information.

The protocol used for this long range communication is called LoRa (for Long Range).

The LPWAN gateway (see Figure 10.13) is in the gateway layer of OpenChirp.

The gateway layer communicates over a constrained network (LoRA) to the actuators and sensors – the LPWAN nodes. The gateway layer also communicates over an unconstrained network to the agent layer. The agent layer is where useful applications reside. In the agent layer we find MQTT brokers, databases and web applications. Visualization tools, data analysis tools, and machine learning applications may reside there as well.

In the exercises, we ask that you compare and contrast this architecture with some others that you may be using or developing on.

Sketch of Carnegie Mellon's OpenChirp Architecture

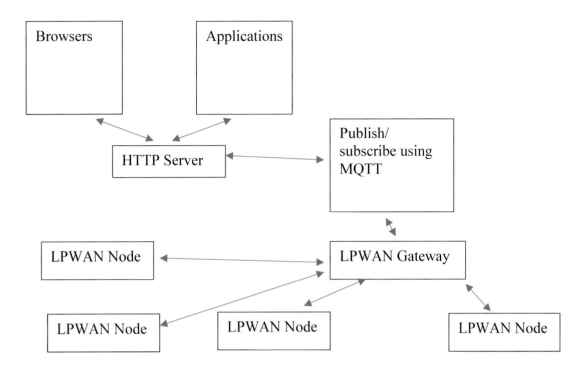

Figure 10.13 Sketch of CMU's OpenChirp System Architecture

Check Your Understanding

1. Modify the firmware in Part 1 so that it reports on how deep the sensor is placed in the water. For example, if the sensor is submerged only slightly, report "Slightly submerged". If the sensor is placed more deeply into the water, it will report "Fully submerged".

2. Modify the Node-RED flow in Part 2 so that it includes a function node between the http-in node and the http-response node. The function node will modify the `msg.payload` property so that the http-response node returns the string "Thank you for the water level value!" to the microcontroller. Show the output on the command line shell with the command `particle serial monitor`.

3. In Part 5, we used the SQL Insert statement. What was the table name that was used in this statement? What were the column names?

4. In Part 5, we used the SQL Create statement. What was the table name that we used? What were the column names? What were the types of data that each column could contain?

5. In Part 5, we used the SQL Select statement. What was the table name? What was the meaning of the asterisk?

6. In Figures 10.5 and 10.12, we viewed the file system as part of a layered architecture. A modern operating system also provides for network communications. Redraw the layered architecture of Figure 10.5 so that it shows how Node-RED communicates with the microcontroller in Part 2.

Make More / Explore Further

1. Use a Large Language model (such as ChatGPT) to research and describe Azure Time Series Insights.

2. Use a Large Language model (such as ChatGPT) to research and describe Amazon Time Stream.

3. Use a Large Language model (such as ChatGPT) to research and describe OpenTSDB.

4. Does Oracle Corporation provide a Time Series database based on NoSQL? Ask ChatGPT.

5. In a programming language of your choice, write a program that is able to read and display the data records in the file named `WaterLevelLog` of Figure 10.4. Each data record will appear as a simple JSON string. The braces will appear just as they do in the file.

6. In a programming language of your choice, write a program that is able to read and display the data records in the file named `WaterLevelLog` of Figure 10.4. But this time, use a library that is able to easily process JSON data. That is, you will be able to drill into the JSON and extract the data by field name. No JSON braces will appear in the output. The output will appear as field name and value pairs.

7. Compare and contrast the OpenChirp architecture with others that are available. Your analysis should include AWS IoT, Google Cloud IoT, and Azure IoT. One additional IoT cloud service (of your own choosing) is also required.

8. Run the command `npm install node-red-openweathermap` and use the `openweathermap` node in the flow of Part 2. If rain is in the forecast the http response to the microcontroller will be "No sprinkler". If rain is not in the forecast and the water level is low, the http response will be "Turn sprinkler on". These responses should be viewable in the serial monitor (we are not using a real sprinkler). You will need to get an API key at `openweathermap.org`.

9. In a programming language of your choice, write code that will display the database created in Part 5. Hint: find a library that supports sqlite.

Summing Up

In this chapter we learned how we can persist and graph IoT data. Since IoT data is often stored with timestamps and queried based on time ranges, a database optimized for time series (a time series database) is appropriate.

We did a quick review of CMU's OpenChirp and we encourage the reader to explore this design.

Looking Ahead

In the next chapter we learn how messy data can be processed with machine learning. Turning again to Node-RED for help, we will incorporate a machine learning node into an IoT system to recognize the presence of humans.

Facial recognition has a wide variety of (positive and negative) use cases.

References

1. "Storm Water Tanks Installation Underway," The Piper, Carnegie Mellon University, June 22, 2016, https://www.cmu.edu/piper/news/archives/2016/june-july/storm-water-tanks.html.
2. U.S. Green Building Council. *LEED Reference Guide for Building Design and Construction*. Washington, D.C.: U.S. Green Building Council, 2013.
3. Dongare, A., et al. 2017. "OpenChirp: A Low-Power Wide-Area Networking Architecture." In *2017 IEEE International Conference on Pervasive Computing and Communications Workshops (PerCom Workshops)*, 569-574. doi:10.1109/PERCOMW.2017.7917625.

Chapter Appendix

```
// WaterSensorWithHTTP firmware
// Guide to Internet of Things
// Chapter 10
// Part 2 WaterSensorWithHTTP.ino

// WaterSensorWithHTTP firmware
// Library: HttpClient included in the Web IDE

// This #include statement was automatically added by the Particle
IDE.
#include <HttpClient.h>

// Define the http variable to be of type HttpClient.
 HttpClient http;

 // We always pass Http headers on each request to the Http Server.
 // Here, we only define a single header. The NULL, NULL pair is used
 // to terminate the list of headers.

 // The Content-Type header is used to inform the server
 // of the type of message that it will be receiving. Here,
 // we tell the server to expect to receive data marked up in
 // JSON.

 http_header_t headers[] = {
    { "Content-Type", "application/json" },
    { NULL, NULL }
 };

 // Here we define structures to hold the request and the response
data.
 // These are declared with types defined in the header file included
above.

 http_request_t request;
 http_response_t response;

// The setup() function runs once when the microcontroller boots up.
 void setup() {

    // The IP address of the server running on our machine.
    // Do not use localhost. The microcontroller would attempt
    // to visit itself with localhost.
    request.ip = IPAddress(192,168,86,25);
```

```
  // Specify the port that our server is listening on.
  // This Node-RED instance is listening on port 1880.
  request.port = 1880;

  Serial.begin(9600);

}

// Provided with a response, display it to the command line
interface.
void printResponse(http_response_t &response) {
  Serial.println("HTTP Response: ");
  Serial.println(response.status);
  Serial.println(response.body);
}

// Post a water value message to the server
void doPostRequest(int waterValue) {

  // Define a character array large enought to hold the integer
  // represented as a string.
  char waterValueStr[10];
  // Use sprintf to print a formatted string into the char array.
  // The sprintf function is being used to create a string from the
integer.
  sprintf(waterValueStr, "%d", waterValue);

  // Specify the URL in the HTTP request.
  request.path = "/stormWaterReading";

  // Build the JSON request
  char json[1000] = "{\"stormWaterValue\":\"";
  // Add the water measurement
  strcat(json,waterValueStr);
  // add the JSON ending
  strcat(json,"\"}");
  // assign the JSON string to the HTTP request body
  request.body = json;
  // post the request
  http.post(request, response, headers);
  // show response
  printResponse(response);

}
```

```
// A0 is conected to the signal pin on the DGZZI Water Level Sensor
const int waterLevelPin = A0;
// We want a report on the level every 5 seconds
const int NUMSECONDS = 5;
int timeCtr = 0;
// Use an int to hold the water level
int waterValue = 0;

// Use the command line and the command:
// "particle serial monitor"
// to view the Serial.println values.
// The loop() function is called repeatedly by the operating system.
void loop() {

    //Make a report every 5 seconds
    if (timeCtr <= millis()) {
        // get the value from A0
        waterValue = analogRead(waterLevelPin);
        // display on the command line
        Serial.println(waterValue);
        // Make an HTTP call
        doPostRequest(waterValue);
        // update timeCtr to be 5 seconds greater than current time
        timeCtr = millis() + (NUMSECONDS * 1000);
    }
}
```

CHAPTER 11

Machine Learning and Facial Recognition

This chapter covers

   Using Node-RED to Recognize Faces
   Interpreting Facial Recognition Data
   Responding to Facial Recognition Data

```
Facial Req. Report
Name: John Smith
Age: 36
Height: 6'1"
Weight: 185lbs
Criminal History: None
```

Things can be programmed to recognize faces

"Science, my lad, has been built upon many errors; but they are errors which it was good to fall into, for they led to the truth."

Jules Verne

How do know that you're looking at a person's face? Is it the shape of the head? The position of the eyes? What if you look at Picasso's *Tête de Femme* painting? Is that a face? Is it spooky to see an upside-down image of someone's face? How close must a face be in order for you to recognize it? How easy is it for someone to disguise their face? Can you look at a face and see only shapes and colors, forgetting that it's a person's face?

The detection of faces, shapes, written text, spoken text, musical compositions, commercial products, and other such things isn't difficult for human beings. But programming software to detect these things is a very challenging problem. In the second half of the 20th century, computer professionals and other specialists made tiny steps toward imitating human intelligence. It wasn't until the 21st century that their efforts with Machine Learning (ML) became reliable enough for common, everyday use.

In the 2010s, the packaging of ML services became commonplace. Without very much understanding of the low-level details, people could connect pre-built components to create their own artificially intelligent applications. In this chapter, you'll use your computer's webcam to send images to a freely-available facial recognition node. You'll analyze the output from that node and send a result to your Photon 2.

Part 1: Capturing your webcam's output

Our goal is to create a Node-RED subflow to repeatedly take pictures with your laptop's webcam.

What you need:
- Node-RED running on your computer
- An Apple or Windows machine with a webcam

What to do:
1. Install the ui-webcam node in Node-RED with the following shell command:

```
npm i node-red-node-ui-webcam
```

2. Install the image-output node in Node-RED with the following shell command:

```
npm i node-red-contrib-image-output
```

3. Run Node-RED from a shell:

```
node-red
```

4. With a browser, visit Node-RED at this URL:

```
http://127.0.0.1:1880/
```

5. Within Node-RED, click the hamburger icon in the upper-right corner. Select Manage Palette in the resulting drop-down list..

6. In the resulting User Settings / Palette list, select the Install tab.

7. In the Search Modules text field, type *ui-webcam*. As a result, an entry labeled node-red-node-ui-webcam appears.

8. In the node-red-node-ui-webcam entry, click the Install button.

9. In the Search Modules text field, type *image-output*. As a result, an entry labeled node-red-contrib-image-output appears.

10. In the node-red-contrib-image-output entry, click the Install button.

11. Click Close to dismiss the User Settings / Palette list.

12. From the Node-Red palette, drag and drop the following four nodes: inject, webcam, function, and image.

13. Connect the nodes as shown in Figure 11.1:

Figure 11.1 The webcam subflow

14. In the "Inject node", set msg.capture to true.

15. At the bottom of the 'inject node' editing panel, set the node to fire every 2 seconds as in Figure 11.2:

Figure 11.2 Injecting every 2 seconds

16. Set the webcam node's properties as shown in Figure 11.3:

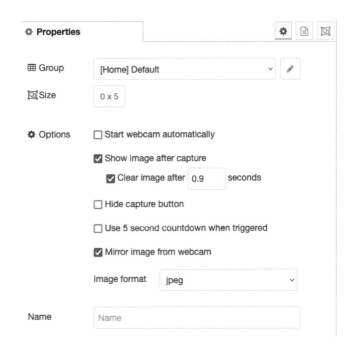

Figure 11.3 Configure the webcam node

17. In the 'function' node's property sheet, click the On Message tab.

18. In the On Message tab's text area, type the following code:

```
global.set('image', msg.payload);
return msg;
```

19. Set the 'image preview' node's properties as shown in Figure 11.4:

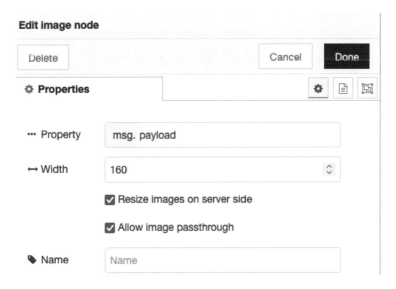

Figure 11.4 Configure the image preview node

20. To start testing what you've done so far, deploy this flow.

21. Look for a down-arrow icon along the rightmost edge of the Node-RED window. Click this icon to reveal a dropdown list containing a Dashboard item. (See Figure 11.5.)

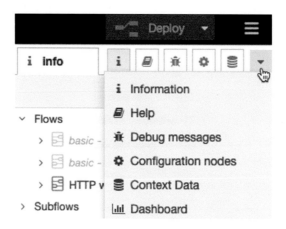

Figure 11.5 Finding the Dashboard item

22. Click the Dashboard item. In the resulting panel, look for an "arrow pointing out of a square" icon. (See Figure 11.6.)

Figure 11.6 Opening the dashboard

23. Clicking the "arrow pointing out of a square" icon opens a new tab in your web browser. This new tab is the Node-RED dashboard. At first, the dashboard displays a box containing a camera icon,

    If your computer has more than one camera, look for a dropdown box near the camera icon. Using this dropdown box, you can select the camera that Node-RED will use.

24. Click the camera icon.

25. After clicking the camera icon, your web browser asks for your permission to use your laptop's camera. Make sure that the camera you want to use is the

one that's selected in the permissions dialog box. Then click the permissions box's Allow button. If all goes well, you should see the image taken by your laptop's camera in the dashboard.

26. In your web browser, return to the Node-RED flow page. Below the 'image preview' node, you see a copy of your webcam's image. (See Figure 11.7.)

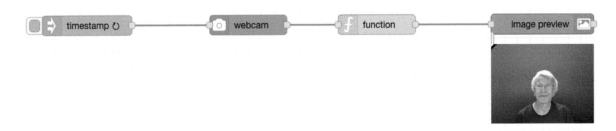

Figure 11.7 An author testing his own instructions

What Did You Do, and How Did You Do It?

In Node-RED, the *dashboard* is a web page for displaying data created by one or more nodes. The look of the dashboard is anything a developer wants it to be because the dashboard can be designed the same way any web page is designed. In Part 1 of this chapter, you install a node that grabs images from your webcam and displays them on a simple dashboard page. All that functionality is built into the webcam node.

In the meantime, a function node runs code to capture the images that are displayed on the dashboard. The statement

```
global.set('image', msg.payload);
```

tells Node-RED to assign the name 'image' to whatever picture appears in the dashboard. It's like an assignment statement:

```
image = msg.payload;   // Sorry, this wouldn't quite work.
```

This assignment is updated every 2 seconds because of the inject node's 'repeat' property.

The strange wording with 'global.set' comes from the way Node-RED handles names. When you set a name's value, you can use 'global.set', 'context.set', or 'flow.set'. Remember that, in the Node-RED window nodes may appear on different tabs. Each of these tabs is called a *flow*, and the set of all flows is called the *canvas*.

- With 'global.set', a name applies everywhere in your canvas.

When one node stores a webcam picture by calling global.set('image', msg.payload), any other node can retrieve that picture by calling global.get('image').

- With 'context.set', a name applies only in the node in which it's defined.

  When one node stores a number by calling context.set('amount', 42), no other node can retrieve that number by calling context.get('amount').

  If one node calls context.set('amount', 42), and another node calls context.set('amount', 99), both nodes can call context.get('amount'). But then, one of the nodes gets the value 42, and the other node gets the value 99.

- With 'flow.set', a name applies only in nodes in flow in which it's defined.

  Nodes in different flows on the same canvas cannot retrieve the assigned value.

In Part 1, we make 'image' refer to the picture on the dashboard because we want to feed that picture to one of the nodes in Part 2.

Part 2: Finding a face

In this part, we detect the presence or absence of a face in the image taken by your laptop's webcam.

What you need:
- Node-RED running the flow from Part 1

What to do:
1. Install the facial-recognition node in Node-RED with the following shell command:

```
npm install node-red-contrib-facial-recognition
```

2. Within Node-RED, click the hamburger icon in the upper-right corner. Select Manage Palette in the resulting drop-down list..

3. In the resulting User Settings / Palette list, select the Install tab.

4. In the Search Modules text field, type *facial-recognition*. As a result, an entry labeled node-red-contrib-facial-recognition appears.

5. In the node-red-contrib-facial-recognition entry, click the Install button.

6. Click Close to dismiss the User Settings / Palette list.

7. From the Node-Red palette, drag and drop the following four nodes: inject, function, facial recognition, and a second function node.

8. Connect the nodes as shown in Figure 11.8:

Figure 11.8 The webcam subflow

These four nodes are on the same page (the same flow) as the nodes in Part 1, but these nodes aren't connected to any of the nodes you added in Part 1.

9. At the bottom of the 'inject node' editing panel, set the node to fire every 2 seconds as in Figure 11.2.

10. In the first (leftmost) 'function' node's property sheet, click the On Message tab.

11. In the On Message tab's text area, type the following code:

```
msg.payload = global.get('image');
return msg;
```

12. Set the facial-recognition node's properties as shown in Figure 11.9.

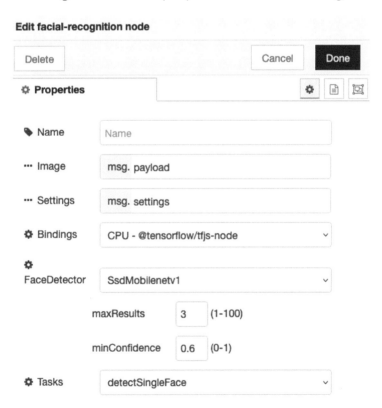

Figure 11.9 The facial-recognition node's properties

13. In the second (rightmost) 'function' node's property sheet, click the On Message tab.

14. In the On Message tab's text area, type the following code:

```
p = msg.payload;

if (p.hasOwnProperty("Result") && p.Result != undefined) {
    global.set("isFace", 1);
    console.log("face detected");
} else {
    global.set("isFace", 0);
    console.log("no face");
}

return msg;
```

15. To start testing what you've done so far, deploy this flow along with the nodes from Part 1 of this chapter.

16. In your web browser, revisit the Node-RED dashboard tab. Click the camera icon and, if necessary, allow your web browser to use your laptop's camera. Once again, you should see the image from your laptop's camera in the dashboard's window.

17. Return to the shell from which you launched Node-RED near the start of Part 1 in this chapter. You should see the messages *face detected* and *no face* appearing in that window. The message *face detected* indicates that Node-RED's facial-recognition node found a face in your webcam's image. The message *no face* indicates that it didn't.

What Did You Do, and How Did You Do It?

When you store some information, you can retrieve that information later. In the function node of Part 1, you called

```
global.set('image', msg.payload);
```

to associate the word 'image' with the picture that appears in the Node-RED dashboard. This picture comes from your computer's webcam. The picture may or may not contain a face.

In Step 2, a function node retrieves that picture by calling

```
msg.payload = global.get('image');
```

This code makes the webcam's picture available to whatever node receives the function node's message. In the flow of Step 2, the receiving node happens to be a 'facial-recognition' node. The 'facial-recognition' node makes use of a machine learning library named TensorFlow.

Machine Learning

Some problems can always be solved by following step-by-step instructions. Think about the problem of computing payments on a loan. You're given the initial loan amount, the number of payments, and the interest rate for each payment. You may not like doing the arithmetic. But, if you're patient, you can do the calculations and come up with the correct answer. If you're not sure how to do the calculations, someone can write explicit instructions for you to follow. If the instructions are unambiguous, and you follow the instructions faithfully, you always come up with the correct answer.

Compare this with another kind of problem - a problem that can't realistically be solved by following step-by-step instructions. Which of the scratches in Figure 11.10 represent the letter S?

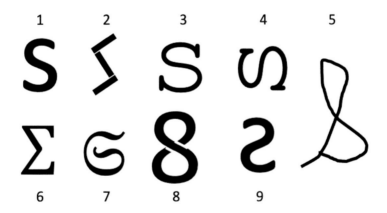

Figure 11.10 The letter S?

Without some extra guidance, it's difficult to agree on the number of S letters in Figure 11.10. Is number 2 a letter S or a playing piece in a game? Are numbers 4 and 9 letters? Does number 6, the Greek letter sigma, count as an S? What about number 7, the Fraktur symbol for S? Number 8 may be a letter S, but it may also be a digit 8. How do you know where a symbol stops being an S and starts being an 8?

You may answer that we can make a set of rules for deciding all possible scribbles to classify each as a letter S or not a letter S. But that approach is impractical. With hundreds of pixels in each scribble, the number of all possible scribbles would be astronomical. And yet, we as humans can usually tell a letter S from some other kind of marking.

Specialists in the field of *Artificial Intelligence* (AI) look for ways to get computers to solve difficult problems. In this case, a difficult problem is one that meets two criteria:

- Humans solve the problem without relying on a specific, unambiguous set of instructions.

- It's not practical to have a computer solve the problem by following a specific, unambiguous set of instructions.

The most recent advances in AI involve *Machine Learning* (ML). With Machine Learning, you don't give a computer a set of rules. Instead, you give a computer many examples. For example, you may show the computer's camera 1000 images that look like the marks in Figure 11.10. For each image, the computer guesses whether the image contains the letter S or not. In a version of the procedure called *Supervised Machine Learning*, you may give some kind of feedback to the computer after each guess. "Yes," the computer's guess about mark number 3 in Figure 11.10 was correct. "No," the computer's guess about mark number 4 in Figure 11.10 was not correct. The researchers program the computer to adjust its own rules and thus "learn" from its mistakes.

How can a computer adjust its own rules? In what form are these rules recorded? One very fruitful approach has come from studies of the human brain. In the mid-1940s, researchers developed a theoretical model of the human brain. A human brain consists of neurons, each of which has several inputs and one output. Neurons are attached to one another in many different ways, but the basic idea is in Figure 11.11.

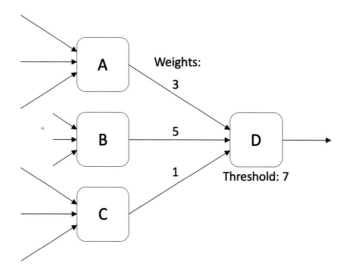

Figure 11.11 A simple neural network.

Figure 11.11 shows four neurons labeled A, B, C, and D. (Luckily, there's no neuron labeled with a dubious letter S!) The inputs to neuron D come from the three other neurons in the figure. In the simplest of all models, each neuron either *fires* or *doesn't fire*. If it helps, you can think of a neuron's output as either 0 or 1. A neuron that doesn't fire outputs 0, and a neuron that fires outputs 1.

In Figure 11.11, each input to neuron D has a number called a *weight*, and the D neuron has a number called its *threshold*. Now imagine these scenarios:

- Neurons A and B fire, but neuron C doesn't fire.

    Then neuron D fires, because the sum of the weights of neurons A and B is 8, which is greater than D's threshold 7.

- Neurons B and C fire, but neuron A doesn't fire.

    Then neuron D doesn't fire, because the sum of the weights of neurons B and C is 6, which is smaller than D's threshold 7.

An *artificial neural network* is software or hardware that simulates the behavior of neurons in the human brain. The network starts with some choice of weights and thresholds. As the network receives feedback ("Yes," you guessed correctly or "No," you didn't guess correctly) the network tries adjusting its own weights and thresholds. If the adjustment results in fewer correct guesses, the network undoes the adjustment's changes. But, if the adjustment results in more correct guesses, the network keeps the adjustment's changes and makes more changes as it receives more feedback.

By adjusting the weights and thresholds of its own neurons, a neural network *learns* to classify things like letters, traffic lights in reCAPTCHA tests, and yes, even peoples' faces.

Node-RED's facial-recognition analyzes your webcam's image by calling on a code library named TensorFlow. You can read about it by visiting tensorflow.org. Using the TenforFlow library of functions, the facial-recognition node creates a report with information about the image. The last function node in Part 2 receives this report.

The facial recognition node's report

The facial-recognition node's report is a JSON file. When the node detects a face, JSON the file looks something like this:

```
{
  "Result": {
    "detection": . . .,
      . . .
    "expressions": {
      "neutral": 0.9831507802009583,
      "happy": 0.0005548514309339225,
```

```
        "sad": 0.016226721927523613,
        "angry": 0.000021951811504550278,
        "fearful": 1.6472910147058428e-7,
        "disgusted": 0.00004416248702909797974,
        "surprised": 0.0000015125023082873668
    },
    "gender": "male",
    "genderProbability": 0.999609649181366,
    "age": 41.08097839355469
    . . .
    }
    . . .
}
```

When the node doesn't detect a face, you get

```
{
  "Result": undefined,
  . . .
}
```

In Step 13 of this part, the code

```
if (p.hasOwnProperty("Result") && p.Result != undefined) {
    global.set("isFace", 1);
} else {
    global.set("isFace", 0);
}
```

checks to see if a face was detected, and sets a global name "isFace" to 1 or 0 depending on the answer.

Part 3: Responding to a web request

In this part, we respond to a web request for information about the image in your laptop's webcam. The request can come from a web browser or from some other source.

What you need:
 - Node-RED running the nodes from Parts 1 and 2.

What to do:

1. Within Node-RED, click the hamburger icon in the upper-right corner. Select Manage Palette in the resulting drop-down list..

2. In the resulting User Settings / Palette list, select the Install tab.

3. In the Search Modules text field, type *http*. As a result, an entry that's simply labeled node-red appears.

4. In the node-red entry, click the Install button.

5. Click Close to dismiss the User Settings / Palette list.

6. From the Node-Red palette, drag and drop the following three nodes: http in, function, and http response.

7. Connect the nodes as shown in Figure 11.12:

Figure 11.12 Responding to an HTTP request

8. In the leftmost http node's property sheet, set the Method property to GET and set the URL property to /monitor (starting with a slash).

9. In the On Message tab of the function node's property sheet type the following code:

```
msg.payload = global.get("isFace");
return msg;
```

10. To start testing your work, deploy the flow that contains your work from Parts 1, 2, and 3 of this chapter.

11. In your web browser, revisit the Node-RED dashboard tab. Click the camera icon and, if necessary, allow your web browser to use your laptop's camera. Once again, you should see the image from your laptop's camera in the dashboard's window.

12. In your web browser, open a new tab and visit:

```
http://localhost:1880/monitor
```

As a result, the browser should display the number 0 or the number 1. The number 0 means that the facial-recognition node did not detect a face, and the number 1 means that it did. (If you want to update the number in the browser window, refresh the browser page.)

What Did You Do, and How Did You Do It?

This part of your project configures Node-RED to respond to HTTP requests. In Figure 11.10,

- The '[get] monitor' node tells Node-RED to respond when it receives a request like the one in Step 12.

- The 'function' node retrieves the 1 or 0 that was produced in Step 2, and passes that value on to the 'http' node.

- The 'http' node sends the 1 or 0 back to whatever software sent the request. In Step 12, that software is your computer's web browser. But in Part 4, that software lives on your Photon 2.

Part 4: Sending face-detection information to the Photon 2

In this part, the Photon 2's LED shows different colors depending on whether a face does or doesn't appear in your laptop's webcam.

What you need:

- Node-RED running the flows from Parts 1, 2, and 3.
- A Photon 2 connected to the same network as your laptop.

What to do:

1. Create the flows described in Parts 1, 2, and 3, of this chapter.

2. Deploy these flows as described in Parts 1, 2, and 3.

3. Visit your account at Particle.io and create a file named FaceRecognitionHttpClient.

4. Click the library ICON on the left side of the Particle IDE. Search for the HttpClient library.

5. Include this HttpClient library into the FaceRecognitionHttpClient firmware.

6. Copy and paste the code from shown below into the file FaceRecognitionHttpClient.

7. Before flashing this code to your Photon 2, change the IP address in the code to your own IP address. You should not use 'IPAddress(192,168,50,135)' here. You will need to find the IP address on your system. On a Mac, select System Preferences/Settings and search for IPv4. On a Windows computer, find Settings, then select Network & Internet, then select Ethernet or Wi-Fi. Under Properties, look for IPv4.

```
// File name: FaceRecognitionHttpClient

// Guide to Internet of Things Chapter 11 Part 4
// Sends GET requests to the http server.
// Sets the Particle's status LED color:
//   Green when a face is detected,
//   Red when no face is detected.

// To compile this code, you must first choose Libraries
// and search for the HttpClient library in the Particle IDE.
// The library must be added to this project before flashing
// the code to the device.

// This #include statement was automatically added by the Particle IDE when
// the HttpClient library was included in this project.
#include <HttpClient.h>

 HttpClient http;
 http_request_t request;
 http_response_t response;

 http_header_t headers[] = {
    { "Content-Type", "application/json" },
    { NULL, NULL }
 };

 // So we can avoid using sleep()
 unsigned long loop timer;

 LEDStatus status;

 void setup() {
   status.setActive(LED_PRIORITY_IMPORTANT);

   // This program assumes a server is available and can receive
   // HTTP Post messages such as:
   // http://192.168.50.135:1880/monitor
   request.ip = IPAddress(192,168,50,135); // ** REPLACE THESE NUMBERS **
   request.port = 1880;
   request.path = "/monitor";

   // Find the time
   loop_timer = millis();
 }

 // Provided with a response, set the color of the status LED
```

```
void setLEDColor(http_response_t &response) {
  if (response.body == "1") {
    status.setColor(RGB_COLOR_GREEN);
  } else if (response.body == "0")  {
    status.setColor(RGB_COLOR_RED);
  } else {
    status.setColor(RGB_COLOR_YELLOW);
  }
}

// Send a GET request to the server
void doGetRequest() {
  http.get(request, response, headers);
  setLEDColor(response);
}

// Every 2 seconds, perform a GET request
void loop() {
  if(millis() - loop_timer >= 2000UL) {
      loop_timer = millis();
      doGetRequest();
  }
}
```

8. After flashing your firmware, watch your Photon 2 device's status LED. When there's a face within view of your laptop's webcam, the LED turns green within 4 seconds. When there's no face, the LED turns red.

What Did You Do, and How Did You Do It?

This step's firmware is very much like the firmware in Chapter 3. Every two seconds, Photon 2 does what your web browser would do when your browser visits http://192.168.50.135:1880/monitor. (Remember! Step 7 says you'll probably have to change the numbers 50 and 135 to get this to work. You may also have to change 192 and 168.)

In Part 3, you told Node-RED to send either 0 or 1 in response to such a request. So your Photon 2 receives the number 0 or 1, where 0 means "there's no face in the webcam image", and 1 means "there's a face." An `if` statement in this part's firmware sets the Photon 2's status LED to either red (for no face), green (for face), or yellow (in cases where something goes wrong).

The entire routine, from Part 1 to Part 4, depends on three repeating timers - two in Node-RED's inject nodes, and one in the Photon 2's firmware. So the Photon 2's status LED may not change immediately when you move your face to (or away from) the webcam. In this chapter's instructions, each timer interval is set to 2 seconds, but you can change that if you want. The shorter the intervals, the more immediate the Photon 2's response will be.

But of course, there's a tradeoff. Shorter intervals mean more processing effort. On a slow processor, very short timer intervals may be unrealistic. The best way to select timer intervals involves an estimate of the degree of responsiveness that a particular application requires. For example, an app that monitors your home's front door might wait ten seconds or more between the processing of images. But a camera that tracks the entrance to a high-security governmental facility may require the analysis of the image every tenth of a second.

Check Your Understanding (Activities)

1. Modify the application so that values other than 1 and 0 indicate the presence or absense of a face.

2. Experiment with the time intervals in the inject nodes and the Photon 2 firmware. How quickly can you make the status LED react before some part of the system becomes overworked and sluggish?

3. Name three real-life situations in which you'd want the Photon 2's light to change almost immediately when a face appears or stops appearing. Name three other situations in which you'd tolerate a very long time interval because the Photon 2's light changes.

4. Perform experiments to find out how well the facial recognition node works with faces turned at various angles. Does the software work if a face is titlted sideways? What about a face that's pointed to the left? How much of your face can you cover with your hand and still have the software recognize it as a face?

Make More / Explore Further (Problems)

1. Some generative AI tools, such as DALL-E, create images upon request. Use one of these tools to create an image of a face. Does your Node-RED work from this chapter recognize it as a face?

   If not, what can you do to make the image more recognizable?

   If Node-RED recognizes the generated image as a face, change the instruction you give to the AI tool. Have it generate an image that looks to you like a face but yields the "no face" message from Node-RED. What kinds of variations on face features does Node-RED successfully recognize?

2. The JSON output from the facial recognition node contains an estimate of the person's age. Modify the application so that it responds differently when it sees people of different ages. For example, make the status LED glow green for faces under 30 and yellow for faces over 30.

3. The JSON output from the facial recognition node attempts to quantify a face's expressions. It assigns numerical values to qualities such as happiness, sadness, anger, and so on. Modify your code so that it makes use of these values. Then test the recognition node's accuracy by posing in front of your webcam.

As a follow-up experiment, have several different people pose in front of your webcam. Is the recognition software more accurate with some peoples' faces than with others?

When you pose for the camera, you're probably faking one emotion or another. What happens when you use photographs of people who are genuinely feeling happy, sad, angry, or some other way? Are the software's estimates more accurate when you do this?

4. Many social scientists claim that today's facial recognition software suffers from racial bias, gender bias, and other forms of bias. Can you devise experiments to test for bias in this chapter's facial recognition software?

5. The facial recognition node that you used in this chapter has many useful options. Figure 11.13 shows some of the settings in the node's Properties list.

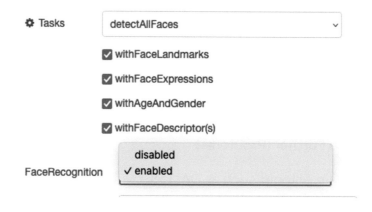

Figure 11.12 Responding to an HTTP request

The facial recognition node can look for more one face in a single webcam image. It can also attempt to distinguish one person's face from another person's face. Enhance your software to take advantage of some of these capabilities.

Summing Up

In this chapter, we plugged facial recognition software into a Node-RED application. The software relies on decades of work by researchers in Artificial Intelligence. The software mimics the neurons in the human brain to perform tasks that would be difficult to codify as a set of rules. Like the human brain, the software adjusts its own characteristics (weights and thresholds) to inch its way toward an effective solution.

This way of solving problems can be applied to other domains. Instead of recognizing the presence or absence of a face, the software can be trained to recognize words in a language, oncoming vehicles, or patterns from signals from distant galaxies.

Our Node-RED software included an HTTP server. The server sends out one of two messages - 0 for "no face", and 1 for "face." We can query this server from any software attached to our network, so we programmed the Photon 2 to send repeated HTTP requests. In this simple exercise, we made the Photon 2's status LED change color when the webcam's face status changed. We could have programmed the Photon 2 to react in many other ways. The range of practical applications is endless.

Looking Ahead

Web 1.0 was all about reading data from the web. Web 2.0 allowed us to both read and write - creating social networks. In Web 3.0, the user is able to own resources - including digital money. In the next chapter, we will learn how an IoT device can be paid for services.

CHAPTER 12

Blockchains and IoT

This chapter covers
- **Digital payments to unattended devices**
- **Cryptocurrency wallets**
- **Using an Ethereum blockchain simulator**
- **Programming with ethers**

A machine that charges for use

"The importance of money flows from it being a link between the present and the future."

John Maynard Keynes

An unattended device that receives payments for services

Have you ever used coin operated binoculars at a city or mountain overlook? It makes good sense. Rather than using tax dollars to pay for the service, only the individuals who want to see the sites up close are required to pay a small fee.

This is an unattended device that receives payments for services. The problem is that, in this case, the payments are in cash. Dollars and change need to be manufactured, transported, and disposed of. All of which has an environmental cost. Think of the vehicles needed to gather the coins from the binoculars.

Many unattended payment systems are going cashless. Electric vehicle charging stations or parking meters often use credit or debit cards for digital payments.

Credit and debit cards are part of centralized payment systems. In this chapter, we will build a decentralized digital payment system using IoT and Web 3.0 technologies.

The original World Wide Web, Web 1.0, was all about reading data from the internet. Web 2.0 was about reading as well as writing data to the internet - think Facebook and X (formerly Twitter). Web 3.0 is about reading and writing as well as ownership.

What if unattended devices were able to monitor funds on a blockchain?

In this chapter, you will build a blockchain based system that will allow a device to provide a simple service – but only if the device is first paid in a cryptocurrency.

Our goal is for a Photon 2 microcontroller to recognize when a payment has been made to its account on the Ethereum[2] network. It will respond to the payment by turning on a light for a certain number of seconds. The Photon 2, in our example, will charge 1 ETH per second of light. At current prices, this is very expensive but it is free when using a blockchain simulator.

A blockchain simulator, Hardhat, is used to hold a single instance blockchain. MetaMask, a cryptocurrency wallet, is used to transfer funds from one account to another on Hardhat. A node.js web application, using the ethers middleware library, reads from Hardhat and makes the balance information available to a Wi-Fi enabled Particle Photon 2. The Photon 2 is assigned one of the addresses available on Hardhat and has that address stored in its firmware.

Part 1: Hardhat and MetaMask

What you need:

- Computer running node.js
- Hardhat – directions follow
- MetaMask – directions follow

What to do:

1.Install and run a single instance blockchain - Hardhat.

    a. Create an empty project directory named Ch12_hardhat.

    b. Change directory (cd) into the project directory.

```
cd Ch12_hardhat
```

    c. Build a package.json file (holding important information about this project) by running the following command. Hit return and take the defaults provided.

```
npm init
```

    d. Now, from within the project directory, install hardhat:
```
npm install --save-dev hardhat
```

    e. Next, within the project directory, initialize Hardhat with the Node Package Execute (npx) command and choose to "Create an empty hardhat.config.js".

```
npx hardhat init
```

f. Within the project directory, install the Hardhat toolbox:

    npm install --save-dev @nomicfoundation/hardhat-toolbox

g. Copy the following to the hardhat.config.js file. Note that we are using 31337 as the chain ID and http://127.0.0.1:8545 as the URL. Note too that this is http and NOT https. The initialBaseFeePerGas is set to 0 for testing with MetaMask and Hardhat. This file may also be found at this URL:

    https://github.com/mm6/Ch12_code_hardhat/blob/main/hardhat.config.js

```
require("@nomicfoundation/hardhat-toolbox");
/** @type import('hardhat/config').HardhatUserConfig */
module.exports = {
  defaultNetwork: "localhost",
  networks: {
    hardhat: {
      initialBaseFeePerGas: 0,
      chainId: 31337
    },
    localhost: {
      url: "http://127.0.0.1:8545"
    }
  },
  solidity: "0.5.14",
};
```

h. Within the project directory, execute the following command to start a JSON-RPC server that will run on top of the Hardhat Ethereum Virtual Machine. After startup, this server will become available at http://127.0.0.1:8545. It will allow remote procedure calls (RPCs) to this URL. We will use RPC's to visit this port with a wallet (MetaMask) and a web application. But it will not be usable with a standard HTTP GET request from a browser.

    npx hardhat node

i. This server will display 20 accounts. These are "Account 0" through "Account 19". You should be able to see the public and private keys associated with each account. Leave this server running. Our next activity is to connect to it using MetaMask.

2. Install Google Chrome (MetaMask does not run on Safari).

Visit `https://www.google.com/chrome/downloads/`

3. Install a cryptocurrency wallet - MetaMask for Chrome:

   a. Visit `https://metamask.io/download/`

   b. During the MetaMask installation, you will be given a 12 word pass phrase. This is your Secret Recovery Phrase and is used to generate your private keys. Keep a copy of this phrase safe.

   c. After installing MetaMask in the Chrome browser, read over the following brief cheat sheet guide to MetaMask. Note that you may need to reset the nonce before retrying after a failed transaction.

MetaMask Cheat Sheet Guide

MetaMask is self-custodial (keeps private keys local) by design.

The Secret Recovery Phrase (SRP) is used to generate public and private key pairs.

A user might have many key pairs derived from the same recovery phrase.

In the top right corner is a three dot menu or vertical ellipsis.

Under the three dots menu we find the following selected options:

  Account details

    Change the name on the account

    View the public key

    Copy the public key

    View the private key if you have the password

  Settings

    Network

    Add a Network

      For Hardhat, set New RPC URL to: http://localhost:8545 and chain

      ID to 31337. The chain ID is used to distinguish between chains, is included in signatures, and provides replay protection. The currency symbol is ETH.

Snaps are third-party extensions to MetaMask

Just to the left of three dots menu:

Shows accounts connected

These web sites will have access to your public key (only!) of your accounts.

We are not connecting our account in this project.

In the middle of the wallet is the main page with several options:

Account name

Public key (with a copy icon)

Balance in ETH

Balance in USD may be visible

Under tokens (notice ETH counts as "Tokens")

Import Tokens (custom token)

A coin contract deployed to Hardhat counts as a "custom token".

A user may enter a contract address (the address of the token)

Enter token symbol

Enter token decimals for tokens with fractional parts

Under Activity

Recent activities on this account

By selecting the drop down arrow in the middle of the page:

Select an account

Options appearing: Buy & sell, send, swap, bridge, portfolio

The bridge option requires that you have tokens on the source and destination network.

To change tokens from one blockchain to another, we need to connect

to a bridge service.

MetaMask does not currently work with Bitcoin or non-ethereum blockchains.

Many Bitcoin wallets exist, e.g. see BitCoinWallet.com.

The portfolio option allows you to view several accounts at once.

Settings/Advanced/Clear Activity Tab data to reset the nonce and failed activities.

Settings/Advanced/Clear Activity Tab is useful when debugging.

You may need to clear the nonce if you get a failed transaction. Each time you start

the server, it wants the first nonce to be zero. This is useful when experimenting with

MetaMask.

Select account, note three dot drop down:

The "Select an Account" page has a three dot menu next to each account.

Select Account Details and change the name on an account or access its public key

via copy and paste or a QR code.

Remove account is an option only for accounts that were imported with private keys.

Remove account is not an option for accounts created by the recovery phrase.

Near the bottom is the Add account or hardware wallet option

Add a new account (based on your secret phrase)

Import an account

You will need the account's private key.

Add Hardware wallet

This option will allow you to store private keys offline.

Top left drop down

  The button on the bottom allows us to Add a network

    Under Settings there are many options. Some are discussed here:

    General

      Currency conversion

      Primary currency

    Networks

      In order to add Harhat:

      Add a Network/Add a network manually

  Security and Privacy

      Reveal secret recovery phrase (SRP)

      SRP is deterministic and may be used to generate many key pairs (without

      randomness).

  Show test networks

      Turn on when using Hardhat network for testing

4. Connect MetaMask to Hardhat.

Like Bitcoin, Ethereum can be used as a simple payment network. In this part of the project, we experiment with using MetaMask for sending ETH from one account (we need to be in possession of the sender's private key for signing) to another receiver account (we need the public address of the receiver).

  a. Using MetaMask, add a network manually. We want to select the Hardhat Network. You will need to point to the location where you started the server (http://127.0.0.1:8545) and will need to set the chain ID to 31337. Use the cheat sheet for guidance.

    b. From the shell where you started the server (the project directory), copy the private key of the first account to the clipboard and import this key into MetaMask. Name this new account "Alice".

    c. From the shell where you started the server, copy the private key of the second account to the clipboard and import this key into MetaMask. Name this new account "Bob". Alice and Bob should each show 10,000 ETH. These account balances are provided by Hardhat.

5. For practice, send 10 ETH from the first account to the second account by performing a send operation in MetaMask. We are sending from the first Hardhat account (whose private key is in MetaMask) to the second Hardhat account. To do this, we need the public address of the second account. Copy the public address of the second account from Hardhat and paste it into MetaMask as the destination of the send operation.

In Parts 2 and 3, we will use the second account on Hardhat as the account of the microcontroller. We will use the first account on Hardhat as the payer account.

What Did You Do, and How Did You Do It?

You installed MetaMask which runs in the browser. This software uses the operating systems as a source of entropy to randomly select from a list of 2048 words. Thus, each word represents 11 bits of information. Recall our discussion of entropy in Chapter 3 and note that $\text{Log}_2 2048 = 11$.

The series of random words is used as a seed to mechanically generate an Ethereum master private key of 256 bits. From this master private key, many new private keys can be generated in a hierarchical manner. Thus, one wallet, such as MetaMask, may hold many private keys. Each of these keys is used to control an Ethereum account.

Asymmetric Key Cryptography and Signatures

In Chapter 3, we discussed symmetric key cryptography. In symmetric key cryptography, both the sender of a message, say Bob, and the receiver of a messages, say Alice, must be in possession of the same key. Bob encrypts the message with the key and Alice is able to decrypt the message with the same key. In Chapter 3, we used the one-time pad and the Tiny Encryption Algorithm (TEA) to perform symmetric key encryption and decryption.

In this chapter, we are using asymmetric key cryptography. In asymmetric key cryptography, each player has two keys that are created as a pair and are mathematically related to each other. Each player has a private key that is kept private and not shared with others. Each player also has a related public key which can be made available to anyone.

Asymmetric key cryptography may be used for encrypting a message or for signing a message. The message that we want to encrypt with asymmetric key cryptography is often a symmetric key.

Suppose Bob wants to encrypt a message and send it to Alice using asymmetric key cryptography. Bob will use Alice's public key to encrypt the message and Alice will use her private key to decrypt the message. The message might be a normal message like "Hello Alice". But note that Bob might also do this in order to transfer a symmetric key to Alice. After decrypting the message with her private key, both players will hold the same symmetric key. They may use that key for subsequent encryption. This is often done because symmetric key cryptography is typically far faster than asymmetric key cryptography. We are using asymmetric key cryptography to establish a shared secret – the shared symmetric key. We are using the shared symmetric key for the bulk of the encryption.

In this chapter, we are not using asymmetric key encryption. Instead, we are using the MetaMask wallet to sign messages (transactions) and an Ethereum client, Hardhat, to verify that the messages were signed and refer to a particular account.

Signatures

In general, suppose Bob wants to sign a message. He wants anyone who is interested to be able to see that the message was signed with his private key without, of course, revealing his private key to anyone. This can be done with asymmetric key cryptography. He can take the message and compute a cryptographic hash of the message. He can then encrypt the hash with his private key. This encrypted hash can be used to verify that Bob signed the message. A signature verification process will proceed by computing a new hash of the message and comparing that new hash with the result of decrypting the encrypted hash using Bob's public key. If the new hash matches the decrypted hash, then Bob's key was used to sign the message.

In the example in this chapter, MetaMask holds the private key used for signing transactions. The wallet transfers the associated public key and the signed transaction to an Ethereum client. The Ethereum client is able to verify that the transaction was signed by the holder of the private key.

Referring to the top left of Figure 12.1, the MetaMask wallet is illustrated. This wallet software is able to communicate with an Ethereum client. The wallet contains three important integers. Perhaps the most important is the private key. This key is created using techniques from Elliptic Curve Cryptography (ECC). This key should, of course, be kept private and is not normally transmitted onto a network. It is used to sign transactions so that a receiver may verify that a transaction emanated from a particular key. The holder of the private key is able to move money from the account associated with the private key to another account. Said another way, the holder of the private key is able to spend cash from its account.

ECC Public Key and Private Keys

In Ethereum, using ECC, the private key is used to generate a public key that is mathematically associated with its private key. The wallet transmits its public key, in the clear (unencrypted), along with a signed request to move money from an account it controls. A receiver, an Ethereum node such as Hardhat, uses the received public key to verify that the originator of the transaction signed the transaction with the corresponding private key.

Some readers may be familiar with the important role that digital certificates play in public key cryptography more generally. Certificates are used to associate or bind a public key with an individual or organization. In Ethereum, no certificates are necessary. There are no organizations or individuals behind transactions, only private keys.

Suppose we have two players, Alice and Bob, and Bob wants to move some funds from Alice's account to his own. Bob is not able to move money from Alice's account to Bob's account because Bob is not (or, hopefully not) in possession of Alice's private key. If he does not have Alice's private key, he cannot sign a message pretending to be Alice.

That is why you copied the private key of the first account from Hardhat and pasted it into MetaMask. MetaMask would be unable to sign a transaction that transfers the first account's funds without the private key of the first account. Since Hardhat is a testing platform, it allows you access to private keys. This is not normally the case when we step out of the testing environment. Private keys are normally kept secret.

Bob is able to move money from Bob's account to Alice's account if Bob has his private key and is willing and able to sign off on the transaction. He must also have sufficient funds in his most recent account balance and he must know Alice's Ethereum address.

Ethereum Addresses

This brings us to the third important integer found in an Ethereum wallet - the address of the account controlled by the private key in the wallet. The Ethereum account address is mathematically derived from the public key. Others may transfer funds to the account if they are in possession of the account address.

That is why, when you transferred 10 ETH from the first account to the second account, that you copied the address of the second account into MetaMask.

In summary, Bob's private key is used to generate his public key and his account address. The public key and account address are available to the Ethereum client. The public key will be used to verify that the transaction request is coming from the holder of the corresponding private key and the account address is used to lookup Bob's account balance.

Part 2: Using Web3 to examine account balances

What you need:

- Node.js
- express
- ethers
- Completion of Part 1

What to do:

1. We need to build a web site that is able to respond to a browser (or, a Photon 2) and return the balance of an account.

2. Using a new command line shell, cd into the project directory (Ch12_hardhat).

3. From the command line run the following commands:

```
npm install express
npm install ethers@5.7.2
```

4. Create a file named index.js in the project directory. It is available at the following URL and is also available in the chapter appendix.

https://github.com/sn-code-inside/guide-to-iot/blob/main/Ch12_code/index.js

6. With Hardhat running in a separate shell, execute the JavaScript file using node.js.

```
node index.js
```

7. Visit the web site with one of the account addresses as shown next (replace the account address shown with the second account address from Hardhat):

```
http://localhost:3000/getBalance/0x5E99d7c0694F70859C8E0c2Fc048bae
B3b56cfc5
```

8. The account address and balance should be visible on the browser.

What Did You Do, and How Did You Do It?

The reader should review the code in `index.js`. You will note that, for the first time in this book, we make use of the ethers library. This library allows the JavaScript developer to make calls to an Ethereum node such as Hardhat. Behind the scenes, the ethers middleware is creating a message

in the JSON RPC format and transmitting that message over TCP/IP. Before this code will run, we needed to install the ethers library in a directory called node_modules. This we did when we ran `npm install ethers@5.7.2`
.

We also installed `Express`. We did this so that it would be an easy matter to provide a web service. The service that we provide fetches the account balance associated with an account address on Hardhat. We can make an HTTP call to this service using a browser or, perhaps, a device such as a microcontroller. We will do that next.

Part 3: Making Digital Payments to a Microcontroller's account

What you need

- d. Particle Photon 2
- e. Completion of Part 1 and Part 2

What to do

1. You will need a copy of the code in blockchain-payment.ino. The file `blockchain-payment.ino` may be found in the chapter appendix and at this URL:

https://github.com/sn-code-inside/guide-to-iot/blob/main/Ch12_code/blockchain-payment.ino

2. Within this firmware, be sure to replace the account address provided with an account address that will represent the Photon 2's balance. This will be the account address of the second account on Hardhat. Recall that we are using the first account to make payments and the second account to maintain the balance of our microcontroller.

3. Make sure that Hardhat is running and that MetaMask has the private key of the first account in Hardhat.

4. Use the Particle Web IDE and flash the code to your Photon 2.

5. Study the code. Upon startup, the firmware fetches the current balance from the blockchain. It does this by preparing the HTTP request and calling:

prevBalance = callAndGetTruncatedEthBalance();

6. The LED on the Photon 2 will turn on for about 1 second for each additional eth that is transferred to its account.

7. Use MetaMask and transfer 10 ETH to the second account.

4. If a payment in ETH has been made to the account address found in the firmware, the Photon 2's light turns on for 10 seconds. Additional payments result in more light.

What did you do and how did you do it?

Referring to the bottom left of Figure 12.1, the microcontroller is illustrated. It controls a light (illustrating a simple service) and is able to make HTTP requests to the web application. The microcontroller is fitted with an Ethereum account address. One might imagine many such devices, each with its own account. If money is deposited to a particular account then and only then will it perform a particular service.

In this chapter, we are not connecting to a real Ethereum client. Instead, we are connecting to a local instance of Hardhat. Hardhat acts as a simulator of an Ethereum node and is often used by developers to test code before connecting to the Ethereum mainnet.

Agreement on account balances

In traditional banking, customers find that they have one balance for each account that they control. The same must hold for decentralized systems such as Ethereum. Each of the computers in the peer-to-peer network (see Figure 12.1) must each have a copy of the same balance for each account. How is this accomplished? In computer science, this is the famous problem of distributed consensus.

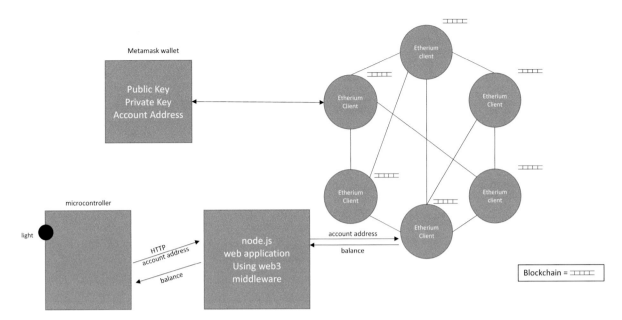

System Architecture Figure 12.1

Referring to the right side of Figure 12.1, the Ethereum peer-to-peer networks is illustrated. Each Ethereum client (peer) maintains its own copy of a list of blocks linked together by cryptographic hashes - forming a blockchain. We discuss cryptographic hashes in a section below. Each block also has references to account balances. These balances must each be the same on each peer.

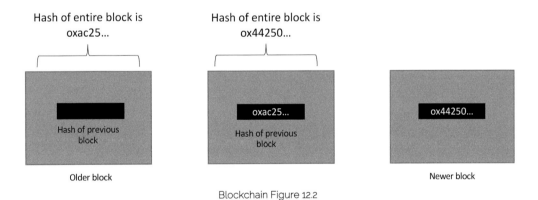

Blockchain Figure 12.2

See Figure 12.2. It is important that each chain of blocks be identical on each of the Ethereum clients. Account balances may be accessed by examining references made from within a block. See Figure 12.3. The peer-to-peer protocol running on the peer-to-peer network, whether based on proof-of-work or proof-of-stake, is designed to keep the many thousands of peers in agreement on the value of account balances. In this way, the system presents a single view of each account balance. The Ethereum peers provide a distributed and decentralized ledger of accounts and account balances.

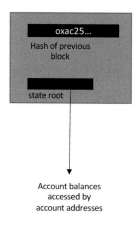

Block Figure 12.3

Referring to the bottom middle of Figure 12.1 the Node.js web application is illustrated. This is a standard HTTP service that utilizes an ethers (Web3 middleware) object in order to communicate with one of the many Ethereum clients. In our case, we are communicating with the Hardhat client. Unlike a real Ethereum client, Hardhat is not connected to the peer-to-peer network.

Consensus

A consensus protocol among a set of peers in a peer-to-peer network is a conversation among the peers designed in such a way that the network reaches consensus on a particular proposed value. Some of these protocols, for example Paxos and Raft, are designed to reach agreement among non-faulty nodes even if some of the other nodes in the network are faulty. Still other protocols, such as the Practical Byzantine Fault Tolerance protocol (PBFT), go further. These are designed to reach agreement among non-faulty and non-malicious nodes even if some of the other nodes *are* maliciously trying to subvert the protocol.

Neither Bitcoin[1] or Ethereum[2] use Paxos, Raft, or PBFT to reach consensus. These well-established protocols are mentioned here so that the reader is aware of them and is aware that the problem of distributed consensus has alternative characterizations and solutions. Some were designed to work in the presence of failing machines. Others take on the additional task of working in the presence of malicious adversaries.

In Ethereum and Bitcoin, large amounts of money are at stake. Large amounts of money attract malicious players. Ethereum and Bitcoin were designed to work in the presence of such adversaries.

Proof of work

Bitcoin (and prior versions of Ethereum) consensus is based on proof-of-work. While many peers may be collecting transactions and organizing them into blocks, only one peer is selected to contribute its block to the blockchain. This "special peer" is selected by a competitive process and gets to tell all of the other peers which is the next block to adopt. In this way, everyone on the network ends up with the exact same chain as all of the others. All of the peers have the exact same block added to the chain because each peer received that block from the same special peer.

To clarify, suppose all of the peers in Figure 12.1 start off with the exact same blockchain and that we are using proof-of-work consensus. Each peer collects transaction messages from users of the network. Each peer checks that the transactions are signed and valid (a client may not transfer money from one account to another unless it has the money to spend and has signed and approved of the transfer) and adds the transactions to a block that the peer will propose to be adopted by all of the other peers. In order to incentivize the peers to perform this work, there is money added to the account of the peer whose block is finally accepted by all of the others. In Bitcoin, this is called a COINBASE payment. How do we choose which peer is the special peer whose block will be accepted by all of the others? How do we choose that peer that will receive the COINBASE payment? There is serious money at stake. This special peer is chosen because it is the first to solve a very particular mathematical puzzle. The peer that is chosen as "special" is the peer that solves the puzzle first and is able to prove to the other peers that it has worked hard to do so. This procedure is sometimes called "Nakamoto Consensus".

Without the requirement of proof, anyone could attempt to claim the prize. Suppose you walk into a lottery office and claim to have won the billion dollar prize. The people who run the lottery will want to see your ticket. They want proof that you won. It must be clear to them that the ticket has not been tampered with!

In order to explain this process more fully, we turn our attention to the way Bitcoin uses cryptographic hashing to perform proof-of-work. For reasons described below, recent versions of Ethereum have moved away from this approach.

Cryptographic Hashing

As we have seen Chapter 3, cryptography can be used to encrypt messages. Encryption is a mathematical technique used so that an eavesdropper is unable to read messages that are being transmitted or stored.

And as we discussed above, cryptography can also be used to sign messages. This technique is used so that a receiver of a message can quickly verify that the message sender is in possession of a particular key.

Another major application of cryptography is cryptographic hashing. This is NOT the same as encryption.

The best way to get some familiarity with this important and fundamental concept is by working with it.

Secure Hash Algorithm 256 (SHA-256)

Visit this web site and experiment with SHA-256:

```
https://emn178.github.io/online-tools/sha256.html
```

Let's define a *message* as a variable length string of characters. We will call the cryptographic hash of a message a *digest*.

Notice that the SHA-256 hash of the message:

```
guidetointernetofthings
```

is the digest

```
626f40e0fb45077e4646297742c4913d50efb9acfb7b1ff634c21aa9b49594cb
```

And notice that the hash of

```
guidetointernetofthings35
```

is the digest

```
074ae934f4fe92a17fa04b9e8eacb7c545faa6ae4f1d4733ba6adfdd44c73a08.
```

And notice the number 35 tagged on at the end of the message. This is called a *nonce*. The hash of this message (including the nonce) has a leading hexadecimal 0. Try it! Now, suppose we want more than one 0. Here is a puzzle for you to solve:

Find the smallest positive integer (nonce) that can be appended to the string `guidetointernetofthings` so that the hash of `guidetointernetofthings` along with the nonce produces a hash with two leading hex zeroes. Start with `guidetointernetofthings1`. Try `guidetointernetofthings2` and so on until you find a hash with two leading hexadecimal 0's. It may take several minutes to discover this nonce. It is important to give this exercise a try. If you do not have the time to perform this work, the answer is mentioned in the Make Explore further section. The answer should be enough to convince you (prove) that someone (the author) actually performed this work

The only known way to solve the problem of finding these leading zeroes is with brute force. In blockchain parlance, this brute force activity that you just performed is called proof-of-work. It can be solved in a reasonable amount of time only if the number of required 0's is small.

Each SHA-256 message produces a single, deterministic, seemingly random output. The hash of guidetointernetofthings35 will always be the same.

Notice how the message can vary in size but the output is of fixed length. The message might be small or a large data file. The message might even be an entire block of transactions.

Here is another hash, this one taken from the Bitcoin blockchain. The message being hashed (a block) is not shown. Only the result of hashing the block is shown.

```
0000000000000000000073f86dbc03d7b9709d44dd6b5bef6eb0c6af00a9e97ee
```

Note all of the leading 0's. There was a lot of brute force work applied to the message that produced this hash. A very fast computer might take two weeks to find such a hash - by varying a nonce as you did above by hand. While two weeks is the average time needed by a random peer, the Bitcoin network (as a whole) produces a block every ten minutes or so. There are many nodes trying to win the race. One will get lucky and get there first.

This is the mindless mathematical puzzle that each peer is trying to solve.

In Bitcoin, the number of zeros required to win the race is established by noting how fast new blocks are being produced. If valid blocks are arriving faster than every ten minutes, the software in each node knows to increase the number of zeroes required. If valid blocks are arriving less often than one every ten minutes, the number of required zeroes is reduced.

Referring again to Figure 12.1, the nodes with copies of the blockchain are furiously competing to see which one wins the race to find a nonce (the nonce is placed within the new block) that causes the hashing algorithm to generate an appropriate number of zeroes. If a node finds a solution to the puzzle, it broadcasts that solution to the other nodes. These other nodes check that the hash is correct and that the transactions within the block are valid – all transactions are properly signed and no one is allowed to spend the same coin twice. If everything checks out then the new block is adopted by everyone and the winner of the contest is paid. The payment itself is found in the new block – a COINBASE transaction paying the winning node.

It only requires one hash computation to verify that the winner is, in fact, a real winner. It takes a very large number of hash computations to arrive at the correct number of zeros.

Account Balances

Ethereum holds account balances as shown in Figure 12.3. An account address is associated with a particular balance. This is called an account based system and is similar to the way a bank maintains account balances.

Bitcoin uses account history, also known as provenance, to determine which account owns what. For example, in Bitcoin, if there is a transaction that says that Alice gives 2 BTC to Bob and another transaction that says Charlie gives 1 BTC to Bob, then Bob may spend 3 BTC. Of course, this assumes that there is no prior transaction that has Bob spending any of those proceeds. Bitcoin will look for that and will not permit Bob to spend the bitcoins a second time.

Proof-of-stake

In September of 2022 Ethereum transitioned away from proof-of-work and adopted a proof-of-stake approach. One of the reasons for this transition is to protect the environment. Proof-of-work has been shown to be a very large waste of resources. No useful work (outside of supporting the protocol) is performed by proof-of-work computations. Yet, it consumes a large amount of electricity (comparable to nation states). In addition, proof-of-work consumes time and slows down the overall network. For fast and environmentally clean transaction processing, something else is needed.

In proof-of-stake consensus, the special node that is selected to produce the next block is chosen based upon some randomness and on how much wealth the node controls. There is no competitive game played by all of the nodes. Nodes with significant wealth are more likely to be chosen as the special node. Winners are incentivized to behave properly and to help ensure the health of the network. They earn fees for producing valid blocks and also have the most to lose if the network is corrupted.

In Ethereum's version of proof-of-stake (there are others), a node that wants to be a part of the block selection process must stake (or, put in escrow) 32 eth. At the time of writing, 32 ETH is valued at about 70,000 USD. If the node behaves poorly then a portion of the staked ETH may be taken from the node. If the node performs well, rewards may be earned.

Proof-of-stake blockchains are generally faster and are far friendlier to the environment than proof-of-work style blockchains.

Check Your Understanding

1. Using MetaMask and Hardhat, transfer 1/10 of 1 ETH from the first account to the second account.
2. Using MetaMask and Hardhat, add the third account's private key to MetaMask – so that it, along with the first account, can make payments to the second account.
3. Using MetaMask and Hardhat, have the third account pay the second account .25 Eth. See Question 2.
4. Modify your firmware so that it turns the light on for 1 second for each 0.5 ETH added to its account.
5. Using the Blockchain explorer at https://www.blockchain.com/explorer, find the block whose hash is

```
00000000000000000000073f86dbc03d7b9709d44dd6b5bef6eb0c6af00a9e97
ee
```

6. Using the Blockchain explorer and the hash in question 5, determine if this a Bitcoin or Ethereum hash.
7. Using the Blockchain explorer, how much money (in USD) did the miner earn by solving the puzzle on the block in question 5?
8. Using the Blockchain explorer, what is the identity of the miner that mined the block in question 5?
9. Using the Blockchain explorer, how many transactions were included in the block named in question 5 ? (The name of a block is its cryptographic hash.)
10. Using the Blockchain explorer and the block from question 5, what was the destination address of the COINBASE transaction? A COINBASE transaction is the transaction that pays the miner for solving the puzzle.
11. Using the Blockchain explorer and the block from question 5, use your phone to scan the QR code associated with the COINBASE transaction. What value is stored in the QR code?
12. How could the QR code in question 11 be used? That is, describe a Bitcoin use case that would involve the use of such a QR code. Your answer must refer to the application discussed in this chapter.

Make More / Explore Further

1. Research Pennsylvania's E-ZPass system. How does it differ from the system built in this chapter? How is it the same?
2. Smart city projects can be expensive. Describe how such projects might be paid for.
3. How does the system built in this chapter differ from traditional electronic payment schemes? How is it the same?
4. Ask ChatGPT to compare Bitcoin with Ethereum in terms of environmental friendliness?
5. Describe how coin operated binoculars could be redesigned using the ideas from this chapter. What type of networking would make sense? What cost savings could be achieved? How would the system be paid for?
6. The URL of the bitcoin block explorer is here: https://www.blockchain.com/btc/blocks
Visit the bitcoin block explorer and determine the *block height* of the block with this hash
`00000000000000000000073f86dbc03d7b9709d44dd6b5bef6eb0c6af00a9e97ee.`
7. Which is greater, the number of SHA-256 hashes or the number of atoms in the earth? You need to research this a bit. Provide a brief explanation.
8. In the proof-of-work exercise, you should have found that the nonce 139 will produce two hexadecimal 0's to start the digest. Write a program (in your

language of choice) that finds a nonce for four hexadecimal 0's to start the digest.

9. Configure your Photon 2 hardware (use a light sensor) so that it is able to detect when a room light is turned on or off. When the light is switched from on to off, make a small payment to an address on Hardhat – you will need to use ethers and Node.js. The private key (for signing) must be stored in Node.js.

10. Ask ChatGPT to discuss the benefits of a peer-to-peer decentralized system over a centralized client server system. Do you agree?

Summing Up

In this chapter we built a simple microcontroller application that monitors a blockchain for payment. The microcontroller only provides a service if a sufficient amount of cryptocurrency has been deposited to its account. We used Hardhat to simulate the Ethereum blockchain and MetaMask, a cryptocurrency wallet, to make payments. Node.js and ethers were used to build a web application that was directly queried by the microcontroller.

Digital payments may be more friendly to our environment than cash payments. Digital payments may be centralized or decentralized. In this chapter, we worked with a decentralized payment system.

Looking Ahead

This is the end of our book but not the end of IoT. New sensors, actuators, and networks will be coming and so will new applications that use them. Security concerns will be ever-present and we will need to be vigilant and keep up our guard.

We say "goodbye" and hope that you will one day design IoT architectures and systems that promote a sustainable world.

References

[1] Nakamoto, Satoshi. "Bitcoin: A Peer-to-Peer Electronic Cash System." Bitcoin.org. Accessed July 24, 2023. https://bitcoin.org/en/bitcoin-paper
[2] Buterin, Vitalik. "Ethereum Whitepaper." Ethereum.org. Last updated May 10, 2023. Accessed July 24, 2023. https://ethereum.org/en/whitepaper/

Chapter Appendix

```
// Guide to Internet of Things
// Chapter 12 Unattended digital payments
// Part 1
// index.js

// This JavaScript program runs in Node.js. It communicates with a
// local instance of the Ethereum blockchain simulated by Hardhat.
// It provides a web service that takes, as input, on the URL, the
// public address of an Ethereum account (from Hardhat). It returns
// a JSON string holding the account address and the current balance
// in ETH.

// Before running, be sure to install version 5.7.2 of ethers
// by running:
// npm install ethers@5.7.2

// After starting this program, use a browser to visit with a URL like
// this:
//
// http://localhost:3000/getBalance/0x64f63F50074A514E8A6De7d073C5932997C6951c
// The hexadecimal value is an Ethereum address from Hardhat.
// Be sure to use your own address from a running instance of Hardhat.

// This code simply reads the account balance from the blockchain.
// It maintains no private key and, therefore, cannot transfeer funds.
// Use a wallet, such as MetaMask, to transfer funds into an account
// read by this program.
// The program uses Node.js, Express and ethers to run.
// Run at the command prompt with:
// node index.js
// Visit at http://localhost:3000/getBalance/AccountID
// Note: the AccountID is copied and pasted from a running Hardhat nstance.
// From a browser, use the address of an account in the URL to see the account's
// balance.

// Use Express
const express = require('express');
app = express();
// Listen on port 3000
const port = 3000;
// Access needed middleware libraries
const { ethers, JsonRpcProvider } = require("ethers");

// Get the balance for an account from Hardhat using ethers.
async function retrieveBalance(account,myCallBack) {
  const provider = new
ethers.providers.JsonRpcProvider("http://localhost:8545");
  // Replace with the address that you want to check the balance of.
  const address = "0xf39Fd6e51aad88F6F4ce6aB8827279cffFb92266";
  const balance = await provider.getBalance(address);
  const etherString = ethers.utils.formatEther(balance);
```

```
    console.log(`The balance of ${address} is ${etherString} ETH`);
    myCallBack(balance);
}

// Initial values
var balance = 0;
var account;
var response;

// This function runs after a response from the Ethereum blockchain.
function handleResponse(balance) {
    // We want a JSON response. Build an object and the stringify to json.
    let returnObject = new Object();
    returnObject.account = account;
    returnObject.balance = balance.toString();
    response.send(JSON.stringify(returnObject));
}

// Respond to an HTTP get request from a browser or a microcontroller.
app.get('/getBalance/:account', (req, res) => {
    // The callback will send the response when its ready.
    // Here, we make the response object global.
    response = res;
    // Place the account ID in the global variable account.
    account = req.params.account;
    // Call to make the query.
    retrieveBalance(req.params.account,handleResponse);

})

// When we run this code, we see this message on how to use the program.
app.listen(port, () => {
    console.log(`Blochain query listening for GET at
http://localhost:${port}/getBalance/accountID`);
})
```

```
// Guide to Internet of Things
// Chapter 12
// Part 2 blockchain-payment.ino

/* This program is designed to demonstrate a simple, unattended digital
      payment service.
It periodically checks a web service to see if money has been paid to its
      Ethereum account.
If the program detects an increase in its Ethereum balance, it turns on
      its D7 LED for a
certain number of seconds. The number of seconds the LED is on
      corresponds to the amount
of increase that was paid to its account. For each ETH, we get 1 second
      of light.
```

```
Before flashing the program to a Particle Photon 2 microcontroller, make
      two changes:

(1) Change the IP address to the correct address of the machine where the
      web service is running.
    Currently, it is set with char myHost[] = "192.168.86.250";
(2) Change the Ethereum account address to the address of the
      microcontroller's
Ethereum account. Currently, it is set with
char pathWithEthereumAddress[] =
      "/getBalance/0xf39Fd6e51aad88F6F4ce6aB8827279cfffFb92266";

*/


// This program will make HTTP requests to a web service.
#include <HttpClient.h>
// Standard Particle header.
#include "Particle.h"

// This is the light this program will control.
const pin_t MY_LED = D7;


// http will be of class HttpClient.
HttpClient http;

// An array of structs is used to represent the http header message sent
      to the server.
// We expect to receive a JSON response.
http_header_t headers[] = {

    { "Content-Type", "application/json" },
    { "Accept" , "application/json" },
    { "Accept" , "*/*"},
    // null terminate the array
    { NULL, NULL }
};

// A request will include the headers
http_request_t request;
// Get an HTTP response with JSON
http_response_t response;

// Service  IP location. This will normally need to change.
char myHost[] = "192.168.86.250";
// Service port
int port = 3000;

// This is the path to Node.js service.
// Specify the microcontroller's Ethereum account address on the path.
```

```
// This will normally need to change.

char pathWithEthereumAddress[] =
      "/getBalance/0xf39Fd6e51aad88F6F4ce6aB8827279cffFb92266";

// Handle time values.
// oldCallTime is used for timing the calls to the servie.
unsigned int oldCallTime = 0;
// oldSecondsTime is used check the LED every second.
unsigned int oldSecondsTime = 0;

// We will make a remote call every 5 seconds
unsigned int callInterval = 5000;
// And check the light every one second
unsigned int secondInterval = 1000;


// Hold Ethereum balance
int prevBalance = 0;
// Add to secondsBucket if we see an increase in the controller's
      account.
int secondsBucket = 0;

// We will fill up these arrays from the response.
// We want the address and the balance on the account.
char addr[1000];
char balance[1000];

// Do this on start up.
// Note that we make a call for the initial balance on startup.
// The light will come on when there is an increase in the balance.
void setup() {

    Serial.begin(9600);
    request.hostname = myHost;
    request.port = port;
    request.path = pathWithEthereumAddress;
    pinMode(MY_LED, OUTPUT);
    // Turn light off
    digitalWrite(MY_LED, LOW);
    // get initial balance fro the blockchain
    prevBalance = callAndGetTruncatedEthBalance();
}


void loop() {


    // Every second take 1 away from the seconds bucket or set it to 0.
    // If there are seconds in the bucket, turn the light on.
    // If there are no seconds left in the bucket, turn the light off.
```

```
    if (millis() - oldSecondsTime >= secondInterval) {

        if (secondsBucket > 0) {
            digitalWrite(MY_LED, HIGH);
            secondsBucket = secondsBucket - 1;
        }
        else {
            digitalWrite(MY_LED, LOW);
            secondsBucket = 0;
        }

        oldSecondsTime = millis();
    }


    // Every 5 seconds (callInterval) make a call to the service
    // and if we have an increase, place seconds in the seconds bucket.
    if (millis() - oldCallTime >= callInterval) {

        int bal = callAndGetTruncatedEthBalance();
        // If there is an increase, add seconds to the bucket.
        if(bal > prevBalance) {
            secondsBucket = secondsBucket + (bal - prevBalance);
        }
        // The previous balance becomes the new balance.
        prevBalance = bal;
        // Update oldCallTime with new time
        oldCallTime = millis();
    } // end if

}
// Make a call to a web application to
// learn the balance in Eth of this account.

int callAndGetTruncatedEthBalance() {

        // result will hold the new balance
        int result = 0;

        // Make the HTTP Get request and include the Ethereum address.
        http.get(request, response, headers);

        // If all went well...
        if(response.status == 200) {

            JSONValue outerObj = JSONValue::parseCopy(response.body);
            JSONObjectIterator iter(outerObj);

            // More than one name-value pair is returned so use
            // while rather than if.
            while (iter.next())
```

```
                {
                if(iter.name() == "Account")
                {
                    strcpy(addr,iter.value().toString().data());
                    Serial.printf("Account address: %s", addr);
                }
                if (iter.name() == "balance") {
                    strcpy(balance,iter.value().toString().data());
                    result = balanceTruncatedToEth(balance);
                    // Serial.printf("Balance truncated to Eth %d", result
    );
                }
            } // end while
        } // end if
        else {
            Serial.println("Response not 200");
            result = -1;
        }

        return result;
}

// Balances are returned with positions for full eth followed by 18
// positions
// for fractions of an eth. Here, we remove the 18 positions from
    consideration.
int balanceTruncatedToEth(char *balanceAsString) {

    int len = strlen(balanceAsString);      // len of entire string
    int ethCharactersLen = len - 18;        // len of charaters
        representing Eth

    if(ethCharactersLen <= 0) return 0;     // handle case where we have
        no full eth

    char* substr = (char *) malloc(ethCharactersLen + 1);   // make room
        plus one for null
    strncpy(substr, balanceAsString, ethCharactersLen);   // copy Eth
        characters
    substr[ethCharactersLen] = '\0';    // null terminate

    int result = atoi(substr); // convert ascii to int

    free(substr); // free temporary memory created with malloc

    return result;  // return the number of Eth
}
```